MW00613780

COLORADO GUN LAW

Armed And Educated

A Complete Guide To Gun Law In Colorado

2016 Edition

By Attorneys Douglas Richards,
Stanley Marks, and Christopher Ferraro

Copyright © 2016 by Stanley Marie, LLC
First Printing

All rights reserved. No part of this book may be reproduced in any form or by any means without permission in writing from the publisher.

Written by Douglas Richards, Stanley Marks & Christopher Ferraro and published in the United States of America
By U.S. Law Shield
ISBN 978-0-692-64072-2

To order additional books by phone or for wholesale orders call (877) 448-6839.

TABLE OF CONTENTS

PREFACE

As lawyers with years of representing law-abiding gun owners in cases all over the State of Colorado, we have seen how well-intended folks exercising their Second Amendment rights get mixed up in the legal system through just plain not understanding the law. For that reason, we set about creating a one volume resource that provides any gun owner with a base level of knowledge about laws that gun owners need to know.

The law can be complicated, overlapping, hard to understand, and in some cases, completely arbitrary to the point of confusion. Laws are often written by lawyers for lawyers or are the result of political compromises generating confusing laws that the courts are left to interpret. After years of legal work in the arena of firearms law, we found there did not exist a resource that explained gun law in a manner that was easy for everyone to understand, because understanding the law goes far beyond just reading statutes or regulations. If you do not know either the process by which the law is being administered or how the courts are interpreting the meaning of the law, then you don't understand the full legal story.

That is why we wrote *Colorado Gun Law: Armed And Educated*. It is a one volume guide to the minimum law every gun owner needs to know to stay legal. Whenever appropriate, we tried to present useful analysis and real world applications. Our goal was to explain the "law" so gun owners who wanted to could inform and educate themselves. Thousands of attorney hours have gone into producing this resource, always with the goal in mind of education. Our collective legal experience has taught us well that anyone can become ensnared in the legal system. Many people firmly believe that "it" can't happen to them. Even people that have never been in trouble before find themselves in the world of law, lawyers, and law enforcement through ignorance of the law.

We are committed to helping protect Second Amendment rights for all legal gun owners. It is our passion and our mission. We want people to know the law, because only through eternal vigilance will we protect our cherished right to bear arms. If you own a gun, the laws concerning firearms and their use apply to you. Ignorance of the law is not a valid legal excuse. Therefore, if you want to stay legal, know the law!

CHAPTER ONE
BRIEF LEGAL HISTORY OF THE RIGHT TO BEAR ARMS AND THE LAWS REGULATING FIREARMS

I. Introduction and overview

To fully understand gun rights today in Colorado or the United States, one should start first at the beginning: the formation document for our federal government, the United States Constitution. The Constitution was written without any enumerated guaranteed individual rights. The founding fathers thought it obvious and apparent that individuals had rights; therefore, there was no reason to elucidate them in a document that was supposed to control the government. James Madison also thought that by naming certain rights, it would imply that those were the only rights an individual possessed. After much discussion, and a complete change of opinion by Madison, the lack of enumerated rights was remedied in the first Congressional session and the state ratification process. When the dust settled, ten amendments were added to the Constitution; these ten amendments are the Bill of Rights. It is the Second Amendment that concerns firearms specifically, though throughout this book we will reference many others, including the Fourth and Fifth Amendment that both affect your rights to bear arms and the fundamental rights for us all.

II. Do I have a constitutional right as an individual to keep and bear arms?

Yes; the United States Supreme Court has decided that an individual has a constitutionally given right to keep and bear arms that flows from the Second Amendment, which states simply:

> *A well-regulated Militia, being necessary to the security of a free State, the right of the people to keep and bear Arms, shall not be infringed.*

From a plain reading, there are two important parts to this amendment: first, that a well-regulated militia is necessary to the security of a free state, and second, that there is a right of the people to keep and bear arms. For years, before the issue was decided, anti-gun activists have tried to argue that the Second Amendment only applied to "militias" and not to individuals. Luckily, this argument is not the law. Nevertheless, despite the Supreme Court rulings stating otherwise, this myth seems to persist. What do these parts of the Second Amendment mean? Are they the same, or are they different?

A. _What is a "Well-Regulated Militia?"_

As we discussed earlier, the first part of the Second Amendment references a "well-regulated militia." What is a well-regulated militia? The U.S. Supreme Court has held what this phrase does and does not mean. In 1939, in the case of _United States v. Miller_, 307 U.S. 174 (1939) (ironically, a ruling that upheld firearms regulation), the court defined a Militia as comprising "all males physically capable of acting in concert for the common defense." Based on how the amendment was drafted, the Court stated, it was clear that the Militia pre-dated Article I of the Constitution, because unlike armies and navies, it did not have to be created by Congress. What then is "well-regulated" per the court? It is exactly what it sounds like: the imposition of discipline and training. So, is this just the National Guard? No.

In the case of _D.C. v. Heller_, 554 U.S. 570 (2008), the Supreme Court stated that the well-regulated militia is not the state's military forces, but a separate entity altogether. The Supreme Court stated that the word "militia" referred to the body of the people, and they—the people—were required to keep a centralized government in check. The Supreme Court considered and rejected the position that the National Guard is the current militia under the Second Amendment.

B. *How has the phrase "right to keep and bear arms" been interpreted by the courts?*

One of the first cases to directly deal with the Second Amendment was *United States v. Miller*. In *Miller*, the Supreme Court found that the National Firearms Act ("NFA"), which imposed registration requirements on machine guns, short-barreled weapons, destructive devices, and other similarly unique firearms, did not violate the Second Amendment. The Court used the reasoning that possession of weapons regulated by the NFA did not reasonably relate to the preservation or efficiency of a well-regulated militia, therefore, the NFA was held constitutional.

Court fight where it all began: *United States v. Miller*

United States v. Miller (1939)

The facts:

Defendants, Miller and Layton, transported a double barrel 12-gauge shotgun with a barrel length of less than 18 inches from Oklahoma to Arkansas, and were being prosecuted under the National Firearms Act (which required certain types of firearms to be registered and a tax to be paid). Defendants challenged the NFA as an unconstitutional violation of the Second Amendment.

The legal holdings:

Upheld the National Firearms Act as Constitutional.

An interesting quirk of history in the Miller case (and not a shining moment for the legal system) is that Miller's attorney never appeared at the arguments before the U.S. Supreme Court because he was court-appointed and had not been paid. There was no written brief and no legal representation at oral arguments by the party arguing that the law was unconstitutional. The Court only heard the government's side. To make matters worse, Miller was shot to death before the decision was rendered.

C. *69 years later, the Supreme Court interprets the Second Amendment again: D.C. v. Heller*

It would be 69 years after *Miller* until the U.S. Supreme Court addressed the Second Amendment directly again, except this time the Court would hear both the government's and the defendant's arguments. Fortunately, freedom and Second Amendment rights prevailed in court that day. The Court held that individuals have a right to keep and bear arms.

District of Columbia v. Heller (2008)

The Facts

Heller applied for a handgun ownership permit and was denied; without such a permit, D.C. required that all firearms (including rifles and shotguns) be kept unloaded and disassembled, or bound by a trigger lock, even in a person's own home.

The Legal Holdings

1. The Supreme Court found that the Second Amendment protects an individual right of firearms ownership for purposes of self-defense, not connected with any militia or military purposes; it further elaborated that individual self-defense is 'the central component" of the Second Amendment. Further, handguns are the primary defensive weapon of choice and are protected by the Second Amendment.

2. A well-regulated militia is not the state's military forces.

3. The Court also discussed what the phrase "bear arms" meant: "wear, bear, or carry... upon the person or in clothing or in a pocket, for the purpose... of being armed and ready for offensive or defensive action in a case of conflict with another person."

4. The D.C. regulation was held to be unconstitutional.

5. The Court concluded that like other rights, the right to bear arms is not completely absolute. Reasonable provisions and restrictions have been upheld.

Keep in mind *D.C. v. Heller* was a split 5-4 decision; only one justice away from a completely different outcome, where the Second Amendment (according to the dissent) had "outlived its usefulness and should be ignored."

D. *Can states ignore the Second Amendment? McDonald v. City of Chicago*

D.C. v. Heller was fantastic, but there was a slight quirk: The District of Columbia is under the exclusive jurisdiction of Congress and is not part of any state. Therefore, the case shed no light on the question of what states can do when it comes to regulating or banning firearms. How do state constitutions interact with the Second Amendment and can states ban guns outright? *McDonald v. City of Chicago* sought to answer these questions.

McDonald v. City of Chicago, 561 U.S. 742(2010)
The Facts
McDonald v. City of Chicago was decided in 2010; Chicago ordinance banned handgun possession (among other gun regulations). McDonald was a 76-year-old retired maintenance engineer who wanted a handgun for self-defense. Chicago required that all handguns had to be registered, but refused all handgun registration after a 1982 citywide handgun ban.
The Legal Holdings
The Supreme Court held that the Second Amendment is fully applicable to the States and that individual self-defense is "the central component" of the Second Amendment. Therefore, the Second Amendment prohibits states from enacting bans on handguns for self-protection in the home.

E. *Legal limitations of the right to keep and bear arms*

The U.S. Supreme Court has stated: "Of course the right [to keep and bear arms] was not unlimited, just as the First Amendment's right of free speech was not." Courts may have struggled over the years with what the Second Amendment means, but they have been resolute that there is an element of self-defense. The *Heller* Court stated that, "The Second Amendment does not protect the right to carry arms for any sort of confrontation," focusing their decision on self-defense. Further, the *Miller* Court stated that the weapons protected were those "in common use at the time" of the decision. This is supported by historical traditions of prohibiting the carry of "dangerous and unusual weapons" that are commonly used by criminals offensively, as opposed to by law-abiding citizens for defensive purposes.

The Second Amendment does not protect against prohibitions on firearm possession by felons and the mentally ill; *Heller* made this point in its decision, and many circuit court cases such as *U.S. v. Everist* follow the same reasoning. The Court of Appeals in *U.S. v. Everist* states that the Second Amendment is subject to, "limited narrowly tailored specific exceptions or restrictions for particular cases that are reasonable; it is clear that felons, infants and those of unsound mind may be prohibited from possessing firearms." *U.S. v. Everist*, 368 F.3d 517, 519 (5th Cir. 2004). Along this same train of thought, the *Heller* Court did not want to eliminate laws that imposed conditions and qualifications on the commercial sales of firearms.

Practical Legal Tip:

Currently, the two most important court decisions fortifying our gun rights are *Heller* and *McDonald*. But those cases were very, very close to going the other way! Both were decided by a 5-4 majority, meaning that if only one other Supreme Court Justice had decided differently, our individual right to possess and carry firearms could have been severely limited. -*Doug*

It also does not mean that the Second Amendment includes the right to carry anywhere a person wants. The *Heller* Court stated that their opinion was not meant to allow the carrying of firearms in sensitive places such as schools and certain government buildings.

III. Major firearms statutes every gun owner needs to know

At the Federal level, there are plenty of laws and regulations that concern firearms, but this section will focus on some of the more major legislative actions that all gun owners need to know.

A. *Gun Control Act of 1968*

The Gun Control Act of 1968 ("GCA") was enacted by Congress to "provide for better control of the interstate traffic of firearms." This law is primarily focused on regulating interstate commerce in firearms by generally prohibiting interstate firearms transfers except among licensed manufacturers, dealers, and importers, however, interstate commerce has been held by the courts to include nearly everything. It also contains classes of individuals to whom firearms should not be sold. For the specifics of who can and can't purchase a firearm, please refer to Chapter Three. Among other things, the GCA created the Federal Firearms License ("FFL") system, imposed importation restrictions on military surplus rifles (adding a "sporting purpose test" and a "points system" for handguns), and marking requirements.

B. *The Brady Handgun Violence Prevention Act*

The Brady Handgun Violence Prevention Act, commonly referred to as the Brady Law, instituted federal background checks (the National Instant Criminal Background Check System or NICS) for firearm purchasers in the United States. It also prohibited certain persons from purchasing firearms; for more information on who can or can't purchase a firearm, see Chapter Three.

C. *The Firearm Owners' Protection Act*

The Firearm Owners' Protection Act ("FOPA") revised many provisions of the original Gun Control Act, including "reforms" on the inspection of FFLs. This same Act updated the list of individuals prohibited from purchasing firearms that was introduced by the GCA. The FOPA also banned the ownership by civilians of any machine gun that was not registered under the NFA as of May 19, 1986. FOPA created what is called a "safe passage" provision of the law, which allows for traveling across states with a firearm. Finally, FOPA prohibited a registry for non-NFA items that directly linked firearms to their owners.

D. *The Public Safety and Recreational Firearms Use Protection Act*

The Public Safety and Recreational Firearms Use Protection Act, commonly referred to as the *Federal Assault Weapons Ban*, was a subsection of the Violent Crime Control and Law Enforcement Act of 1994. It banned outright the manufacture and transfer of certain semi-automatic firearms and magazines. This ban grandfathered-in previously legally owned weapons, but no prohibited firearm could be acquired or manufactured after September 13, 1994. With great foresight, the drafters of this law included a so-called "sunset provision," that stated the ban would expire ten years later unless renewed. The ban expired in 2004, and all attempts to renew have been unsuccessful.

E. *The National Firearms Act*

The National Firearms Act ("NFA") regulates and imposes a statutory excise tax on the manufacture and transfer of certain types of firearms and weapons: machine guns, short-barreled weapons, suppressors, explosive devices, and "any other weapons" (AOWs can range from everyday objects that are actually firearms, such as an umbrella that can fire a round, to other weapons the ATF decides to place in this category). The tax is $200 if you make or transfer an item (other than for the transfer of AOWs); the tax for transferring AOWs is $5. The NFA is also referred to as Title II of the federal firearms laws. For more information on how to navigate the NFA while remaining legal, please see Chapter Fourteen.

IV. Do Coloradans have a right to keep and bear arms in the Colorado Constitution?

Yes. The Colorado Constitution acknowledges the right to keep and bear arms in Article II, Section 13. This provision of the Colorado Constitution has never been amended. Article II, Section 13 reads:

> *The right of no person to keep and bear arms in defense of his home, person and property, or in aid of the civil power when thereto legally summoned, shall be called in question; but nothing herein contained shall be construed to justify the practice of carrying concealed weapons.*
>
> *Colo. Const. art. II, § 13*

The more observant will notice that, as opposed to the Second Amendment of the United States Constitution, Colorado's version specifies that the right is defensive in nature and does not extend to the carrying of concealed weapons. Chapters Four through Seven of this book fully cover all of the ways a Coloradan may legally use a weapon "in defense of his home, person and property, or in aid of the civil power when thereto legally summoned." Chapters Eight and Nine fully cover Colorado's laws on concealed carry.

A. *Can Colorado prohibit local municipalities from making certain gun laws?*

Yes. The Colorado Legislature can and does prohibit local municipalities from making certain gun laws by the legal doctrine known as "preemption." A preemption statute is a mechanism by which the Colorado legislature sets certain areas off limits to local governments, which helps ensure the uniformity of law across the state, in this case, firearms law.

B. *What local governments may not regulate*

Several of Colorado's preemption statutes state what areas of firearm law municipalities are not allowed to regulate. Colorado Revised Statutes section 29-11.7-102 prevents local governments from maintaining a list or other form or record or database of:

- Persons who purchase or exchange firearms or who leave firearms for repair or sale on consignment;
- Persons who transfer firearms, unless the persons are federally licensed firearms dealers; [or]
- The descriptions, including serial numbers, of firearms purchased, transferred, exchanged, or left for repair or sale on consignment.

Under section 18-12-201 of the Colorado Revised Statutes, the state has complete authority over the issuance of permits to carry concealed handguns for self-defense. Therefore, local governments are prohibited from creating their own permitting regimes. See Chapters Eight and Nine for more information on concealed-carry permits.

Section 29-11.7-103 of the Colorado Revised Statutes prohibits local governments from enacting "an ordinance, regulation, or other law that prohibits the sale, purchase, or possession of a firearm that a person may lawfully sell, purchase, or possess under state or federal law."

Section 18-12-105.6 of the Colorado Revised Statutes prevents local governments from passing "local ordinances regarding firearms in private vehicles." Specifically, "no municipality, county, or city and county shall have the authority to enact or enforce any ordinance or resolution that would restrict a person's ability to travel with a weapon in a private automobile or other private means of conveyance for hunting or for lawful protection of a person's or another's person or property while traveling into, through, or within, a municipal, county, or city and county jurisdiction, regardless of the number of times the person stops in a jurisdiction."

With the exception of a formal written complaint of a resident of the jurisdiction who lived there prior to January 1, 1985, section 25-12-109 of the Colorado Revised Statutes prohibits local governments from seeking a criminal or civil penalty against a sport shooting range or its owners or operators on the grounds of noise emanating from such range that results from the normal operation or use of the qualifying shooting range. Under this section, a "qualifying sport shooting range" "means any public or private establishment, whether operating for profit or not for profit, that operates an area for the discharge or other use of firearms or other equipment" for various types of" recreational or competitive shooting, or professional training."

Lastly, section 30-15-302 of the Colorado Revised Statutes prohibits the "board of county commissioners of any county" from preventing "the discharge of any firearm in shooting galleries or in any private grounds or residence" in unincorporated territory, "under circumstances when such firearm can be discharged in such a manner as to prevent" the bullet from leaving the limits of such "shooting gallery, grounds, or residence." Notice that this limitation only applies to areas that are unincorporated, that is, areas of the county that are not part of a town or city. Further, under section 30-15-302, a board of county commissioners may not prohibit the discharge of firearms in unincorporated territory if the territory in question "has an average population density" of less than "one hundred persons per square mile."

C. *What local governments may regulate*

Local municipalities under state law are empowered to and may regulate the following:

- The discharge of firearms within unincorporated areas of a county with "an average population density" of "one hundred persons per square mile," or more. This power to regulate is subject to other limitations, as explained above. *See* Colorado Revised Statutes sections 30-15-302 and 30-15-303;
- Noise pollution, except in the case of sports shooting ranges, as explained above. *See* Colorado Revised Statutes sections 25-12-103, 25-12-104, and 25-12-105;
- The "open carrying of a firearm in a building or specific area." The local government must post signs on the building or area which inform people that the open carry of firearms is prohibited in that building or area. *See* Colorado Revised Statutes section 29-11.7-104; or
- The use of firearms on "public recreation lands and facilities" owned and operated by a county. *See* Colorado Revised Statutes section 29-7-101.

In addition to these regulatory powers specifically granted by statute to local governments, Colorado Revised Statutes section 31-15-103 grants municipalities the "power to make and publish ordinances not inconsistent with the laws of this state . . . which are necessary and proper to provide for the safety, preserve the health, promote the prosperity, and improve the morals, order, comfort, and convenience of such municipality and [its] inhabitants." This general grant of authority to pass ordinances is limited to laws that are consistent with the laws of Colorado. When determining whether an ordinance is consistent with state law, a court will consider whether the subject matter of the ordinance was one of "local concern, statewide concern, or mixed local and statewide concern." *See, e.g., Webb v. City of Black Hawk*, 295 P.3d 480, 485-86 (Colo. 2013). If a matter is of local concern, then the local ordinance preempts state law on the subject. *Id.* Alternatively, if the matter is of statewide concern, the ordinance is preempted by state law on the subject. *Id.* Finally, if the matter is of mixed local and statewide concern, then the ordinance is only allowed to the extent that it doesn't conflict with state law on the matter. *Id.*

In practice, a court will examine each city ordinance regulating firearms on a case-by-case basis to determine if a conflict with state law exists. For example, following the state's enactment of several preemption statutes, in 2004, the City of Denver sued the state to determine the validity of several city ordinances. City and County of Denver v. State, No. 03-CV-3809, 2004 WL 5212983 (Colo. Dist. Ct. Nov. 5, 2004). One of Denver's ordinances prohibited open carry anywhere in the city. The court held that, even though section 29-11.7-104 only allows local governments to restrict open carry in buildings and specific areas where notices have been posted, Denver could prevent open carry throughout the city because of the city's unique character as "the most densely populated area of Colorado," which meant that open carry was a matter of local concern in Denver. *Id.* Similarly, the court also upheld Denver's ordinance banning the sale or possession of "assault weapons" and "Saturday night special[s]" on the basis that Denver's unique character makes such weapons a matter of local concern. *Id.* The court held this despite the fact that section 29-11.7-103 of the Colorado Revised Statutes prohibits local governments from passing ordinances that restrict the sale or possession of firearms that are allowable under state law, which includes "assault weapons" and "Saturday night special[s]." *Id.* It may seem that this decision effectively does away with state preemption on firearm law; however, the court clearly indicates that it reached its decision based on the uniqueness of Denver. It remains to be seen if another municipality could successfully argue that similar ordinances covered matters of local concern.

CHAPTER TWO
LEGAL DEFINITIONS AND CLASSIFICATIONS OF FIREARMS: WHAT IS LEGAL?

I. Introduction and overview

Before discussing the law of firearms and all its different facets, it is important first to understand what the law defines as a "firearm." Firearms laws are governed on both the federal and state levels; therefore, throughout this chapter we will explore the interactions federal and state law have on the purchase and possession of firearms.

A. *What is a firearm?*
Federal definition

Under the federal law, a firearm is defined as "any weapon (including a starter gun) which will or is designed to or may readily be converted to expel a projectile by the action of an explosive." 18 U.S.C. § 921(a)(3). The federal definition of a firearm also includes the frame or receiver of any such weapon, any firearm muffler or silencer, or any "destructive device." This is similar to the Colorado definition, but not exactly the same.

Colorado definition

In the State of Colorado, for purposes of applying state and not federal law, a firearm is defined by section 18-1-901(3)(h) of the Colorado Revised Statutes. This section defines a firearm as "any handgun, automatic, revolver, pistol, rifle, shotgun, or other instrument or device capable or intended to be capable of discharging bullets, cartridges, or other explosive charges."

Why might it be important to know the different ways the term "firearm" is defined under federal and state law? It is because if a person finds themselves charged with a crime by federal authorities, the federal definition of a firearm will apply. Likewise, if the charge is under a violation of state law, then the Colorado definition will apply. Thus, the primary difference in the definitions and their impact on a defendant charged with a crime involving a firearm lies with how a person may be in trouble with the law. As we will see in the next section, the definitions of what does and does not constitute a firearm, although similar in many aspects, contain an array of differences that make violating the law unwittingly easy.

B. *Definitions for handguns, rifles, and shotguns*

In addition to defining what constitutes a firearm, federal and Colorado law further classify and define firearms into categories of handguns and long guns (rifles and shotguns). This section will provide an overview of how federal and state laws classify firearms as well as the physical requirements for a firearm to be legal.

1. What is a handgun?

Ultimately, looking at the federal definition, the term handgun simply refers to any firearm that is designed to be fired by using only one hand. While it is true that most individuals will use two hands when firing a handgun for safety and accuracy purposes, the emphasis in the legal definition of a handgun rests purely in its design to be held or fired with a single hand. Conversely, Colorado law focuses more on the barrel length than hand configuration.

Federal definition

The United States Code of Federal Regulations defines a handgun as "(a) any firearm which has a short stock and is designed to be held and fired by the use of a single hand; and (b) any combination of parts from which a firearm described in paragraph (a) can be assembled." 27 CFR § 478.11.

Colorado definition

Under Colorado law, handguns are defined by section 18-12-101 of the Colorado Revised Statutes. A handgun "means a pistol, revolver, or other firearm of any description, loaded or unloaded, from which any shot, bullet, or other missile can be discharged, the length of the barrel of which, not including any revolving, detachable, or magazine breech, does not exceed twelve inches."

2. <u>What is a rifle?</u>

Federal law defines a rifle as "a weapon designed or redesigned, made or remade, and intended to be fired from the shoulder, and designed or redesigned and made or remade to use the energy of the explosive in a fixed metallic cartridge to fire only a single projectile through a rifled bore for each single pull of the trigger." 27 CFR § 478.11. In addition, a legal rifle must have a barrel length of 16 inches or greater, and includes any weapon made from a rifle which is at least 26 inches overall in length. Colorado law does not provide a definition for a rifle, but it does classify illegal short-barreled firearms, including rifles in the same manner as the federal definition. *See* Colorado Revised Statutes § 18-12-101(h).

Minimum lengths

In order for a rifle to not be subject to the National Firearms Act or classified as a short-barreled firearm under Colorado law, it must have a <u>barrel</u> of at least 16 inches in length. The ATF procedure for measuring barrel length is accomplished by measuring from the closed bolt (or breech-face) to the furthermost end of the barrel or permanently attached muzzle device. Below is an example of a rifle that does not meet the minimum barrel length requirement after measurement:

The barrel is measured by inserting a dowel rod into the barrel until the rod stops against the bolt or breech-face. The rod is then marked at the furthermost end of the barrel or permanently attached muzzle device, withdrawn from the barrel, and then measured. Any measurement of less than 16 inches will classify the rifle as being short-barreled under Colorado and federal law and subject the firearm to the NFA. For short-barreled rifles and other non-compliant firearms, *see* Chapter Fourteen, which discusses the NFA. *Note:* for overall length, rifles with collapsible/folding-stocks are measured from the "extreme ends," unless the stock is "easily detachable," in which case it is measured without the stock.

3. What is a shotgun?

The federal definition of a shotgun is "a weapon designed or redesigned, made or remade, and intended to be fired from the shoulder, and designed or redesigned and made or remade to use the energy of the explosive in a fixed shotgun shell to fire through a smooth bore either a number of ball shot or a single projectile for each single pull of the trigger." 27 CFR § 478.11. Like rifles, legal shotguns have requirements for minimum barrel and overall lengths. Shotgun barrels must be at least 18 inches long and must also comply with the same 26 inch overall length requirement. Under Colorado law, shotguns are classified in the same manner as they are under federal law. *See* Colorado Revised Statutes § 18-12-101(i).

Minimum lengths

In order for a shotgun to not be subject to the National Firearms Act or classified as a short-barreled firearm under Colorado law, it must have a barrel of at least 18 inches in length. The ATF procedure for measuring the barrel length of a shotgun is the same as it is for a rifle. Below is an example of a shotgun that does not meet the minimum barrel length requirement after measurement:

Any measurement of less than 18 inches will classify the shotgun as a short-barreled weapon and illegal under Colorado and federal law unless the requirements of the NFA are satisfied. For short-barreled shotguns and other non-compliant firearms, *see* Chapter Fourteen. *Note:* the collapsible/folding-stock rule that applies to rifles applies to shotguns as well.

C. *Antique firearms and replica firearms*
When is a firearm not legally a "firearm?" It is when the law defines it as not being one, such as with "antique" firearms.

1. Federal definition of "antique firearm"
1898 or prior
The federal definition of firearm under Title 18, Section 921 of the United States Code excludes "antique firearms." Even though an antique firearm still functions ballistically similar to a "modern" firearm, under federal law, antique firearms are regulated differently, if at all. An antique firearm under federal law includes any firearm with a matchlock, flintlock, or percussion cap, or similar type of ignition system manufactured in or before 1898 or any replica of a firearm just described so long as the replica "is not designed or redesigned for using rimfire or conventional centerfire fixed ammunition, or uses rimfire or centerfire ammunition that is no longer manufactured in the United States and is not readily available in ordinary channels of commerce." 18 U.S.C. §§ 921(16)(A) and (B). So, an "antique firearm" is not a "firearm" for purposes of federal regulation.

Muzzle loading
In addition, federal law does not consider "any muzzle loading rifle, muzzle loading shotgun, or muzzle loading pistol, which is designed to use black powder, or a black powder substitute, and which cannot use fixed ammunition" as a firearm. Be aware, however, that the term "antique firearm" does not include any weapon which incorporates a firearm frame or receiver, any firearm which is converted into a muzzle loading weapon, or any muzzle loading weapon which can be readily converted to fire fixed ammunition by replacing the barrel, bolt, breechlock, or any combination of these parts. 18 U.S.C. § 921(a)(16)(C).

2. Colorado definition of "antique firearm"
Colorado defines "antique firearm" simply by citing the federal definition. *See* Colorado Revised Statutes sections 12-26.1-105 and 18-12-112. These two statutes exempt transfers of "antique firearms" from background check requirements for purchases at gun shows and for private transfers. *See id.*

D. *What firearms are illegal?*
Under Colorado Revised Statutes § 18-12-102, certain firearms are prohibited or illegal under Colorado law. These firearms include:

- machine guns;
- short-barreled firearms; and
- firearm silencers or suppressors.

This section also makes illegal other weapons such as metallic knuckles, ballistic knives, blackjacks, gas guns, gravity knives and switchblades. However, a person may have a defense to prosecution under state law if he or she has complied with the requirements of the National Firearms Act (*see* Chapter Fourteen for more information on the NFA).

Under federal law, the same firearms that are prohibited weapons under state law are regulated by the National Firearms Act. These firearms include:

- short-barreled shotguns;
- short-barreled rifles;
- machine guns;
- firearm silencers or suppressors;
- weapons or devices capable of being concealed on the person from which a shot can be fired;
- pistols or revolvers having a smooth bore (as opposed to rifled bore) barrel designed to fire a fixed shotgun shell;
- pistols or revolvers with a vertical handgrip;
- destructive devices; and
- weapons classified as "Any Other Weapon," or AOWs.

See 26 U.S.C. § 5845. For more information on these weapons, *see* Chapter Fourteen discussing the National Firearms Act.

On the surface, the prohibited firearms list is similar between both federal and state law with the primary difference existing merely in classification only (federal law classifies most of these items as firearms whereas Colorado classifies the items not as firearms but as dangerous or illegal weapons). However, although these firearms and/or weapons are prohibited by statute, it does not mean a person absolutely cannot possess one. Many of these weapons may be legally possessed with proper documentation under the National Firearms Act. For more information on these prohibited weapons and the NFA, *see* Chapter Fourteen.

E.   *How big of a gun can a person possess?*
Federal law dictates that any firearm which has any barrel with a bore of more than one-half inch in diameter is a "destructive device" and is subject to the National Firearms Act. Possession of any such firearm without the proper paperwork associated with NFA firearms is illegal. Note, however, that some shotguns are

regulated differently. For more information on destructive devices and the NFA, *see* Chapter Fourteen.

II. Ammunition and the law

No discussion concerning firearms laws would be complete without examining laws concerning the ammunition that goes into a firearm. Just like firearms, the law regulates the possession, sale, and even composition of "legal" ammunition. This section addresses the essential aspects of the law concerning ammunition and what gun owners need to know, both under federal and Colorado law.

A. *How does the law define ammunition?*

Under federal law, the term ammunition is defined under 18 U.S.C. § 921(a)(17)(A) and means "ammunition or cartridge cases, primers, bullets, or propellant powder designed for use in any firearm." Thus, the federal definition of ammunition includes the finished product and all of the components in making a round of ammunition. However, the federal definition of ammunition does not include (1) any shotgun shot or pellet not designed for use as the single, complete projectile load for one shotgun hull or casing, nor (2) any unloaded, non-metallic shotgun hull or casing not having a primer. *See* 27 CFR § 478.11. In other words, individual ammunition components are legally defined as ammunition themselves, even if they are simply parts, except that shotgun ammunition components, if not completely assembled, are not ammunition. Under Colorado law, there is no statutory definition for mere "ammunition" of any kind.

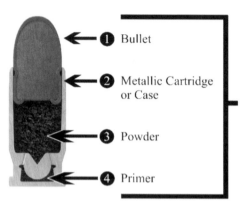

1. Bullet

2. Metallic Cartridge or Case

3. Powder

4. Primer

A complete round of ammunition or any enumerated sub-component is ammunition as defined in federal law.

B. *Is there a difference in ammunition that is used in different types of firearms?*

Yes. Ammunition can be divided into two classifications: ammunition for handguns and ammunition for long guns. Long gun ammunition can be further divided into ammunition for rifles and ammunition for shotguns.

Handgun ammunition means ammunition that is meant to be fired from a handgun, and it comes in many different calibers. Rifle ammunition is meant to be fired from a rifle and is similar to handgun ammunition in that it comes in many different calibers. Shotgun ammunition, on the other hand, comes in self-contained cartridges loaded with some form of shot or a shotgun slug which is designed to be fired from a shotgun.

Practical Legal Tip:

Even with firearms, having the right tool for the job is important. Practically speaking, you should choose the firearm and ammo that you feel most comfortable using. At the end of the day, <u>why</u> you started shooting is always more important than <u>what</u> you chose to shoot with. *-Stanley*

C. *What ammunition is illegal?*

Armor-piercing handgun ammunition is the only ammunition which has explicit prohibitions under federal law. The federal definition of armor-piercing ammunition is found in 18 U.S.C. § 921(a)(17)(B) and means "[1] a projectile or projectile core which may be used in a handgun and which is constructed entirely (excluding the presence of traces of other substances) from one or a combination of tungsten alloys, steel, iron, brass, bronze, beryllium copper, or depleted uranium; or [2] a full jacketed projectile larger than .22 caliber designed and intended for use in a handgun and whose jacket has a weight of more than 25% of the total weight of the projectile."

Under federal law, while there is no blanket prohibition on the mere possession of armor-piercing ammunition, it is prohibited under four conditions:

1. *Prohibition one: it is illegal to make or import armor-piercing ammunition.* Under 18 U.S.C. § 922(a)(7) it is unlawful for any person to manufacture or import armor-piercing ammunition unless (1) the manufacture of such ammunition is for the use of the United States, any department or agency of the United States, any state, or any department, agency, or political subdivision of a state; (2) the manufacture of such ammunition is for the purpose of exportation; or (3) the manufacture or importation of such ammunition is for the purpose of testing or experimentation and has been authorized by the United States Attorney General.

2. *Prohibition two: it is illegal for manufacturers and importers to sell or deliver armor-piercing ammunition.* Federal law states that it is unlawful for any manufacturer or importer to sell or deliver armor-piercing ammunition unless such sale or delivery is (1) for the use of the United States, any department or agency of the United States, any state, or any department, agency, or political subdivision of a state; (2) for the purpose of exportation; or (3) for the purpose of testing

or experimentation and has been authorized by the United States Attorney General. *See* 18 U.S.C. § 922(a)(8).

3. *Prohibition three: an FFL or other license-holder cannot sell or deliver armor-piercing ammunition without the proper documentation.* Under 18 U.S.C. § 922(b)(5), it is unlawful for any licensed importer, licensed manufacturer, licensed dealer, or licensed collector to sell or deliver armor-piercing ammunition to any person unless the licensee notes in his records, as required under 18 U.S.C. § 923, the name, age, and place of residence of such person if the person is an individual, or the identity and principal and local places of business of such person if the person is a corporation or other business entity.

4. *Prohibition four: it is illegal to possess armor-piercing ammunition if a person is involved in a crime of violence or a drug-trafficking crime.* Pursuant to 18 U.S.C. § 924(c)(5), it is unlawful for "any person who, during and in relation to any crime of violence or drug trafficking crime (including a crime of violence or drug trafficking crime that provides for an enhanced punishment if committed by the use of a deadly or dangerous weapon or device) for which the person may be prosecuted in a court of the United States, use or carries armor piercing ammunition." Individuals who use or carry armor-piercing ammunition in the commission of a crime of violence or during a drug-trafficking crime are subject to heightened sentencing standards should they be found guilty.

As you can see, while possession of armor-piercing ammunition itself is not illegal, obtaining armor-piercing ammunition without violating one of the foregoing prohibitions is almost impossible.

By definition, it should be noted that not all ammunition that *can* pierce armor is actually armor-piercing. The federal definition contains specific requirements for the composition of a particular round of in order to make it armor-piercing. Federal law requires that the ammunition be comprised of certain alloys. For instance, 5.7 millimeter ammunition for an FN57 handgun or a PS90 rifle, while capable of piercing armor based on its size and velocity, is not ammunition that is armor-piercing as defined under the law because such ammunition, sold commercially, is primarily for sporting purposes according to the ATF.

PS90

D. *Does modifying traditional ammunition make it illegal?*

No, outside of armor-piercing ammunition, there is no handgun or long gun ammunition that is prohibited under the federal law. In fact, there are many examples of hollow-point rounds which are modified in a way to become more lethal such as the R.I.P. ammunition, Black Talons, *etc.*, which star outward upon impact in order to do more internal damage. Such ammunition, though it looks different from traditional ammunition rounds, is perfectly legal.

Factory and Expanded Hollow Point Rounds

E. *Is it legal to use ammunition that works in both handguns and rifles?*

Yes, except for armor-piercing ammunition that is used principally in handguns. This is because the federal definition of armor-piercing ammunition contemplates handguns only. Armor-piercing ammunition for a rifle is perfectly legal, though it may complicate matters at trial in trying to demonstrate to the jury any differentiation. Beyond armor-piercing ammunition, it is legal to use ammunition that is available in common calibers and that functions in both handguns and rifles.

With a solid understanding of what is and is not a firearm and ammunition, as well as what firearms and ammunition a person may legally possess without the necessity of obtaining additional documentation, we are now ready to move to the next chapter discussing the purchase and possession of firearms.

CHAPTER THREE
PURCHASING, TRANSFERRING, AND POSSESSING FIREARMS

I. Laws of purchasing and possessing: the basics

The laws of purchasing, selling, gifting, or otherwise transferring a firearm are distinct and different from the laws of possessing a firearm. It may be legal for someone to possess a firearm, and it still be illegal for them to "purchase" the firearm. Further, each of these sets of laws for "purchasing" or "possessing" has a federal and a state component both of which must be satisfied in order to start on the right side of the law.

On the federal level, the Bureau of Alcohol, Tobacco, Firearms and Explosives ("ATF") is charged with regulating firearms including sales, purchases, and transfers through Federal Firearms Licensees ("FFLs" or "dealers"), however, a multitude of federal agencies can be involved in any given firearms law investigation or police function most currently falling under a branch of the U.S. Department of Homeland Security.

A. *What is an FFL?*

A FFL, or Federal Firearms License, is a license required by federal law for those persons or entities that are engaged in the business of buying and selling firearms. A federal firearms licensee is often called an "FFL" or "dealer." When an individual purchases, sells, or transfers a firearm through a dealer, the FFL and the individual must both comply with specific federal law requirements, paperwork, and procedures concerning the buying, selling, or transferring of those firearms. These requirements will be addressed throughout this chapter.

B. *Who must obtain an FFL?*

Federal law requires a federal firearms license if a person is engaged in business as a firearms dealer, manufacturer, or importer. For the purposes of our discussion in this chapter, a person is engaged in the business when the person "devotes time, attention, and labor to dealing in firearms as a regular course of trade or business with the principal objective of livelihood and profit through the repetitive purchase and resale of firearms, but such term shall not include a person who makes occasional sales, exchanges, or purchases of firearms for the enhancement of a personal collection or for a hobby, or who sells all or part of his personal collection of firearms." 18 U.S.C. § 921(a)(21)(C).

C. *What is a private sale?*
A private sale is just what it sounds like: a sale, purchase, or transfer of a firearm by parties that are not licensed dealers. A private sale is perfectly legal for both handguns and long guns in Colorado, as long as all other legal requirements are met. We will discuss the ins-and-outs of private sales in greater detail in this chapter under Section IV.

D. *What is the legal age to purchase and possess a firearm?*
Federal law controls all FFL firearms transactions and requires that a person be 21 years of age or older before they may purchase a handgun or 18 for the purchase of a long gun.

Under federal law, a person must be at least 18 years of age in order to possess a handgun or ammunition for a handgun. *See* 18 U.S.C. § 922(x)(2). Unlike the law on purchasing a long gun, there is no federal age requirement for the possession of a rifle or shotgun.

E. *What is the legal age to possess a firearm under Colorado Law?*
Because of the way Colorado law is constructed, it makes the most sense to discuss the legal age of possession before talking about the legal age to purchase firearms. Colorado Revised Statutes section 18-12-108.5 prohibits anyone under the age of 18 from possessing a handgun, with some exceptions. Persons

under the age of 18, called "juveniles" by the law, are excepted from Section 18-12-108.5 if they are:

- In attendance at a hunter's safety course or a firearms safety course;
- Lawfully practicing with a firearm or target shooting at an authorized shooting range or in an area where the discharge of a firearm is not prohibited;
- Engaging in an organized competition involving the use of a firearm or participating in or practicing for a performance put on by a non-profit organization that uses firearms as part of the performance;
- Hunting or trapping with a valid license;
- Traveling with an unloaded handgun to any of the above allowed activities;
- Located on the real property of their parent, guardian, or grandparent, and have the permission of a parent or guardian to possess a handgun; or
- Located in their own residence and have the permission of their parent or guardian to possess a handgun for lawful use in self-defense.

What constitutes lawful use in self-defense is covered fully in Chapters Four through Seven. Notice that Section 18-12-108.5 prohibits the possession of handguns only. This section does not apply to other types of firearms.

F. _What is the legal age to purchase a firearm under Colorado law?_
In Colorado law establishes the minimum age to purchase a handgun through reference to the possession statute, section 18-12-108.5, explained above. Under Colorado Revised Statutes section 18-12-108.7, a person who "intentionally, knowingly, or recklessly provides a handgun . . . to any person under the age of 18," in violation of section 18-12-108.5, commits a class 4 felony.

Section 18-12-108.7(3) does allow juveniles to purchase firearms other than handguns with the consent of their parent or legal guardian. However, selling a firearm other than a handgun to a juvenile without the consent of their parent or legal guardian is a class 1 misdemeanor.

G. *Criminal liability for allowing a juvenile access to a firearm*

In addition to governing sales of firearms to juveniles, section 18-12-108.7 also covers non-sale transfers of firearms to juveniles. Just as with sales, any person who "intentionally, knowingly, or recklessly" provides a handgun to a juvenile in violation of section 18-12-108.5 commits a class 4 felony. Also, under section 18-12-108.7(3), it is a class 1 misdemeanor to transfer possession of a firearm other than a handgun to a juvenile without the consent of that juvenile's parent or legal guardian.

In addition, under section 18-12-108.7, if a person knows that a juvenile's conduct violates section 18-12-108.5 and they fail to "make reasonable efforts" to prevent the violation, that person is guilty of "permitting a juvenile to possess a handgun," a class 4 felony. However, a person who permits a juvenile to possess a handgun cannot be charged with a crime under this section if that person "believes that [the] juvenile will physically harm the person if the person attempts to disarm the juvenile or prevent the juvenile from committing a violation of section 18-12-108.5."

II. **Federal law disqualifications for purchasing and possessing firearms**

Federal law lists categories of persons disqualified from legally purchasing and possessing a firearm. This list comprises disqualifications that come from several different pieces of federal legislation including the Gun Control Act of 1968, the Brady Handgun Violence Protection Act, and the Violence Against Women Act. If a person buys or attempts to buy a firearm from an FFL, they must not be disqualified under any of the laws. Before an FFL may sell or otherwise transfer a firearm, the purchaser must fill out an ATF Form 4473. This form makes inquiries into criteria that may disqualify a person to purchase a firearm under federal law. These disqualifications include:

1. if the person is not the actual purchaser of the firearm— also known as a "straw man purchaser;"
2. if the person is under indictment or information in any court for a felony or any other crime for which the judge could imprison the person for more than one year;
3. if the person has ever been convicted in any court for a felony or other crime for which the judge could imprison the person for more than one year;
4. if the person is a fugitive from justice;
5. if the person is an unlawful user of, or addicted to, marijuana, or any depressant, stimulant, narcotic drug, or controlled substance;
6. if the person has ever been adjudicated as mentally defective or has been committed to a mental institution;
7. if the person has been dishonorably discharged from the Armed Forces;
8. if the person is subject to an active protective order restraining the person from harassing, stalking, or threatening the person's child, or an intimate partner or child of such partner;
9. if the person has been convicted in any court for a misdemeanor crime of domestic violence;
10. if the person has ever renounced their United States citizenship;
11. if the person is an alien illegally in the United States; and
12. if the person is admitted under a non-immigrant visa and does not qualify for an exception.

The purchaser must legally affirm that they are not subject to any of the criteria listed above before they may purchase a firearm. If a prospective purchaser answers any question on the form in a manner that indicates they are legally disqualified, it is illegal for the FFL to sell that person the firearm, and it is illegal for the purchaser to complete the transaction or possess the firearm.

A. _Understanding who is disqualified_
   1. Can I buy a firearm for another person?

No. This would be a "straw man" purchase. In order to legally purchase a firearm from a dealer, you must be the "actual purchaser or transferee." If you are not the actual purchaser or transferee, it is illegal for you to complete the transfer or sale under federal law. Purchases for third persons are often called "straw man" purchases and are illegal. If you are not the actual purchaser, beware!

In fact, the ATF has a campaign called "Don't Lie for the Other Guy" that is targeted at (as they term it on their website) detection and deterrence of "straw man" purchases. The ATF website lists numerous examples of prosecutions for "straw man" purchases and a United States Supreme Court case examined and upheld federal law on this matter. _Abramski v. United States_, 134 S.Ct. 2259 (2014).

So who is the "actual" buyer or transferee so as not to be a "straw man?" The ATF states that you are the actual "transferee/buyer if you are purchasing the firearm for yourself or otherwise acquiring the firearm for yourself (_e.g._, redeeming the firearm from pawn/retrieving it from consignment, firearm raffle winner)." The ATF goes on to state "you are also the actual transferee/buyer if you are legitimately purchasing the firearm as a gift for a third party."

Example:

> _Mr. Smith asks Mr. Jones to purchase a firearm for Mr. Smith. Mr. Smith gives Mr. Jones the money for the firearm. Mr. Jones then buys the firearm with Mr. Smith's money and gives Mr. Smith the firearm._

Mr. Jones is not the "actual buyer" (he is legally a "straw man") of the firearm and if Mr. Jones indicates that he is the "actual buyer" of the firearm on ATF Form 4473, he has committed a federal crime. The Supreme Court ruling in *Abramski*, however, did not make "gifts" of firearms illegal.

When completing ATF Form 4473: if a person checks "yes" to the box asking if the person is the "actual purchaser," then that person cannot have engaged in a separate transaction to sell or transfer the firearm privately. Please note: The Supreme Court's ruling held that a person cannot legally purchase a firearm on behalf of another even if the person receiving the firearm would not otherwise be prohibited from making the purchase themselves. So don't buy a firearm for another person no matter how good a friend, relative, or person they are—it is a crime!

FREQUENTLY ASKED QUESTIONS FROM ATF WEBSITE
Q: May I buy a firearm from an FFL as a "gift" for another person?   **A**: Yes.
Editor's note: Instead of the previous example where Mr. Smith paid Mr. Jones to purchase a firearm for him, if Mr. Jones decides to buy a firearm with his own money and then give the firearm to Mr. Smith as a present, then Mr. Jones is the actual buyer/transferee of the firearm. Since Mr. Jones is the actual buyer, there exists no sham or "strawman," and the purchase is legal.
Q: May a parent or guardian purchase a firearm as a gift for a juvenile?   **A**: Yes, however, possession of handguns by juveniles is generally unlawful under federal law. Juveniles may only receive and possess handguns with the written permission of a parent or guardian for limited purposes, *e.g.*, employment, ranching, farming, target practice, or hunting.

See www.atf.gov.

2. A person cannot purchase a firearm if they have been convicted or are under "indictment or information" for a felony or certain misdemeanors

If a person has been convicted of a felony or other crime for which a judge may sentence, or could have sentenced the person to more than one year imprisonment, that person may not legally purchase a firearm (unless the crime was a state misdemeanor punishable by imprisonment of two years or less). *See* 18 U.S.C. § 921(a)(20)(B). Likewise, if a person is under "indictment" or "information" for a felony, or any other crime for which a judge may sentence the person to more than one year imprisonment, that person is disqualified from purchasing a firearm. An "indictment" or "information" is a formal accusation of a crime punishable by imprisonment for a term exceeding one year. It is important to point out that the actual sentence received is not the determining factor for disqualification, rather, it is the possible maximum sentence. A person may have only been sentenced to 30 days imprisonment, but if the crime for which they were charged allowed a maximum penalty of five years, then that person is disqualified. *See Schrader v. Holder*, 831 F.Supp.2d 304 (D.D.C. 2011, *aff'd*, 704 F.3d 980 (D.C. Cir. 2013)).

3. What does it mean to be a "fugitive from justice" so as to be disqualified from purchasing a firearm?

A "fugitive from justice" is a person who, after having committed a crime, flees from the jurisdiction of the court where the crime was committed. A fugitive from justice may also be a person who goes into hiding to avoid facing charges for the crime of which he or she is accused. Such individuals are not eligible to purchase or possess firearms.

4. Unlawful users of or persons addicted to drugs are disqualified from purchasing firearms

Federal law is very broad in that it disqualifies persons from the purchase of firearms if they are either users of or addicted to marijuana or any depressant, stimulant, narcotic drug, or any controlled substance. Under federal law, an "addict" is defined as a person that "habitually uses any narcotic so as to endanger the public morals, health, safety, or welfare, or who is so far addicted to the use of narcotic drugs as to have lost the power of self-control with reference to his addiction." 21 U.S.C. § 802(1).

However, in using the terms "users of," no such frequency or dependence seems contemplated in the words, nor did Congress give further guidance. Illegal users and addicts are prohibited from purchasing firearms from any person under federal law, and are likewise prohibited from possessing firearms. *See* 18 U.S.C. §§ 922(d) and (g).

5. A person can't legally buy or possess firearms if they are "mentally defective"

What does "mentally defective" mean? A person is considered to have been adjudicated as "mentally defective" if there has been a "determination by a court, board, commission, or other lawful authority that a person, as a result of marked subnormal intelligence, or mental illness, incompetency, condition, or disease: is a danger to himself or others, or lacks the mental capacity to contract or manage his own affairs." The term "mentally defective" includes "a finding of insanity by a court in a criminal case, and those persons found incompetent to stand trial or found not guilty by reason of insanity or lack of mental responsibility." 27 CFR § 478.11.

"Mentally defective" also includes a person who has been committed to a mental institution by a court, board, commission, or other lawful authority, or a commitment to a mental institution involuntarily. The term includes commitment for mental defectiveness or mental illness, and also includes commitment for other reasons, such as drug use. However, it does not include a person in a mental institution for observation or a voluntary admission to a mental institution. Individuals who have been adjudicated as mentally defective are also prohibited from possessing firearms under federal law. *See* 18 U.S.C. § 922(g)(4).

6. <u>A person subject to a restraining order may not purchase or possess a firearm</u>

Under 18 U.S.C. § 922(g)(8), firearms may not be sold to or received by person subject to a court order that: (a) was issued after a hearing which the person received actual notice of and had an opportunity to participate in; (b) restrains the person from harassing, stalking, or threatening an intimate partner or child of such intimate partner or person, or engaging in other conduct that would place an intimate partner in reasonable fear of bodily injury to the partner or child; and (c) includes a finding that such person represents a credible threat to the physical safety of such intimate partner or child; <u>or</u> by its terms explicitly prohibits the use, attempted use, or threatened use of physical force against such intimate partner or child that a person would reasonably be expected to cause bodily injury. An "intimate partner" of a person is the spouse or former spouse of the person, the parent of a child of the person, or an individual who cohabitates with the person.

7. <u>Domestic violence issues and disqualifications</u>

A person who has ever been convicted of the crime of domestic violence may not purchase or possess firearms under federal law. These restrictions were passed in what is known as the *Violence Against Women Act* in 1994 and amended in 1996. This is an often misunderstood law, and, in fact, the ATF has numerous "Frequently Asked Questions" concerning this disqualification on its website: www.atf.gov. The ATF does a good job of explaining the scope of this subject in their FAQs. Due to the complexity of this issue, the ATF examples are included here:

FREQUENTLY ASKED QUESTIONS FROM ATF WEBSITE
Q: What is a "misdemeanor crime of domestic violence?"
A: A "misdemeanor crime of domestic violence" means an offense that:
1. is a misdemeanor under federal or State law;
2. has, as an element, the use or attempted use of physical force, or the threatened use of a deadly weapon; and

3. was committed by a current or former spouse, parent, or guardian of the victim, by a person with whom the victim shares a child in common, by a person who is cohabiting with or has cohabited with the victim as a spouse, parent, or guardian, or by a person similarly situated to a spouse, parent, or guardian of the victim.

However, a person is not considered to have been convicted of a misdemeanor crime of domestic violence unless:

1. the person was represented by counsel in the case, or knowingly and intelligently waived the right of counsel in the case; and
2. in the case of a prosecution for which a person was entitled to a jury trial in the jurisdiction in which the case was tried, either;
   1. the case was tried by a jury; or
   2. the person knowingly and intelligently waived the right to have the case tried by a jury, by guilty plea or otherwise.

In addition, a conviction would not be disabling if it has been expunged or set aside, or is an offense for which the person has been pardoned or has had civil rights restored (if the law of the jurisdiction in which the proceedings were held provides for the loss of civil rights upon conviction for such an offense) unless the pardon, expunction, or restoration of civil rights expressly provides that the person may not ship, transport, possess, or receive firearms, and the person is not otherwise prohibited by the law of the jurisdiction in which the proceedings were held from receiving or possessing firearms. 18 U.S.C. 921(a)(33), 27 CFR 478.11.

Editor's note: A significant number of people make the mistake of overlooking or forgetting about a court issue or family law judicial proceeding. However, if you meet the above criteria, you are federally disqualified from possessing a firearm. The fact that it may have happened a long time ago, or that you did not understand the ramifications, is legally irrelevant.

Q: What is the effective date of this disability?
A: The law was effective September 30, 1996. However, the prohibition applies to persons convicted of such misdemeanors at any time, even if the conviction occurred prior to the law's effective date.

Editor's note: For those wondering why this is not an unconstitutional *ex-post facto* law, multiple federal appeals courts have ruled against that argument and the Supreme Court has consistently declined to review any of those cases, effectively accepting the ruling of the courts of appeals and upholding the law.

Q: X was convicted of misdemeanor assault on October 10, 1996, for beating his wife. Assault has as an element the use of physical force, but is not specifically a domestic violence offense. May X lawfully possess firearms or ammunition?
A: No. X may not legally possess firearms or ammunition. 18 U.S.C. 922(g)(9), 27 CFR 478.32(a)(9).

Editor's note: In this situation because X's conviction for assault was against a person in the statute's protected class, the conviction would be, for purposes of firearms purchasing disqualification, a domestic violence conviction.

Q: X was convicted of a misdemeanor crime of domestic violence on September 20, 1996, 10 days before the effective date of the statute. He possesses a firearm on October 10, 2004. Does X lawfully possess the firearm?
A: No. If a person was convicted of a misdemeanor crime of domestic violence at any time, he or she may not lawfully possess firearms or ammunition on or after September 30, 1996. 18 U.S.C. 922(g)(9), 27 CFR 478.32(a)(9).
Q: In determining whether a conviction in a State court is a "conviction" of a misdemeanor crime of domestic violence, does Federal or State law apply?

A: State law applies. Therefore, if the State does not consider the person to be convicted, the person would not have the Federal disability. 18 U.S.C. 921(a)(33), 27 CFR 478.11.

Q: Is a person who received "probation before judgment" or some other type of deferred adjudication subject to the disability?
A: What is a conviction is determined by the law of the jurisdiction in which the proceedings were held. If the State law where the proceedings were held does not consider probation before judgment or deferred adjudication to be a conviction, the person would not be subject to the disability. 18 U.S.C. 921(a)(33), 27 CFR 478.11.

Q: What State and local offenses are "misdemeanors" for purposes of 18 U.S.C. 922(d)(9) and (g)(9)?
A: The definition of misdemeanor crime of domestic violence in the GCA (the Gun Control Act of 1968) includes any offense classified as a "misdemeanor" under Federal or State law. In States that do not classify offenses as misdemeanors, the definition includes any State or local offense punishable by imprisonment for a term of 1 year or less or punishable by a fine. For example, if State A has an offense classified as a "domestic violence misdemeanor" that is punishable by up to five years imprisonment, it would be a misdemeanor crime of domestic violence. If State B does not characterize offenses as misdemeanors, but has a domestic violence offense that is punishable by no more than one year imprisonment, this offense would be a misdemeanor crime of domestic violence. 18 U.S.C. 921(a)(33), 27 CFR 478.11.

Q: Are local criminal ordinances "misdemeanors under State law" for purposes of sections 922(d)(9) and (g)(9)?
A: Yes, assuming a violation of the ordinance meets the definition of "misdemeanor crime of domestic violence" in all other respects.

Q: In order for an offense to qualify as a "misdemeanor crime of domestic violence," does it have to have as an element the relationship part of the definition (e.g., committed by a spouse, parent, or guardian)?
A: No. The "as an element" language in the definition of "misdemeanor crime of domestic violence" only applies to the use of force provision of the statute and not the relationship provision. However, to be disabling, the offense must have been committed by one of the defined parties. 18 U.S.C. 921(a)(33), 27 CFR 478.11.

Editor's note: This basically means that if illegal force was used against another person, regardless of the language in the underlying statute, if the illegal force was used against a member of the protected class under the statute, federal law will deem this as satisfying the requirements and disqualify the individual from purchasing and possessing firearms.

Q: What should an individual do if he or she has been convicted of a misdemeanor crime of domestic violence?
A: Individuals subject to this disability should immediately dispose of their firearms and ammunition. ATF recommends that such persons transfer their firearms and ammunition to a third party who may lawfully receive and possess them, such as their attorney, a local police agency, or a Federal firearms dealer. The continued possession of firearms and ammunition by persons under this disability is a violation of law and may subject the possessor to criminal penalties. In addition, such firearms and ammunition are subject to seizure and forfeiture. 18 U.S.C. 922(g)(9) and 924(d)(1), 27 CFR 478.152.

Q: Does the disability apply to law enforcement officers?
A: Yes. The Gun Control Act was amended so that employees of government agencies convicted of misdemeanor crimes of domestic violence would not be exempt from disabilities with respect to their receipt or possession of firearms or ammunition. Thus, law enforcement officers and other government officials

who have been convicted of a disqualifying misdemeanor may not lawfully possess or receive firearms or ammunition for any purpose, including performance of their official duties. The disability applies to firearms and ammunition issued by government agencies, purchased by government employees for use in performing their official duties, and personal firearms and ammunition possessed by such employees. 18 U.S.C. 922(g)(9) and 925(a)(1), 27 CFR 478.32(a)(9) and 478.141.

Q: Is an individual who has been pardoned, or whose conviction was expunged or set aside, or whose civil rights have been restored, considered convicted of a misdemeanor crime of domestic violence?

A: No, as long as the pardon, expungement, or restoration does not expressly provide that the person may not ship, transport, possess, or receive firearms.

See www.atf.gov.

Practical Legal Tip:

If you or a loved one are going through court proceedings involving family issues and a restraining or protective order is entered in your case, it can suspend your ability to purchase or possess firearms. Language in the court order prohibiting any acts of family violence whether or not family violence actually occurred, make it so the person whom the other impacts is legally barred from the purchase or possession of any firearm. Believe it or not, the Family Courts have the ability to suspend your Second Amendment rights. *-Chris*

8. Illegal aliens or aliens admitted under a non-immigrant visa

Persons who are illegally in the United States may not legally purchase, possess, or transport firearms. Generally, non-immigrant aliens are also prohibited from legally purchasing, possessing, or transporting firearms.

Exceptions for nonimmigrant aliens

However, a nonimmigrant alien who has been admitted under a nonimmigrant visa is not prohibited from purchasing, receiving, or possessing a firearm if the person falls within one of the following exceptions:

1. if the person was admitted to the United States for lawful hunting or sporting purposes or is in possession of a hunting license or permit lawfully issued in the United States;
2. if the person is an official representative of a foreign government who is accredited to the United States Government or the Government's mission to an international organization having its headquarters in the United States;
3. if the person is an official representative of a foreign government who is *en route* to or from another county to which that alien is accredited;
4. if the person is an official of a foreign government or a distinguished foreign visitor who has been so designated by the Department of State;
5. if the person is a foreign law enforcement officer of a friendly foreign government entering the United States on official law enforcement business;
6. if the person has received a waiver from the prohibition from the Attorney General of the United States.

See 18 U.S.C. § 922(y).

III. Colorado law disqualifications: who cannot buy a firearm under Colorado law?

As mentioned earlier, Colorado has restrictions on the sale, transfer, and possession of firearms that are separate and distinct from the federal restrictions. If a person runs afoul of the law, they could potentially face prosecution in both state and federal court. We have already covered the sale, transfer, and possession of firearms with respect to juveniles. Next, let's examine other restrictions on the sale, transfer, and possession of firearms.

A. *Colorado law disqualifications for "purchasing" a firearm*

Section 18-12-111(1) of the Colorado Revised Statutes makes it a class 4 felony to purchase or otherwise obtain a firearm with the intent to transfer that firearm to a person who the transferor knows or should have known is ineligible to possess a firearm under either federal or state law. Section 18-12-111(2)(a) requires licensed dealers to display a sign warning purchasers of the restrictions imposed by 18-12-111(1).

Although Colorado law does not explicitly state it, any person who is prohibited from possessing a firearm is obviously prohibited from purchasing a firearm. Under section 18-12-108(1) of the Colorado Revised Statutes, this prohibition includes anyone who has been convicted of a felony, or convicted for "attempt or conspiracy to commit a felony," under federal law or the law of any state.

Further, Colorado law follows federal law in preventing domestic violence offenders from purchasing firearms. Section 18-6-801(8) of the Colorado Revised Statutes prohibits a person from purchasing a firearm if that person is convicted of a "misdemeanor crime of domestic violence," as defined under federal law in 18 U.S.C. 921(a)(33), or if that person is convicted of a crime that is punishable by more than one year in prison and includes an "act of domestic violence," as defined in section 18-6-800.3(1) of the Colorado Revised Statutes. Please see the ATF's description of what domestic violence offenses prevent a person from possessing a firearm in part II of this Chapter.

It will be up to a jury to determine, based on the facts of the individual case, whether the crime amounted to a "misdemeanor crime of domestic violence" under federal law, or a crime which included an "act of domestic violence" under state law. If the jury determines that the crime fits either classification, section 18-6-801(8) requires the court to order that the person is prohibited from purchasing a firearm. Also, the court order must prohibit that person from possessing firearms and ammunition. Limits on possession will be covered in the next section below.

In addition, Colorado law prohibits persons who are *accused* of domestic violence from purchasing a firearm while a "civil protection order" remains in effect. *See* C.R.S. 13-14-105.5; U.S.C.A. 922(d)(8) and (g)(8). Civil protection orders may be issued by a judge, at the request of any person, against an adult or a juvenile over the age of ten, to prevent domestic abuse, among other things. *See* 13-14-104.5. Under section 13-14-105.5 of the Colorado Revised Statutes, a person cannot purchase a firearm in Colorado if a court has issued a civil protection order that restrains that person from:

- harassing, stalking or threatening an intimate partner or an intimate partner's child; or
- engaging in conduct that causes an intimate partner to have a reasonable fear of bodily injury for themselves or their child;

and if that order:

- includes a finding that the person represents a credible threat to the physical safety of such intimate partner or child; or

- explicitly prohibits the use, attempted use, or threatened use of physical force against such intimate partner or child that would reasonably be expected to cause bodily injury.

For a person to be denied the right to purchase a firearm, the civil protection order must satisfy at least one of the bullet points from each of the two lists above and the person must have had the opportunity to dispute the order in court. *See* C.R.S. 13-14-105.5 (citing U.S.C.A. 922(d)(8), (g)(8)). Civil protection orders that satisfy these criteria also prevent the accused person from possessing firearms and ammunition, discussed below.

B. *Colorado law disqualifications for "possessing" firearms*
As discussed earlier, in Colorado, it is a crime for any person convicted of a felony, or for attempt or conspiracy to commit a felony, under federal law or the law of any state, to knowingly possess, use, or carry a firearm under section 18-12-108(1) of the Colorado Revised Statutes.

Also as discussed earlier, under section 18-6-801 of the Colorado Revised Statutes, any person convicted of a "misdemeanor crime of domestic violence" as defined by federal law under 18 U.S.C.A. section 921(a)(33), or who is convicted of a crime that is punishable by more than one year in prison and includes an "act of domestic violence," as defined in section 18-6-800.3(1), is prohibited from possessing firearms and ammunition. Further, any person who is subject to a "civil protection order," as explained earlier, is also prohibited from possessing any firearm or ammunition while the order is in effect. In any of these three cases, the person must also relinquish any firearm or ammunition in the person's possession or control to ensure compliance with the prohibition on possession. Sections 18-6-801(b) and 13-14-105.5(c) both provide that relinquishment can be done in one of three ways:

- Through the sale or transfer of the firearm or ammunition to a federally licensed firearms dealer; or
- Through the sale or transfer of the firearm or ammunition to a private party who may legally possess the firearm or ammunition; or
- Through storage of the firearm or ammunition with a law enforcement agency.

For those convicted of a crime involving domestic violence, under section 18-6-801(8)(b), a court may grant up to 72 hours to comply with the relinquishment, but 24 hours is most common. If a defendant is unable to comply with this requirement because they are incarcerated or in custody, the court shall require that the defendant comply within 24 hours of the defendant's release from incarceration or custody. *See* 18-6-801(8)(c). For those subjected to a civil protection order, a court may allow up to 5 days to comply with the relinquishment. *See* 13-14-105.5(2)(b). Just as with a domestic violence conviction, if a person subjected to a civil protection order is unable to comply because they are incarcerated or otherwise in custody, the court shall require that the defendant comply within 24 hours of the defendant's release from incarceration or custody. *See* 13-14-105.5(3).

In Colorado, some private transfers of firearms are subject to a requirement that the receiving party pass a background check. These provisions are found in section 18-12-112 of the Colorado Revised Statutes and are discussed fully in section IV of this Chapter. This requirement is mentioned here because any person who is convicted of a violation of any of the requirements under section 18-12-112, a class 1 misdemeanor, is prohibited from possessing a firearm for two years, beginning on the date of his or her conviction.

Unlike some other states, Colorado does not allow for the automatic restoration of a felon's right to possess firearms after a certain amount of time passes. Rather, felons can only regain their right to possess firearms in Colorado through a pardon. The same is true for those who have lost their gun rights because of a domestic violence related conviction. For those subjected to a civil protection order, their rights are restored when the order expires, provided the protection order was not made permanent. *See* section 13-14-105.5(a)(I). For more on the restoration of gun rights, on both the state and federal level, *see* Chapter Eleven.

In Colorado, there exist laws that prohibit the carrying of firearms into various locations. Location specific prohibitions are covered in Chapter Ten of this book.

IV. Private transfers of firearms
A. *What are the legal restrictions on "private transfers" of firearms?*

Private individuals may legally buy, sell, gift, or otherwise transfer firearms to other private individuals in Colorado. However, when doing so, careful attention needs to be paid to not violate the laws regulating these transactions. So what are the legal restrictions? First, the ATF website has an informative pamphlet entitled "Best Practices: Transfers of Firearms by Private Sellers" located on its website. This pamphlet should be a must-read before entering into a private transfer involving a firearm. So what are the rules in Colorado regarding private transfers?

In part I of this Chapter, we discussed Colorado's restrictions on the possession of handguns by juveniles, covered under section 18-12-108.5 of the Colorado Revised Statutes. Never transfer possession of a handgun permanently to a person under the age of 18 and be wary when allowing a juvenile temporary possession of a handgun. Make sure that the temporary transfer is an allowed exception (as discussed in section I, subsection E of this Chapter), or you will risk a violation of section 18-12-108.7, which is a class 4 felony. Also, remember to get permission from a juvenile's parent or guardian before providing the juvenile with a firearm other than a handgun, as required by section 18-12-108.7(3).

In part III of this Chapter, we discussed Colorado's law restricting the purchase of firearms for the purpose of transferring the firearm to a person who is prohibited from possessing firearms, section 18-12-111(1) of the Colorado Revised Statutes. Do not make the mistake of obtaining a firearm for the purpose of transferring it to a person who you know or should have known was ineligible to possess firearms. Doing so is a felony, which will prevent you from ever possessing a firearm again. Now, let's look at additional restrictions on private firearm transfers that have not yet been covered in this book.

1. <u>Background check requirements</u>

Under section 18-12-112 of the Colorado Revised Statutes, in order for a private transfer of a firearm to be legal in Colorado, the person making the transfer must require that the person receiving the firearm submit to a background check. Once the background check has been performed, the transferor must obtain an approval from the Colorado Bureau of Investigations before making the transfer. See 18-12-112(1)(a)(II).

First, not all private transfers of firearms are subject to the background check requirement. The following transfers are exempt from the background check requirements under section 18-12-112 of the Colorado Revised Statutes:

- Transfers of antique firearms, as described in Chapter Two of this book;
- Bona fide gifts or loans between immediate family members, which only includes "spouses, parents, children, siblings, grandparents, grandchildren, nieces, nephews, first cousins, aunts, and uncles;"
- Any transfers by law, such as through a will;
- As rare as it might be, any *temporary* transfer that occurs in the home of the receiving party because that party reasonably believes it is necessary to prevent imminent death or serious bodily injury to themselves, provided

that the receiving party is not prohibited from possessing firearms;

- A *temporary* transfer at a legally incorporated shooting range;
- A *temporary* transfer at a target shooting competition, authorized by a state agency or a nonprofit organization;
- A *temporary* transfer while hunting, fishing, target shooting, or trapping if the activity is legal in all locations where the receiving party possesses the firearm, and the receiving party holds any license or permit that may be required to engage in the activity;
- A transfer made for the purpose of maintenance or repair of the firearm;
- Any *temporary* transfer that occurs while in the continuous presence of the owner of the firearm; or
- Any *temporary* transfer that lasts not more than 72 hours. (The transferor may be legally liable for damages caused by any unlawful acts the receiving party engages with the firearm in during this time.)

The background check must be done by a licensed gun dealer and the dealer will record the transfer and retain the records in the same way the dealer records every sale the dealer makes. *See* 18-12-112(2)(a), (b). The dealer will then obtain an approval or disapproval from the Colorado Bureau of Investigations and will provide the transferring parties with the results. *See* 18-12-112(2)(c). The dealer may charge no more than ten dollars to perform the background check. *See* 18-12-112(2)(d). If the transfer is approved by the Colorado Bureau of Investigations following the background check, the parties have 30 days to complete the transfer. Failure to do so will require another background check before the transfer can be made. *See* 18-12-112(4). It is a violation of this law to knowingly give false information to a dealer in order to obtain a firearm. *See* 18-12-112(3)(b). Further, it is a violation of this law to accept possession of a firearm without undergoing a background check. *See* 18-12-112(3)(a).

It is extremely important that gun owners pay attention to the provisions of 18-12-112 and follow them whenever they are involved in a private transfer of a firearm. Remember that failure to do so can result in a two year suspension of the offender's gun rights (as explained in Section III, subsection B of this Chapter).

2. Firearm sales at gun shows

In Colorado, under section 12-26.1-101(1) of the Colorado Revised Statutes, a purchaser at a gun show must also undergo a background check and obtain approval from the Colorado Bureau of Investigations before the sale can be finalized. To facilitate the background check process, the gun show promoter must have at least one licensed gun dealer present at the show to carry out background checks. *See* 12-26.1-101(2). Unlike with private transfers outside of a gun show, there are no exceptions to the gun show background check requirement. Even a transfer between immediate family members is subject to a background check at a gun show. *See* 12-26.1-101(3).

A violation of 12-26.1-101 constitutes a class 1 misdemeanor, but does not carry with it any restrictions on an offender's gun rights, unlike a violation of the private transfer law. *See* 12-26.1-101(4).

V. Buying, selling, and transferring through an FFL
A. *Basic procedures*

Persons purchasing firearms through dealers must comply with all legal requirements imposed by federal law. These include both paperwork, and appropriate background checks or screenings to ensure that the purchaser is not prohibited from the purchase or possession of a firearm under federal law.

When purchasing through a dealer, the first thing a prospective buyer will do is select a firearm. Once a selection has been made, the prospective purchaser is required to show proper identification and complete ATF Form 4473. This form requires the applicant, under penalty of law, to provide accurate identifying information, as well as answer certain questions in order to establish whether a person may legally purchase a firearm. The information provided on Form 4473 is then provided to the National Instant Criminal Background Check System (NICS) for processing and approval in order to proceed with the transfer (however, no NICS background may be required if the transferee is legally exempt for reasons such as possessing a state-issued firearms license that qualifies as a replacement. Colorado's Concealed Carry Permits do not currently qualify for this purpose). A FFL dealer can submit the check to NICS either by telephone or through the website and only after the FFL completes all of these steps successfully is a purchaser/transferee allowed to take possession of the firearm.

B. *What is Form 4473?*

ATF Form 4473 is the ATF's form known as a Firearms Transaction Record which must be completed when a person purchases a firearm from an FFL. *See* 27 CFR § 478.124. Form 4473 requires the applicant to provide their name, address, birth date, state of residence, and other information including government issued photo identification. The form also contains information blanks to be filled-in including the NICS background check transaction number, the make, model, and serial number of the firearm to be purchased, and a series of questions that a person must answer. *See* 27 CFR § 478.124(c). This series of questions and the corresponding answers help determine a purchaser's eligibility under federal law to purchase a firearm. Once the form is completed, the prospective purchaser will sign the form and attest that the information provided thereon is truthful and accurate under penalty of federal law. This means that if you lie or make false statements on this form, the Feds can and will prosecute you for a crime!

Likewise, the dealer must also sign Form 4473 and retain it for at least 20 years. The ATF is permitted to inspect, as well as receive a copy of Form 4473 from the dealer both during audits and during the course of a criminal investigation. The 4473 records must be surrendered to the Bureau of Alcohol, Tobacco, Firearms and Explosives in the event the FFL dealer retires or ceases business.

C. *How are background checks administered when purchasing a firearm?*

   1. NICS: National Instant Criminal Background Check System

Background checks by dealers when transferring firearms are completed through the National Instant Criminal Background Check System or NICS, if required, prior to the transfer of a firearm from an FFL dealer to a non-dealer. When the prospective purchaser/transferee's information is given to NICS, the system will check the applicant against at least three different databases containing various types of records. Applicants are checked against the records maintained by the Interstate Identification Index (III) which contains criminal history records, the National Crime Information Center (NCIC) which contains records including warrants and protective orders, as well as the NICS Index which contains records of individuals who are prohibited from purchasing or possessing firearms under either federal or state law. In addition, if the applicant is not a United States Citizen, the application is processed for an Immigration Alien Query (IAQ) through the Department of Homeland Security's Immigration and Customs Enforcement Division.

   2. Responses from NICS

NICS responses to background checks come in three basic forms: proceed, delay, or deny. The "proceed" response allows for the transfer to be completed. The "delay" response means that the transfer may not legally proceed. If the dealer receives a response of "delay," NICS has three business days to research the applicant further. If the dealer has not received a notice that the transfer is denied after the three business days, then the transfer may proceed. "Deny" means the transfer does not take place; a transferee's options after a "deny" are discussed below.

Practical Legal Tip:

Thinking about buying a gun on behalf of your buddy? Not a good idea! One of the purposes of ATF Form 4473 is to conduct a background check on individuals who want to purchase firearms in order to make sure they are legally allowed to do so. Acting as a "strawman" by purchasing it for your buddy circumvents this process and is a crime. -*Doug*

3. <u>What transactions require background checks?</u>

A background check is required before each and every sale or other transfer of a firearm from an FFL to a non-licensee unless an exception is provided under the law. For every transaction that requires a background check, the purchaser/transferee must also complete ATF Form 4473. This includes:

- The sale or trade of a firearm;
- The return of a consigned firearm;
- The redemption of a pawned firearm;
- The loan or rental of a firearm for use off of an FFL's licensed premises; or
- Any other non-exempt transfer of a firearm.

4. <u>What transactions do not require a background check?</u>

A background check is not required under the following circumstances:

- The sale or transfer of a firearm where the transferee presents a valid state permit/license that allows the transferee to carry a firearm from the state where the FFL is located <u>and</u> the state permit/license is recognized by the ATF as a qualifying alternative to the background check requirement (Colorado's Concealed Carry Permits are not valid for this purpose);

- The transfer of a firearm from one FFL to another FFL;
- The return of a repaired firearm to the person from whom it was received;
- The sale of a firearm to a law enforcement agency or a law enforcement officer for official duties if the transaction meets the specific requirements of 27 CFR § 478.134 including providing a signed certification from a person in authority on agency letterhead stating that the officer will use the firearm in official duties and where a records check reveals the officer does not have any misdemeanor convictions for domestic violence;
- The transfer of a replacement firearm of the same kind and type to the person from whom a firearm was received;
- The transfer of a firearm that is subject to the National Firearms Act if the transfer was pre-approved by the ATF.

Note: A Colorado Concealed Carry Permit currently does not qualify as an alternative to the NICS background check requirement. However, permits from some other states are accepted as an alternative to the NICS background check requirement, as long as the license was issued within five years of the date of the transfer. A complete permit chart for all states is available on the ATF's website at www.atf.gov.

5. If a person buys multiple handguns, a dealer must report that person to the ATF

Under federal law, FFLs are required to report to the ATF any sale or transfer of two or more pistols, revolvers, or any combination of pistols and revolvers totaling two or more to an unlicensed (non-FFL) individual that takes place at one time or during any five consecutive business days. This report is made to the ATF on Form 3310.4 and is completed in triplicate with the original copy sent to the ATF, one sent to the designated State police or local law enforcement agency in the jurisdiction where the sale took place, and one retained by the dealer and held for no less than five years.

6. FFLs must report persons who purchase more than one rifle in southwest border states

In Texas, Arizona, New Mexico, and California, dealers are required to report the sale or other transfer of more than one semiautomatic rifle capable of accepting a detachable magazine and with a caliber greater than .22 (including .223 caliber/5.56 millimeter) to an unlicensed person at one time or during any five consecutive business days. *See* 18 U.S.C. § 923(g)(3)(A). This report is made via ATF Form 3310.12 and must be reported no later than the close of business on the day the multiple sale or other disposition took place. This requirement includes (but is not limited to) purchases of popular semi-automatic rifles such as AR-15s, AK-47s, Ruger Mini-14s, and Tavor bullpup rifles.

VI. What if I'm denied the right to purchase a firearm?

A. *If I am denied the right to purchase, how do I appeal?*

Persons who believe they have been erroneously denied or delayed a firearm transfer based on a match to a record returned by the NICS may request an appeal of their "deny" or "delay" decision. All appeal inquiries must be submitted to the NICS Section's Appeal Service Team (AST) in writing, either online or via mail on the FBI's website at www.fbi.gov. An appellant must provide their complete name, complete mailing address, and NICS Transaction Number. For persons appealing a delayed transaction, a fingerprint card is required and must be submitted with the appeal, although the fingerprint card is merely recommended on appeals for denied applications. This may seem counter-intuitive, but it is required per the FBI's website.

B. *What if I keep getting erroneously delayed or denied when I am attempting to buy a firearm?*

Apply for a PIN (personal identification number) that is designed to solve this issue. Some individuals may have a name which is common enough (or happens to be flagged for other reasons) that it causes undue delays or denials in the background check verification process through NICS. For that reason, NICS maintains the Voluntary Appeal File database (VAF) which allows any applicant to apply by submitting an appeal request and then obtain a UPIN or Unique Personal Identification Number. A person who has been cleared through the VAF and receives a UPIN will then be able to use their UPIN when completing Form 4473 in order to help avoid further erroneous denials or extended delays. A person can obtain a UPIN by following the procedures outlined on the FBI's website at www.fbi.gov.

C. *What if I am denied the right to purchase a firearm by the Colorado Bureau of Investigations?*

Background checks for private purchases under Colorado law are governed by section 24-33.5-424 of the Colorado Revised Statutes. As discussed in Section IV, subsection A of this Chapter, if a party is denied the right to purchase a firearm, the results of the background check are provided to that party by the firearms dealer. The denied party may request a review of the denial by the Colorado Bureau of Investigations under section 24-33.5-424(5)(b). Upon request, the Bureau must perform a thorough review of the instant criminal background check records that prompted the denial and must render a final administrative decision within thirty days of the review request. *See* section 24-33.5-424(5)(b)(I) and (II).

A person may also use Rule 106(a)(4) of the Colorado Rules of Civil Procedure to appear before a District Court Judge and argue that the "governmental body or officer" has "abused its discretion" in denying their right to purchase a firearm.

VII. Additional considerations in firearms purchasing and possession laws

A. *How can I legally purchase a firearm from someone in another state?*

Any individual who wishes to purchase a firearm from a person that lives in another state than the purchaser must complete the transaction through an FFL. Sellers or transferors are legally authorized to facilitate a private transaction or transfer by shipping the firearm to the purchaser's FFL in the recipient/buyer's state, where the FFL will complete the transfer process. It is a federal crime to sell or transfer a firearm between persons who are residents of different states, or where a transfer takes place in a state other than the transferee/transferor's singular state of residence.

B. *Can I purchase firearms on the Internet?*

Yes. However, all legal requirements for a transfer must be followed. If the buyer and seller are both residents of Colorado, then the two may lawfully conduct a private sale so long as all other legal issues are satisfied (see our earlier discussion on disqualifications to purchasing and possessing firearms in this Chapter). However, if buyer and seller are not residents of the same state, the transaction can only be legally facilitated through the intervention of an FFL.

C. *Shipping firearms*

    1. Can I ship my firearm through the postal service?

Long guns: yes. Handguns: no. However, under federal law, a non-licensed individual may not transfer (and this would include shipping to someone) a firearm to a non-licensed resident (non-FFL) of another state. However, a non-licensed individual may mail a long gun to a resident of his or her own state, and they may also mail a long gun to an FFL of another state. To that end, the USPS recommends that long guns be mailed via registered mail and that the packaging used to mail the long gun be ambiguous so as to not identify the contents. Handguns are not allowed to be mailed. *See* 18 U.S.C. §§ 1715, 922(a)(3), 922(a)(5), and 922(a)(2)(A). Rather, handguns must be shipped using a common or contract carrier (*e.g.*, UPS or FedEx).

2. Shipping handguns and other firearms through a common or contract carrier

Under federal law, a non-licensed individual may ship a firearm (including a handgun) by a common or contract carrier (*i.e.*, UPS or FedEx) to a resident of his or her own state, or to a licensed individual (FFL) in another state. However, it is illegal to ship any firearm to a non-FFL in another state. It is a requirement that the carrier be notified that the shipment contains a firearm, however, carriers are prohibited from requiring any identifying marks on the package which may be used to identify the contents as containing a firearm. *See* 18 U.S.C. §§ 922(a)(2)(A), 922(a)(3), 922(a)(5), 922(e), 27 CFR 478.31 and 478.30.

D. *Can I ship my firearm to myself for use in another state?*
Yes. In accordance with the law as described in the preceding section, a person may ship a firearm to himself or herself in care of another person in another state where he or she intends to hunt or engage in other lawful activity. The package should be addressed to the owner and persons other than the owner should not open the package and take possession of the firearm.

E. *If I am moving out of Colorado, may I have movers move my firearms?*
Yes, a person who lawfully possesses firearms may transport or ship the firearms interstate when changing the person's state of residence so long as the person complies with the requirements for shipping and transporting firearms as outlined earlier. *See* 18 U.S.C. § 922(e) and 27 CFR § 478.31. However, certain NFA items such as destructive devices, machine guns, short-barreled shotguns or rifles, and so forth require approval from the ATF before they can be moved interstate. *See* 18 U.S.C. § 922(a)(4) and 27 CFR § 478.28. It is important that the person seeking to move the firearms also check state and local laws where the firearms will be relocated to ensure that the movement of the

firearms into the new state does not violate any state law or local ordinance.

F. *May I loan my firearm to another person?*
There is no general prohibition on loaning a firearm to another person, so long as the person receiving the firearm may lawfully possess one. However, remember that Colorado law prohibits providing a handgun to anyone under the age of 18, with a few exceptions, and requires that a person obtain permission from a juvenile's parent or guardian before providing a firearm other than a handgun to the juvenile, as discussed above in part I of this Chapter. Further, as a loan is essentially a temporary transfer, any loan that does not fall under one of the exceptions found in section 18-12-112 is subject to a background check (as discussed in section IV, subsection A of this Chapter). This includes any temporary transfer that is to last longer than 72 hours.

G. *What happens to my firearms when I die?*
Depending on the manner in which a person leaves his or her estate behind, firearms may be bequeathed in a customary manner like other personal property. Under Colorado law, recall that Section 18-12-112(6)(c) exempts a firearm transfer through a will from the background check requirements normally imposed on private transfers. However, firearms held in an estate are still subject to the other state and federal laws of transfer and possession. For example, pursuant to United States Code of Federal Regulations, Title 27, Part 478.30, if the person who would inherit the gun is legally allowed to have a firearm in his or her state, then they can receive it from the estate without going through an FFL. However, each state is permitted to have laws regulating firearms transfers by estates, and some of the more restrictive gun states (*i.e.* New Jersey, Massachusetts, New York, etc.) have these.

Thus, careful consideration needs to be given in estate planning with consideration for firearms law of both the jurisdiction in which the estate is located as well as consideration of who is to receive the firearms.

VIII.   Ammunition: the law of purchasing and possession

A. _Who is legally prohibited from purchasing ammunition under federal law?_

Under federal law, there are six primary situations where a person is prohibited from buying, selling, or possessing ammunition (beyond armor-piercing ammunition which was discussed in Chapter Two).

1. Under 18 U.S.C. § 922(b)(1), it is unlawful for a person to sell long gun ammunition to a person under the age of 18;
2. Under 18 U.S.C. § 922(b)(1), it is unlawful for a person to sell handgun ammunition to a person under the age of 21;
3. Under 18 U.S.C. § 922(x)(2)(B), it is unlawful for a juvenile to possess handgun ammunition;
4. Under 18 U.S.C. § 922(d), it is unlawful to sell ammunition to a person who is prohibited from purchasing firearms;
5. Under 18 U.S.C. § 922(g), it is unlawful for a person who is disqualified from purchasing or possessing firearms to possess firearm ammunition if such ammunition has moved in interstate commerce (which is nearly all ammunition); and
6. Under 18 U.S.C. § 922(h), it is unlawful for a person who is employed by a person who is disqualified from purchasing or possessing ammunition to possess or transport ammunition for the disqualified individual.

For the statutes that involve juveniles, there are a couple of notable exceptions to the law: first, the law against selling handgun ammunition to a juvenile and possession of handgun ammunition by a juvenile does not apply to a temporary transfer of ammunition to a juvenile or to the possession or use of ammunition by a juvenile if the handgun and ammunition are possessed and used by the juvenile in the course of employment, in the course of ranching or farming-related activities at the residence of the juvenile (or on property used for ranching or farming at which the juvenile, with the permission of the property owner or lessee, is performing activities related to the operation of the farm or ranch), target practice, hunting, or a course of instruction in the safe and lawful use of a handgun. The law also does not apply to the temporary transfer to or use of ammunition by a juvenile if the juvenile has been provided with prior written consent by his or her parent or guardian who is not prohibited by federal, state, or local law from possessing firearms. *See* 18 U.S.C. § 922(x)(3).

Additionally, juveniles who (1) are members of the Armed Forces of the United States or the National Guard who possesses or is armed with a handgun in the line of duty, (2) receive ammunition by inheritance, or (3) possess ammunition in the course of self-defense or defense of others are permitted to possess ammunition.

B. *When is a person prohibited from purchasing or possessing ammunition under Colorado law?*

All of the instances in which Colorado law prohibits a person from purchasing or possessing ammunition are covered fully in part III of this Chapter. In short, persons convicted of a "misdemeanor crime of violence" or a crime punishable by more than one year in prison which includes "an act of domestic violence" are prohibited from purchasing or possessing ammunition under section 18-6-801(8) and persons accused of domestic violence who are subjected to a civil protection order are prohibited from purchasing or possessing ammunition under section 13-14-105.5. Please see Part III of this Chapter above for a complete explanation of these laws.

C. *Can a person be disqualified from purchasing ammunition if they are disqualified from purchasing firearms?*

Yes, under federal law. Under 18 U.S.C. § 922(g) it is unlawful for a person who is disqualified from purchasing or possessing firearms if the ammunition has moved in interstate commerce. Since nearly all ammunition or ammunition components move through interstate commerce in one form or another, this disqualification includes essentially all ammunition.

D. *Can a person purchase ammunition that is labeled "law enforcement use only"?*

Yes. Although some handgun ammunition is sold with a label "law enforcement use," such a label has no legal meaning and is only reflective of a company policy or, viewed less positively, as a marketing strategy.

CHAPTER FOUR
WHEN CAN I LEGALLY USE MY GUN: PART I
UNDERSTANDING THE LAW OF JUSTIFICATION
SOME BASIC LEGAL CONCEPTS

I. Ignorance of the law is NO excuse!

Now we start to get into the meat of our discussion: when is it legal to use a gun as a weapon? The purpose of this chapter is to look at the essential, basic legal concepts of the law of when and under what circumstances a person is legally justified in using force or deadly force against other persons or animals. Know when you may legally shoot, because ignorance of the law holds no weight in a courtroom! That is why it is critical you know the law so that you are in the best possible situation to preserve your legal rights if you ever need them.

II. Gun owners need to know Title 18, Article 1, Part 7 of the Colorado Revised Statutes

In Colorado, legal justifications appear in numerous places and areas of the law. Of particular importance to gun owners are the defenses found in Title 18, Article 1, Part 7 of the Colorado Revised Statutes entitled "Justification and Exemptions from Criminal Responsibility" which we cover in detail throughout this book. The text of relevant provisions of that Article of the Colorado Revised Statutes is found in the Appendix.

III. To legally use physical force or deadly physical force, you must be "justified." What is legal justification?

A. *Basic definition of justification: an acceptable excuse*

So, when is it legal to use force or deadly force against another person? When is it legal to even threaten to use force or deadly force against another? The answer is when there is a legal "justification," or defense. A legal justification is an acceptable reason or excuse under the law for taking an action that would otherwise be a crime.

Example:

> Rick is in his suburban back yard with his faithful
> dog when out of nowhere, a coyote appears and
> is about to attack. Rick draws his handgun and
> shoots the coyote.

Rick has discharged his firearm in a public place, which is
ordinarily "disorderly conduct." Why will Rick likely be not guilty
of "disorderly conduct?" Because he was <u>legally justified</u> in
shooting the coyote! That is, the law will likely say the excuse for
discharging the firearm in a public place—protecting himself and
his dog from coyotes—makes Rick's action of discharging a
firearm reasonable and, therefore, legally justified.

Practical Legal Tip:

A <u>defense to prosecution</u> is not the
same as a <u>bar to prosecution</u>. A "bar to
prosecution" is where a person can't be
prosecuted for engaging in certain
conduct, whereas a "defense to
prosecution" allows prosecution for the
conduct, but offers defendants a
justification that must be demonstrated
with evidence in court. *-Stanley*

B. *Basic requirement: you must admit your action*

In legal terms, a legal justification is called an "affirmative
defense." In order to assert an affirmative defense, the accused
person must first admit all of the elements of the crime for which
they are charged. Then, the person must present "some credible
evidence" of justification before a jury will be given an instruction
that "a person is legally justified to use force if..." In plain English,
a person will not be allowed to say "I didn't do it, but if I did do it,
I was justified." You must admit the underlying elements of the
charge.

Example:

> Jane is walking home one night, when a man jumps out of the bushes and demands her purse. Jane pulls out her handgun and points it at the man, who then runs away. Unfortunately, Jane does not call the police, but the criminal immediately does, reporting a crazy woman threatening him with a gun. Jane ends up charged with felony menacing, even though Jane was the victim.

In order for Jane to present an affirmative defense as a legal justification for committing "felony menacing," she must admit in court that she did pull her handgun and point it at the would-be robber. Then, in order for the jury to consider a legal justification defense (*i.e.*, receive a jury instruction from the judge), she must offer some evidence of why she is legally justified under the law for having pulled her weapon (in this example, Jane believed she was being robbed). Once Jane has successfully taken these steps, two things occur. First, Jane is entitled to have the judge instruct the jury that they may find Jane not guilty because she was justified in her action. Second, the prosecution will have the difficult burden of proving beyond a reasonable doubt that Jane was not justified in her use of self-defense. The jury will then decide whether they believe Jane and whether she is guilty or not guilty of the crime of felony menacing.

On the other hand, if Jane does not admit to the elements of the criminal offense she is charged with, she will not be allowed to offer a legal justification defense under Title 18, Article 1, Part 7 of the Colorado Revised Statutes. Legal justification is, therefore, literally the law of "Yes, I did it, BUT...!"

Practical Legal Tip:

A jury instruction is a statement made by the judge to the jury informing them of the law applicable to the case in general, or some aspect of it. -*Chris*

IV. Categories of force for justification under Title 18, Article 1, Part 7

Anytime a person takes a physical action against another person, they have used force. Title 18, Article 1, Part 7 of the Colorado Revised Statutes divides or categorizes uses of force into different levels. Whether or not a use of force was justified under the law often depends on how that force is categorized. These categories, which we will address throughout this book, are: 1) *physical force*, and 2) *deadly physical force*.

A. *What if a person uses greater force than the law allows?*

The use of a legally appropriate level of force is important because if a person uses more force than is "reasonably believed to be necessary" (see Section 4), that person may not be legally justified in using that level of force. It is important to understand the differences in the levels of force and the circumstances under which the law allows the use of each.

For example, if a person uses deadly physical force, and the law allows only for the use of physical force, that person will not be legally justified. Likewise, if a person uses force when no force is legally allowed, that use of force will not be legally justified.

Example:

> *Harry Homeowner looks out his window and sees a person standing on his front lawn. Harry yells at the fellow to get off his land. The fellow on the lawn does not respond. Harry rushes out*

> *to confront the fellow and demands that he*
> *leave Harry's lawn.*

This fellow is now clearly a trespasser! What degree of force may Harry use to remove the trespasser? The law, as discussed later, will show that Harry is only allowed to use force in response to a mere trespasser. If Harry uses deadly physical force against the trespasser, he will not be legally justified and is likely guilty of murder. Ultimately, using the correct degree of force is critical in determining whether a person has committed a crime or a legally justified action. Remember that when you choose to fire your gun, you are often acting in the spur of the moment, with little time to reflect on all of the consequences of your actions. However, in court, the jury will have the benefit of time to analyze every tiny detail of your action. Given this, whenever possible, exercise the utmost care in deciding what degree of force to use, and don't use deadly force unless you absolutely have to.

B. *What is the legal definition of "force?"*
Surprisingly, "force" is not defined in the Colorado Revised Statutes. However, "deadly physical force" *is* defined. Under Title 18, Article 1, Part 7 of the Colorado Revised Statutes, a prerequisite for being able to legally use deadly force is the requirement that the actor must reasonably believe that a lesser degree of force is inadequate. Therefore, one may conclude that mere physical force must be something less than deadly force.

Example:
> *Timmy is being harassed and insulted by a bully,*
> *when the bully suddenly clenches his first and*
> *takes a swing at Timmy, but misses. Timmy*
> *reacts to the swing by punching the bully in the*
> *face.*

The bully's action was a use of force. Even though he missed Timmy, the bully placed Timmy in fear of harm. Timmy's action of striking the bully was likewise a use of force, and as will be discussed later, legally justified because of the bully's use of the same degree of force.

C. _What is deadly force?_

Deadly Physical Force: Colorado Revised Statutes § 18-1-901(d)
"Deadly physical force" means force, the intended, natural, and probable consequence of which is to produce death, and which does, in fact, produce death.

1. Deadly physical force has to have caused death!

On the surface, the legal definition of deadly physical force seems simple. However, the meaning of what is and is not deadly physical force can be legally tricky. An action which would probably cause death is not legally defined as deadly physical force if death does not occur.

Example:

> _Jim is being robbed and beaten by a group of individuals when he manages to draw his handgun and fire it at one of the most aggressive assailants. His shot misses his intended target but breaks the group up, causing the would-be robbers to flee._

In our example, because the bullet did not kill or even strike any of his assailants, Jim did not use deadly physical force. Thus, death is a prerequisite for the existence of deadly physical force. Therefore, in this section of the law, the focus is on the result of the force used rather than the nature of the force itself.

2. "Intended" and "natural, probable consequence" as components of deadly physical force

Deadly physical force, by its legal definition, occurs when a person takes an action that is _intended_ by the actor to cause death, death is a _natural, probable consequence_ of the action, and death actually occurs. This intention to cause death is called a person's mental state. A prosecutor must prove beyond a reasonable doubt that a person possessed a particular mental state applicable to a crime in order to meet the state's burden of proof and convict someone of a crime.

Often a person's intent is easily ascertainable by the circumstances. For example, if a person is the would-be victim of robbery, and the person resists by pulling his or her gun and firing at the robber, killing him, the law will likely find the victim used justifiable deadly physical force, because the victim of the crime resisted and used force with the intent to kill and actually caused the death of the robber.

However, the weapon used is not always dispositive evidence of someone's intent to use deadly physical force. Hammers, toasters, knives, baseball bats, and almost any other object can be capable of causing death under a particular circumstance. The case legally turns, then, on whether death was a "natural, probable consequence" of the force used.

D. _What are threats of force? "Stop or I will..."_
If you are legally justified to use force in any particular situation, it follows then that you may also legally _threaten_ to use force in the same situation. Likewise, if you are justified in using deadly physical force in a particular situation, you may legally threaten the use of deadly physical force in the same situation. It all comes down to whether a jury finds that your actions were reasonable under the circumstances.

Example:
> Billy is walking to his car after work when three individuals with baseball bats confront him in the parking lot and surround him in an aggressive manner. Fearing that they are about to assault him with the bats, Billy draws his gun

and clearly demands that the aggressors leave
him alone, at which point they all flee from the
scene.

Has Billy legally used justified force by showing his gun? Probably yes. Billy's actions amount to felony menacing under section 18-3-206 of the Colorado Revised Statutes. However, Billy can argue that he used a reasonable degree of force in light of his reasonable belief that he faced an imminent physical threat to himself. As with all acts of self-defense, the question for the jury is whether Billy acted reasonable under the circumstances.

E. *Warning shots*

Warning shots get a lot of good folks in legal trouble! Warning shots are commonly portrayed in movies and television as a good idea—and people like to mimic what they see in movies and on TV! What does Colorado law say about warning shots?

1. Are warning shots a use of force?

First, the term "warning shot" does not appear in the Colorado Revised Statutes. However, firing a warning shot can quickly become a violation of the law, whether or not you intended it to. Depending on the location, discharging a weapon is often prohibited by the law (see the Table at the end of Chapter Seven). Further, warning shots can amount to assault with a deadly weapon. If the bullet were to strike a bystander, additional charges could range from assault all the way up to murder, depending on the injury caused. Therefore, a shooter would have to establish that they were justifiably acting in self-defense in order to avoid a conviction.

As with all uses of force in self-defense, the use of a warning shot would be justified if it can be shown to be a reasonable degree of force given the situation. This can be problematic for a defendant. Consider that under section 18-1-704 of the Colorado Revised Statutes, for a person to be justified in using physical force in defense of himself or a third party, that person must reasonably believe that the other person will engage in the "imminent use of unlawful physical force." The use of a warning shot in this situation may call into question whether the use of unlawful force was truly imminent, given that the shooter felt that they could afford the time a warning shot takes.

Further, consider again that warning shots have the opportunity to strike unintended targets directly, through ricochets, or through penetration of a wall or other surfaces. Given all of these considerations, warning shots are almost never the right decision when faced with an attacker.

V.   What does it mean to "reasonably" believe something?

In Colorado law, the legal standard for a justified use of force is generally expressed as a person must "reasonably" believe that the other person is engaged in the use or "imminent" use of unlawful physical force. Further, one may only use the "degree of force" that he "reasonably" believes to be necessary to end the threat.

But what does "reasonable" mean? Further, when is something imminent—and who decides whether it is or not? The answers to these questions are how the legal process decides guilt or justification. For all gun owners, these concepts are critical.

A.   *How does the law determine "reasonable?"*

In determining what is reasonable, the law often uses a standard known as the "reasonable person" standard to evaluate a person's conduct. It uses a hypothetical "reasonable person." Who is a reasonable person, and how does he or she act? Ultimately, a reasonable person is whatever a jury says it is. The legal analysis behind the reasonable person goes like this: if a person used physical force or even deadly physical force, they must act like a reasonable person would have acted under the same or similar circumstances in order to be legally justified. However, if a person fails to act like a reasonable person, their conduct will fall below the acceptable legal standard and will not be justified. The reasonable person standard is the law's attempt to make the concept of reasonableness an objective and measurable test.

Who is this "reasonable person?" The reasonable person is everyman. In effect, the juror will ask: "What would I have done in this situation?" The reasonable person standard is not subjective, which means that the jury will not consider whether the defendant believed he was acting reasonably. Rather, the reasonable person standard is objective, that is, the question is whether the average person would find the action reasonable. If a jury determines that a reasonable person in the same situation would have believed that the degree of force used was necessary to prevent unlawful force, the defendant was justified in that use of force.

Practical Legal Tip:

Throughout this book, we refer to juries making the ultimate determination of fact. There are, however, some limited occasions where a judge makes the determinations. For example, if all parties waive their right to a jury, the Court may conduct what is called a "bench trial." -*Doug*

Keep in mind, however, that judges, juries, and prosecutors are simply human beings, and people can have vastly different ideas of how a reasonable person should act under any given circumstances.

B. *What does "imminent" mean under the law?*
When does someone have a reasonable belief that unlawful use of physical force is <u>imminent</u>? In Colorado, it ultimately may be a

jury that is tasked with determining whether someone had a reasonable belief that the use of unlawful physical force was "imminent." Clearly, the term "imminent" attempts to convey a sense of urgency for the use of force, but again, it usually falls back to the jury to decide if this standard was met in a particular case.

C.   *Self-Defense in One's Home: Colorado's "Make My Day" Law*
Under section 18-1-704.5 of the Colorado Revised Statutes, an occupant of a "dwelling" is justified in using any degree of force, up to and including deadly physical force, against an intruder in the person's dwelling, if they have a reasonable belief that the intruder has or intends on committing a crime against a person or property, and if they have a reasonable belief that the intruder "might use any physical force, no matter how slight, against any occupant."

Under the "Make My Day" law, (which is also covered in depth in Chapter Five), unlike other situations involving self-defense, a person who uses force against an intruder in their home is immune from both criminal prosecution and civil liability. This means that the "Make My Day" defense happens in the preliminary stages of a trial in front of a judge, before a jury has been selected. In addition, the defendant must only prove their justification through preponderance of the evidence. To satisfy preponderance of the evidence, the defendant must only show that it was more likely than not that all of the elements of the defense are satisfied. This is a much easier standard than beyond a reasonable doubt.

Further, "Make My Day" is wholly separate from the typical self-defense justification. If a person fails in their pre-trial attempt to gain immunity from suit through "Make My Day," they may still prevail during the following jury trial through a typical self-defense justification. In this way, "Make My Day" allows a defendant two bites at the apple when they have used physical force against an intruder in their home.

Example:

> *Harry Homeowner is asleep in his house when he hears a noise in his kitchen. Harry enters his kitchen with his .45 drawn and confronts an armed burglar. Harry fires his weapon and the burglar will burgle no more!*

In this situation, was Harry's use of deadly physical force in firing his gun reasonable and therefore justified? Likely yes. Harry is not required to give any warning before employing deadly physical force against an intruder. In this situation, given that the intruder was armed, Harry can likely show that he had a reasonable belief that the intruder had or intended to commit an additional crime against a person or property, and that the intruder might use physical force, no matter how slight, against an occupant. Remember, under "Make My Day," Harry must only show that it was more likely than not that these beliefs were reasonable.

D. *Limits of Colorado's "Make My Day" Law*

As we discussed above, a person may use any degree of force up to, and including, deadly physical force against an intruder in the person's home, provided he has a reasonable belief that the intruder intends to commit another crime in the home and that the intruder might use force. Keep in mind that this only applies to intruders who are inside the home. This does not cover trespassers on land generally, or even trespassers who are on one's porch or patio. A homeowner may still be justified in using force on a trespasser who hasn't entered the home, but he would not be covered under the "Make My Day" law. In situations where the trespasser has not entered the home, the homeowner may only use the degree of force which he reasonably believes necessary, as we discussed above. What exactly counts as being part of a home? Consider whether an attached or unattached garage, a tool shed, a guest house, a mobile home, or a hotel room are part of the home for the purpose of "Make My Day." These interesting questions will be answered in Chapter Five.

VI. **The burden of proof in criminal cases**

In criminal cases, the state attorneys or prosecutors have the burden of proof. This means that it is the State's responsibility to present enough evidence to prove the defendant committed a crime. This burden of proof that the prosecutor bears is a standard called "beyond a reasonable doubt." It is the highest level of proof used in the American justice system. The state's job at trial in attempting to prove the defendant's guilt includes eliminating any reasonable doubt that the defendant's conduct was justified.

We are now ready to look at under what circumstances Colorado law allows a person to use physical force to protect themselves and others in the next chapter.

Practical Legal Tip:

A word about juries. Juries are not "picked" in Colorado. Rather, they are the first twelve people that are not "struck" from the pool of folks called a jury pool. Most of the time, in my opinion, juries get it "right," but after years of practice, some juries' decisions leave you scratching your head... That is why immunity from prosecution under "Make My Day" can be critical. -*Stanley*

CHAPTER FIVE
WHEN CAN I LEGALLY USE MY GUN: PART II
SELF-DEFENSE AND DEFENSE OF OTHERS;
UNDERSTANDING WHEN PHYSICAL FORCE AND
DEADLY PHYSICAL FORCE CAN BE LEGALLY USED
AGAINST ANOTHER PERSON

I. Introduction and overview

The question of "when can a person legally use deadly physical force against another person" is of critical importance if you are a legal Colorado firearms owner. Although a firearm is nothing more than a tool, it is a tool that by its very nature has the ability to deliver deadly physical force. Thus, all responsible firearms owners should understand when they are justified in using physical force and deadly physical force under the law. Failure to understand the law gets lots of good folks in serious trouble!

The primary Colorado statutes dealing with self-defense and defense of other people are contained in two Colorado Revised Statutes Sections:

> 18-1-704: Use of physical force in defense of a person
> 18-1-704.5: Use of deadly physical force against an intruder

The law of justified self-defense is split between the use of deadly force against an intruder in one's own home and all other situations involving the use of physical force in defense of oneself or others. Section 18-1-704.5, also known as "Make My Day," covers the use of deadly physical force against an intruder in one's home. Section 18-1-704 covers the use of physical force in defense of oneself or of a third person outside of the home. Other sections of the Colorado Revised Statutes allow for the justified use of force in other situations. These situations include use of force by law enforcement, in defense of property or premises, while under duress, or when a person uses force because it was the best choice between two evils.

In the previous chapter, several legal concepts, such as reasonableness, the imminent use of unlawful force, and the categorization of physical force and deadly physical force were discussed. Those concepts have practical applications in this chapter. In this chapter, we will expand upon those topics to include when a person may be justified in using physical force or deadly physical force in self-defense, as well as those circumstances when the law specifically prohibits the use of physical force or deadly physical force.

II. Defending oneself or a third person with physical force or deadly physical force

A. *Use of physical force under 18-1-704*

The primary self-defense statute in Colorado is section 18-1-704 of the Colorado Revised Statutes. Section 18-1-704 is all inclusive; it covers the use of both physical force and deadly physical force in defense of oneself or of a third person. Under section 18-1-704, "a person is justified in using physical force upon another person in order to defend himself or a third person from what he reasonably believes to be the use or imminent use of unlawful physical force by that other person, and he may use a degree of force which he reasonably believes to be necessary for that purpose."

Importantly, a person is not justified in using any degree of physical force if he provokes the other person into the use of unlawful force with the intent of using that as a justification to cause the other person bodily injury or death. Similarly, a person is not justified in the use of any degree of physical force if he is the initial aggressor. An initial aggressor can only use physical force "if he withdraws from the encounter and effectively communicates to the other person his intent to" withdraw, and the other person continues to use physical force or threatens to continue.

Who decides whether an actor's belief is or is not reasonable that the other person's use of unlawful force was imminent? Who decides if the degree of force used by someone was reasonable under a particular set of circumstances? The answer to both of these questions is the jury.

Therefore, if a person is facing a criminal charge and claims self-defense under the general self-defense provisions of section 18-1-704, the jury will decide if that person's belief that use of unlawful force by the other person was imminent was or was not reasonable. As can be imagined, this leaves a lot of room for juries to interpret what actions are reasonable or not. It also leaves the door open for legal second-guessing by prosecutors as to when and how much force was used, including arguments that there was no imminent threat, and/or that physical force or deadly physical force was not really justified. If the prosecutor convinces a jury that a person used physical force or deadly physical force in response to a threat that was not imminent, a person's use of physical force or deadly physical force will not be legally justified, and that person will be guilty of using unlawful physical force or deadly physical force.

B. *Use of deadly physical force under 18-1-704*

Under section 18-1-704, one must meet a few requirements to be justified in the use of deadly physical force. First, "deadly physical force may be used only if a person reasonably believes that a lesser degree of force is inadequate." In addition, the user of deadly physical force must meet one of the following requirements: (1) most commonly, "the actor has reasonable ground to believe, and does believe, that he or another person is in imminent danger of being killed or of receiving great bodily injury; or" (2) the other person is using or reasonably appears about to use physical force against an occupant of a dwelling or business establishment while committing or attempting to commit burglary"; or (3) "the other person is committing or reasonably appears about to commit kidnapping," robbery, sexual assault, or assault.

C. _Definitions of the crimes that a person may use deadly physical force to thwart_

As explained above, section 18-1-704 lists several crimes, all felonies, which may justify a person's use of deadly physical force against the person committing them. They are burglary, kidnapping, robbery, sexual assault, and assault. How does the law define these offenses? Like so many things in the law, it may not be as straightforward as expected.

1. Burglary

A person is justified in using deadly physical force if they reasonably believe that a lesser degree of force would be inadequate and the other person is committing or attempting to commit a burglary. Importantly, 18-1-704 lists first, second, and third degree burglary as offenses which may justify the use of deadly physical force. What is burglary?

First let's look at first degree burglary, as defined in section 18-4-202 of the Colorado Revised Statutes. First degree burglary is a rather complicated offense with several elements. After listing the elements, we will examine them each in depth. In order to commit first degree burglary:

- The person must knowingly enter a building or occupied structure unlawfully or he must remain unlawfully in a building or occupied structure unlawfully after a lawful or unlawful entry.
- The person must intend to commit a crime other than trespass, against another person or property, within the building or structure.
- While inside, attempting to enter, or in immediate flight from the building or structure one of the crime's participants assaults or menaces a person, is armed with explosives, uses a deadly weapon, or possesses and threatens to use a deadly weapon.

The first element of first degree burglary requires that the person knowingly, unlawfully enter or unlawfully remain in a building or occupied structure. Notice that a person might enter a building lawfully but then do something, like commit a crime, which makes their presence in the building unlawful. If this occurs, remaining in the building converts a legal entry into a trespass or burglary.

The second element of first degree burglary requires that the person intend to commit a crime, other than trespass, against another person or property, within the building or structure. Often a burglar intends some degree of theft, although they may intend to injure an occupant. However, even the smallest offenses satisfy this requirement. For example, in *People v. Wildhalm*, 991 P.2d 291 (Colo. App. 1999), the court ruled that the violation of a restraining order satisfied this element. Also, notice that the element only requires that the person *intends* to commit a crime. Therefore, this element is satisfied upon making the unlawful entry if the person has the requisite intent. The person does not have to actually attempt the crime at all. Even if the crime the person intends to commit is actually impossible to successfully complete, this element of burglary is satisfied by the intention to commit it. *See People v. Gill*, 506 P.2d 134 (1973).

The third element has two parts. The primary part has to do with a burglar's use or potential use of deadly physical force. To satisfy this part, one of the crime's participants must assault or menace another person, be armed with explosives, use a deadly weapon, or possess and threaten to use a deadly weapon. If there are multiple participants to the crime, only one must satisfy this element for all of the participants to be guilty of first degree burglary. The secondary part of this element has to do with the location where the burglar's use or potential use of deadly physical force occurred. Obviously, if a burglar uses or threatens to use deadly physical force to enter or while within a building or occupied structure, this part of the element is satisfied. The tricky part is what counts as "immediate flight" from the building or occupied structure? In *People v. Fuentes*, 258 P.3d 320 (Colo. App. 2011), the court found that the immediate flight standard is satisfied when the flight occurred close in time to the entry, and that the participant to the crime used or threatened the use of deadly physical force during that flight. The use of deadly physical force happens during the immediate flight if it is "part of a continuous integrated attempt to get away from the building."

Next, let's look at second degree burglary, as defined in section 18-4-203 of the Colorado Revised Statutes. Second degree burglary is the same as first degree burglary except that there is no requirement that deadly physical force has been used or threatened. Therefore, to commit second degree burglary, a person must satisfy only the first two elements of first degree burglary, explained in full above.

Finally, let's look at third degree burglary, as defined in section 18-4-204. In order to commit third degree burglary a person must enter or break into any vault, safe, cash register, coin vending machine, product dispenser, money depository, safety deposit box, coin telephone, coin box, or other apparatus or equipment whether or not coin operated with the intent to commit a crime.

Recall that section 18-1-704 justifies the use of deadly physical force to stop a burglar only if the burglar "reasonably appears about to use physical force against an occupant of a building or occupied structure." This could be an important distinction depending on the facts in a particular situation. For example, if a person knew that the burglar was entering an empty building, he would not be justified in using deadly physical force to stop the burglar.

You may be asking yourself "how am I expected to remember these elements and apply them to a given situation in the heat of the moment when I am witnessing a potential burglary?" Remember that section 18-1-704 only requires that there is a *reasonable appearance* that a person is about to use physical force against an occupant while attempting to commit burglary. As with most legal self-defense issues, whether there was such a reasonable appearance will be a question for a jury.

Example:

> *Jane is returning from a party late at night and parks in her driveway. Out of the corner of her eye, Jane sees a masked man using the butt of a handgun to break the neighbor's window. From inside the neighbor's house, Jane hears a scream. Jane draws her gun and shoots the masked man dead.*

In this example, was Jane justified in her use of deadly physical force against the masked man? Probably yes. Under the circumstances, it was reasonable for Jane to believe that the masked man was actively committing a burglary. The masked man had broken the window, indicating he intended to enter the building. He was masked, which indicates he was likely not welcome in the building and that he intended to commit a crime. The masked man held a gun, satisfying the potential use of deadly force element of burglary. Lastly, because Jane heard a scream, she knew that the neighbor was within and it was reasonable to believe that the armed man was about to use physical force against the neighbor. A jury would likely determine that Jane was justified in her use of deadly physical force. However, juries don't always come to the most obvious conclusion. There is always a risk when it is left to other people to determine the reasonableness of your actions in the heat of the moment.

2. Kidnapping

A person is justified in using deadly physical force if they reasonably believe that a lesser degree of force would be inadequate and the other person is committing or attempting to commit kidnapping. Section 18-1-704 allows for the use of deadly physical force to thwart both first degree and second degree kidnapping. What is kidnapping?

First, let's look at first degree kidnapping. After listing the elements, we will look at each in depth. First degree kidnapping includes both an action element and an intent element. Under section 18-3-301 of the Colorado Revised Statutes, to be guilty of first degree kidnapping:

- A person must either forcibly seize and carry a person from one place to another, entice or persuade a person to go from one place to another, or imprison someone, and;
- Intend to force the victim or any other person to make any concession or give up anything of value in order to secure the release of the victim who is under the perpetrator's actual or apparent control.

The first element is fairly straightforward. The perpetrator has to either forcibly move the victim or entice the victim to go to a location. However, to be guilty of first degree kidnapping, the perpetrator must move the victim with the intention of receiving a ransom or some benefit to secure the victim's release.

Next, let's examine second degree kidnapping. To be guilty of second degree kidnapping under 18-3-302 of the Colorado Revised Statutes, a person must:

- Knowingly seize and carry any person from one place to another, without his consent and without lawful justification, or;
- Take, entice, or decoy any other person's child under 18 with intent to keep or conceal the child from his parent or guardian or with the intent to sell, trade, or barter such child for consideration.

In the first instance, second degree kidnapping is the same as first degree, except that it lacks the intent to receive a ransom or some other benefit. However, if the kidnapping involves a child, then one must also have the intent to sell, trade, or barter the child for compensation of some kind or the intent to keep the child from their parents.

It might not be clear whether a first or second degree kidnapping is occurring when an attacker attempts to abduct a victim. However, under the self-defense statute, it doesn't matter which degree has occurred. Either degree can give a justification for the use of deadly physical force, provided that the defender reasonably believed that no lesser degree of force would have been sufficient to prevent the kidnapping.

Example:
> Jane is out jogging one evening, when a white van pulls up next to her, and a masked man with a gun jumps out, trying to grab her and drag her into his van. Jane pulls out her Glock 42 and fires two shots, killing her attacker.

In this example, was Jane legally justified in her use of deadly physical force against the man? Probably yes. However, a jury would make the final determination on the reasonableness of Jane's actions. Jane was likely reasonable in her belief that the attacker was attempting to commit either first or second degree kidnapping. Given that the attacker had a gun, Jane likely reasonably believed that a lesser degree of force would be inadequate to prevent the kidnapping. These are clear examples, however. We will discuss later how the law is applied in more ambiguous cases.

3. Sexual assault

A person is justified in using deadly physical force if they reasonably believe that a lesser degree of force would be inadequate and the other person is committing or attempting to commit a sexual assault. How does the law define sexual assault?

Section 18-3-402 of the Colorado Revised Statutes defines sexual assault. To be guilty of sexual assault, a person must knowingly inflict sexual intrusion or sexual penetration on a victim and at least one of the following must be true:

- The actor causes the victim to submit by using means that the actor calculated would cause the victim to submit against the victim's will;
- The actor knows that the victim is incapable of appraising the nature of the victim's conduct;
- The actor knows that the victim wrongly believes that the actor is the victim's spouse;
- The victim is less than 15 years old, the actor is at least 4 years older than the victim, and the actor and victim are not married;
- The victim is between 15 and 17 years old, the actor is at least 10 years older than the victim, and the actor and victim are not married;
- The victim is detained by police or in a hospital or other institution, the actor has supervisory or disciplinary authority over the victim and uses that authority to coerce the victim, unless the act is part of a lawful search;
- The actor poses as a medical professional and engages in treatment or examination of the victim for a purpose other than a bona fide medical purpose; or
- The victim is physically helpless and has not consented and the actor knows this.

Most of the situations that constitute a sexual assault involve some kind of abuse of power or false pretenses. A note about the fourth and fifth bullet points above. These two situations focus on the ages of the victim and the actor. Notice that there is no requirement that the actor knows the age of the victim. The only knowledge requirement is the requirement that the actor knowingly engages in the sexual contact. In these scenarios, the victim may misrepresent their age to the actor. This would not protect the actor from a sexual assault charge.

As always, remember that to be justified in using deadly physical force to prevent sexual assault you have to reasonably believe that a sexual assault is occurring or about to occur and you must also reasonably believe that a lesser degree of force would be inadequate to prevent the crime. Again, it will be up to a jury to determine the reasonableness of your actions.

4. Assault

A person is justified in using deadly physical force if they reasonably believe that a lesser degree of force would be inadequate and the other person is committing or attempting to commit an assault. How does the law define assault?

In Colorado, the law distinguishes between first and second degree assault. Both first and second degree assault can provide a justification for the use of deadly physical force under section 18-1-704. Assault is a rather complicated offence with a wide array of differences between first and second degree. Remember that you only need to have a reasonable belief that an assault is occurring or about to occur to be justified in the use of deadly force, provided that you have a reasonable belief that a lesser amount of force would be inadequate to stop the assault.

First let's examine first degree assault, defined in the Colorado Revised Statutes under 18-3-202. A person commits first degree assault if:

- A person intends to cause serious bodily injury to another person, and does cause serious bodily injury to that person with a deadly weapon;
- A person intends to and does seriously and permanently disfigure another person, or destroys, amputates, or permanently disables another person's organ;

- While acting with extreme indifference to human life, a person knowingly engages in conduct which creates a grave risk of death to another person, and thereby causes serious bodily injury to any person; or
- Even without actually causing injury, a person threatens with a deadly weapon with the intent to cause serious bodily injury a peace officer, firefighter, emergency medical service provider, judge, or an officer of the court, if the victim is engaged in performance of their duties, and the person knows this or reasonably should have known.

In most cases, a person must intend to cause serious bodily injury to another person in order to be guilty of first degree assault. The third bullet point above is the exception to that rule. For example, a person who randomly fires a gun into a crowd may not have the intent to cause serious bodily injury to any specific person, but they have acted with extreme indifference to human life and are guilty of assault if they in fact cause a serious injury to someone. The last bullet differs from the other three because a person can be guilty of assault without actually causing an injury when they intend to injure and threaten peace officers and court officials.

Next, let's examine second degree assault, defined in the Colorado Revised Statutes under 18-3-203. A person commits second degree assault if:

- He causes bodily injury to another person with a deadly weapon with the intent to cause bodily injury to that person;
- With intent to prevent a person they knew, or should have known, was a peace officer, firefighter, or emergency medical service provider from performing their lawful duties, he causes bodily injury to any person;
- He recklessly causes serious bodily injury to another person by means of a deadly weapon;

- Without a lawful medical purpose, he causes physical or mental impairment to a person by administering a drug knowingly and without the person's consent; or
- While lawfully confined or in custody, he violently applies physical force against a peace officer, firefighter, emergency medical service provider, judge, officer of the court, or a detention facility employee.

Notice the only difference between the first bullet point and first degree assault is the severity of injury and the intended injury. First degree assault requires serious bodily injury while second degree assault merely requires bodily injury. The second bullet point differs from first degree assault in two ways. First, to be guilty of second degree assault, one must actually cause a bodily injury to a peace officer. Second, second degree assault upon a peace officer does not require a deadly weapon. The third bullet requires recklessness, which is not as egregious as first degree assault's extreme indifference to human life. A person may be reckless when they seriously injure a bystander while firing a gun into the air, for example.

5. Robbery

A person is justified in using deadly physical force if they reasonably believe that a lesser degree of force would be inadequate and the other person is committing or attempting to commit a robbery. Section 18-1-704 allows for the use of deadly physical force to thwart both robbery and aggravated robbery. What is robbery? What is aggravated robbery?

Under section 18-4-301, a person is guilty of robbery when they knowingly take anything of value from another person's body or immediate vicinity by the use of force, threats, or intimidation. Robbery is essentially stealing a person's possessions while they are present through some use of force.

Aggravated robbery, defined in section 18-4-302, uses the exact same elements as robbery but adds the requirement of aggravating factors. To be guilty of aggravated robbery, a person must be committing a robbery or fleeing the scene of a robbery they committed while either:

- Armed with a deadly weapon with intent to kill, maim, or wound the victim or any other person if they resist;
- Knowingly using a deadly weapon to wound or strike the victim or any other person;
- Knowingly using force, threats, or intimidation with a deadly weapon that causes the victim or any other person reasonable fear of death or bodily injury; or
- using any item in a manner that leads any onlooker to reasonably believe it to be a deadly weapon or if he claims to be armed with a deadly weapon (for example: a finger in a coat pocket representing a gun).

To be guilty of aggravated robbery, a robber must take at least one of the above listed actions in addition to the robbery. Now let's consider an example:

Example:

> Tina is on her way home from work. She stops by a local convenience store for some bread and milk. As she enters the store, a masked man suddenly approaches her with a knife, grabs her by the arm, and demands her money. Tina, scared and shaken, remembers her training, opens her purse and pulls a .357 revolver and fires, killing the masked robber.

In this example, because an aggravated robbery was happening, section 18-1-704 allows for Tina's use of deadly physical force, provided that she reasonably believed that a lesser degree of force would be inadequate to prevent the robbery. Thus, her use of deadly force is likely legally justified. What if the example is less clear?

Example:

> *Hank, a 66-year-old disabled man, works downtown. He has to park four blocks from his company's office buildings and has to walk through some rough parts of town in order to get to his car. A man suddenly appears in front of him and says, "Hey man—give me some money!" Hank, feeling very frightened and intimidated, walks on with the now more loud and aggressive panhandler demanding, "Hey! Man! I said give me some money!" Hank now becomes extremely concerned for his safety. About that time, Hank makes a wrong turn into an alley where he is cornered. He again hears, "HEY! MAN! I SAID GIVE ME SOME MONEY!" When Hank turns around, he sees the same man, now very aggressive, with something in his hand.*

Is the panhandler just being annoying, or is Hank about to be the victim of robbery or aggravated robbery? This is the ultimate issue Hank may face if Hank decides to use physical force or even deadly physical force against the alleged aggressor. How will the law evaluate a use of deadly physical force under section 18-1-704?

This is an example with a lot of gray area. The man never verbally threatened Hank, nor did he ever physically touch him. All the man said was "give me some money;" he didn't even demand *all* of Hank's money—just some. Do robbers ever demand just some money? If Hank is in genuine fear of an aggravated robbery, does he have a duty to retreat? What about the fact that Hank was cornered in an alley? If Hank takes out his legally concealed carry pistol and fires it to defend himself, what happens? Was Hank really about to be robbed, or is he a paranoid trigger-happy fellow as the prosecutor may try to portray him? Beyond that, who decides what the facts really were? This goes to show that there are lots of questions and gray area.

If Hank finds himself charged with unlawfully using physical force or deadly physical force against his alleged attacker, he can assert a legal justification based on self-defense under section 18-1-704 of the Colorado Revised Statutes. Again, the law will allow Hank to use physical force or deadly physical force for self-defense when and to the degree he reasonably believes is necessary to prevent an imminent unlawful use of force. Section 18-1-407 of the Colorado Revised Statutes defines "affirmative defense" and lays out how such a defense operates. In this example, under section 18-1-407, before a jury will be allowed to decide if Hank acted in self-defense, Hank must present to the judge "some credible evidence" at trial that he reasonably believed he was about to be robbed (see our discussion of what constitutes "some credible evidence" in the next section).

D. *What is "some credible evidence?"*
So, how much evidence does a person have to offer in a trial to constitute "some credible evidence" in order to be entitled to a jury instruction regarding self-defense? The Colorado Supreme Court held that only "a scintilla of evidence" is needed to trigger an affirmative defense. "Scintilla" is a legal term of art that means even the smallest amount of evidence is enough. *O'Shaughnessy v. People*, 269 P.3d 1233, 1236 (2012).   This means that in court, a defendant can literally offer anything as evidence that raises the issue of self-defense, and he is entitled to receive a jury instruction regarding self-defense under section 18-1-704. The only requirement is that the evidence offered must be related to the incident of self-defense at issue. Whether a

defendant has satisfied the "some credible evidence" standard is a question of law, which means that it is for the judge to determine, not the jury.

The "some credible evidence" requirement may be satisfied where the evidence offered is as simple as the defendant's own testimony, "even if the evidence is improbable." *People v. Johnson*, 327 P.3d 305, 310 (Colo. 2014). In other words, a defendant who testifies in court at his own trial that he was attacked first and feared for his life as a result of the attack has submitted sufficient evidence to be entitled to a jury instruction on self-defense.

Of course, relying on a defendant's testimony to be the sole source of evidence in order to obtain a jury instruction on self-defense can be fraught with peril as well. All defendants have the right *not* to testify at their trial—which can be a sound trial tactic because it prevents the State from examining the defendant under oath and on the witness stand. Once a defendant takes the witness stand, however, that defendant will be subject to examination by not only his attorney, but also by the State. The State's and this cross examination may ultimately contain evidence which sways a jury away from acquitting on self-defense grounds.

Remember Hank's predicament above? Hank may attempt to satisfy the "some credible evidence" requirement by testifying that he was in fear for his safety and had seen the panhandler acting violently on the same street many times in the past. Hank may also say the man raised a weapon in his hand and was moving aggressively toward him, and that the assailant out-weighed Hank by 75 pounds and was about a foot taller. Hank will absolutely testify he felt he was being robbed. If Hank puts forth "some credible evidence" in court that he was the victim of an attempted aggravated robbery, the jury will get to decide if

Hank is credible and if his belief was reasonable, and the law then requires the prosecution to prove beyond a reasonable doubt that Hank did not act in self-defense. However, if Hank's attorney fails to put forth "some credible evidence" that he acted in self-defense, he will not be entitled to a self-defense jury instruction concerning section 18-1-704, and the prosecution will not have the burden to prove beyond a reasonable doubt that Hank did not act in self-defense.

Practical Legal Tip:

My experience as a trial lawyer is that many people serving on juries tend to ignore the rule of "innocent until proven guilty." Even though every person has a Constitutional right to not testify against themselves, by not doing so, it can cloud a juror's mind so as to make the notion of innocent until proven guilty viewed with skepticism. *-Doug*

E.   *"Make My Day"*

Colorado's "Make My Day" law, section 18-1-704.5, introduced in Chapter Four, was created based on a belief by Colorado lawmakers that "the citizens of Colorado have a right to expect absolute safety within their own homes." Recall that under "Make My Day," a person is justified in using any degree of force, up to and including deadly physical force, against an intruder in the person's "dwelling," if they have a reasonable belief that the intruder has or intends on committing a crime (other than the initial trespass) against a person or property inside the dwelling, and if they have a reasonable belief that the intruder "might use any physical force, no matter how slight, against any occupant." When exactly does this apply? The only way to answer this question is to look at the legal definition of dwelling.

1. What is a dwelling under "Make My Day?"

Section 18-1-901 defines "dwelling" as a "building which is used, intended to be used, or usually used by a person for habitation." First, let's consider what types of buildings clearly fall under this definition. Certainly, a person's primary residence, apartment, or condominium is a "dwelling."

Next, let's examine certain types of buildings which Colorado courts have determined are "dwellings" under the Colorado Revised Statutes. First, in *People v. Morales*, 298 P.3d 1000 (Colo. App. 2012), the court determined that an existing home which was under renovation at the time of a burglary was considered a "dwelling" because it was "intended to be used" for habitation in the future. The Colorado Supreme Court, in *People v. Jiminez*, 651 P.2d 395, 396 (Colo. 1982), held that a garage that is attached to a home is also considered part of a "dwelling."

Whether a hotel room or hospital room is a "dwelling" is a little less clear. In *People v. Germany*, 586 P.2d 1006 (Colo. App. 1978), the court recognized that courts in other states have ruled that hotel rooms were "dwellings" because they are "habitually used as a place where persons sleep." Based on this, the court determined that hospital rooms are also "dwellings" because people habitually sleep in them. However, this case was overturned by the Colorado Supreme Court based on errors made by the court on unrelated legal issues. It is likely that a future court would rule that hospital and hotel rooms are "dwellings" based on the rationale in the *Germany* case and in cases from other states, but it is not absolutely certain.

Lastly, let's look at specific parts of buildings which are not considered "dwellings" by Colorado courts. In *People v. Cushinberry*, 855 P.2d 18 (Colo. App. 1992), the court determined that "common areas" of an apartment building, such as a stairwell, were not "dwellings" under "Make My Day." It follows that "common areas" would include lobbies, hallways, laundry rooms and other similar parts of an apartment building.

F. *A person who provokes an attack is not entitled to act in self-defense*

Under section 18-1-704(3)(a), "a person is not justified in using physical force" if "he provokes the use of unlawful physical force by" the other person with the "intent to cause bodily injury or death to another person." If a person provokes another person into the unlawful use of force for the purpose of injuring or killing that person under the guise of self-defense, that person cannot claim self-defense as a justification. The most important thing to understand is that "mere words" generally are not sufficient provocation that would prevent a person from claiming self-defense. *People v. Silva*, 987 P.2d 909, (Colo. App. 1999); *People v. Winn*, 540 P.2d 1114 (Colo. App. 1975).

G. *The "doctrine of no-retreat"*

Many states have "Stand Your Ground" laws which govern whether a person must retreat before using physical force in the face of an attacker. Colorado does not have such a law. Instead, Colorado courts rely on the common law "doctrine of no-retreat." Common law simply means law that is created by courts in the absence of a statute that governs the legal issue.

In Colorado, the doctrine of no-retreat "permits non-aggressors who are otherwise entitled to use physical force in self-defense to do so without first retreating, or seeking safety by means of escape." *People v. Coughlin*, 304 P.3d 575, 587 (Colo. App. 2011). When the court says "non-aggressors," it refers to "initial aggressors" under section 18-1-704, who must retreat and effectively communicate their intent to retreat to the other person. Beyond "initial aggressors," there is no duty to retreat in Colorado. Keep in mind at all times that, although there is not a *duty* to retreat, all of your actions will be examined by a jury to determine if your actions were reasonable. In a situation where retreat would have been easily made without risk of harm to yourself, a prosecutor will certainly question whether your belief that deadly physical force was necessary was reasonable.

H. *"Initial aggressors" under section 18-1-704*

As mentioned above, under 18-1-704, "initial aggressors" are not justified in using physical force in self-defense unless they withdraw from the encounter, effectively communicate their withdrawal to the other person, and the other person continues or threatens to use unlawful physical force.

What makes someone an initial aggressor? An initial aggressor is a person who has "initiated the physical conflict by using or threatening the imminent use of unlawful physical force." *People v. Griffin*, 224 P.3d 292, 300 (Colo. App. 2009). Most commonly, an initial aggressor is someone who uses unlawful force against another person and then realizes they made a mistake. Certainly, a person who provokes another with the intent to injure or kill that person is an initial aggressor. As with provocation, mere words will generally not make someone an initial aggressor. At trial, the jury will examine the actions of the defendant in the context of a particular situation and will determine if that person was an initial aggressor.

What constitutes withdrawal and an effective communication of withdrawal? Again, this will be a question for the jury to determine. As such, any action that could be considered withdrawal may convince a jury that withdrawal occurred. In *People v. Smith*, 682 P.2d 493, 495 (Colo. App. 1983), the court held that simply turning and walking away from the other person could constitute a withdrawal. Further, a withdrawal can be communicated to the other person through body language alone. The *Smith* court held that a jury could find that turning and walking away from a conflict was an effective communication of withdrawal.

I. *Consent to force*

Section 18-1-704(3)(c) prevents a person from claiming self-defense as a justification if the "physical force involved is the product of a combat by agreement not specifically authorized by law. This is best explained with an example.

Example:

> *Andy and Dwight are having an argument about whose favorite football team will win the championship. In the heat of the argument, Andy calls Dwight a derogatory name and Dwight asks if Andy wants to take it outside. Andy agrees and they both begin fighting in the parking lot. Shortly after they begin fighting, the police show up and arrest them for disorderly conduct and assault.*

This statute serves the purpose of preventing individuals who arrange to fight each other from avoiding criminal responsibility for their actions by claiming self-defense. The statute here is clear: if a person agrees to the force used against him or her by another person, that person cannot later claim that he or she fought back in self-defense! To fall under this exception to self-defense, there must have been an agreement to fight between the parties entered into prior to the beginning of combat. *See People v. Cuevas*, 740 P.2d 25, 26 (Colo. App. 1987). This statute also applies to individuals who agree to participate in unlicensed "fight clubs." That now explains why "the first rule of fight club is you do not talk about fight club!"

III. Do I have a legal responsibility to defend another person?

Under Colorado law, the average person has <u>no duty to come to the defense of another</u>, so long as that actor was not the cause of the situation or occurrence. This is true even if a crime is in progress (but note: this lack of a legal duty does not include police officers and other professionals that may have affirmative legal duties to assist). If you see a third person that is the victim of what you believe to be the unlawful use of force or deadly force, you have no legal duty to aid that person—it is your decision. This is equally true if you are legally carrying a gun. But what if you decide to help the third person?

Practical Legal Tip:

The right to remain silent is a fundamental Constitutional right which is why it is so disturbing that in 2010, the US Supreme Court held that you have to say the magic words of "I invoke my right to remain silent and to counsel" in order to trigger it. Seemingly, by the Court's standard, if you don't say the magic words, police could interrogate you until the end of time. *-Chris*

A. *Defense of a third party*

Under Colorado law, the law does not make a distinction between self-defense and defense of a third person. Both are covered under section 18-1-704 and follow the same rules. Therefore, when a person uses physical force or deadly physical force in defense of a third party, the jury will consider whether the degree of force used was reasonable and whether the person reasonably believed that it was necessary to prevent the use or imminent use of unlawful physical force against the third party.

B. *What if the situation is not as I thought it appeared to be?*
A third person and a "Good Samaritan" may not potentially see things as they really are. When a person elects to use force or deadly force to defend a third person, it can all go terribly wrong.

Example:

> Peter, a permitted concealed handgun owner, decides to get some lunch, so he pulls into a local burger joint to eat. He parks and exits his vehicle whereupon he witnesses a man walking out of the restaurant and across the parking lot. Suddenly, another man comes running up and points a gun in the first man's face. Peter, not wanting the man to become a victim of a robbery, drops to one knee while drawing his handgun. Still seeing the gun pointed at the first man, Peter decides to protect the would-be victim of robbery and fires his gun striking the robber.

If there was in fact an armed robbery taking place, Peter's use of deadly force is likely legally justified, because Peter had a reasonable belief that an aggravated robbery was occurring, and Peter would be legally justified in using deadly physical force to stop the aggravated robbery under 18-1-704. Thus, the law will deem Peter's belief that the use of deadly physical force was necessary as reasonable. But what if there was no armed robbery?

In fact, what would happen if in the instant after Peter fires his gun, the man Peter sought to protect immediately turns to help the wounded suspected robber yelling "murderer!" at Peter while screaming in fear and grief, "why did you shoot my friend?" It turns out that there was not robbery, just a couple of fellows were pranking each other, and the gun Peter saw was a toy. How does the law deal with this scenario?

In such a situation, Peter's perspective and knowledge of the situation are very different from the person he sought to defend. The man clearly knew there was no robbery in progress since he recognized his friend, and that it was a prank. However, when a person acts in defense of a third party, just as when they act in self-defense, what matters is whether the actor's belief was reasonable based on their own perception and knowledge of the situation. In this situation, if Peter's belief that an aggravated robbery was in progress was reasonable, then Peter will be legally justified. However, if a jury finds that his belief was unreasonable, Peter will not be legally justified and likely guilty of aggravated assault.

IV. The use of force in preventing suicide

Colorado law provides that a person may be justified in using force to prevent another from committing suicide or inflicting serious bodily injury on themselves. If a person has a reasonable belief that it is necessary to use force in order to prevent another from committing suicide or inflicting serious bodily injury on themselves, then the reasonable use of physical force is justified. Of course, the use of deadly physical force is never justified in that scenario: the purpose of this statute is to preserve life, not end it!

Justified Use of Force to Prevent Suicide or Self-Inflicted Serious Bodily Injury: Co. Revised Statutes § 18-1-703(1)(d)

1. The use of physical force upon another person which would otherwise constitute an offense is justifiable and not criminal under any of the following circumstances:

(d) A person acting under reasonable belief that another person is about to commit suicide or to inflict serious bodily injury upon himself may use reasonable and appropriate physical force upon that person to the extent that it is reasonably necessary to thwart the result.

CHAPTER SIX
WHEN CAN I LEGALLY USE MY GUN: PART III
UNDERSTANDING WHEN DEADLY FORCE
CAN BE USED AGAINST ANIMALS

I. Can I legally use deadly force against animals?

When it comes to the law of use of force and deadly force to defend yourself, others, or property from animal attacks, Colorado law is a hodgepodge of different laws that are not contained in one section of statutes.

A. *No general defense against animals statute*

Colorado has no general self-defense or defense of others statute that deals with animals. There exist statutes that justify conduct against bears, mountain lions, and dogs if necessary to prevent injury to a person, livestock, or damage to property.   The typical laws you would expect to find such as self-defense against an animal attacking a human being don't exist under Colorado law at all!   What this means is that one may not find specific legal justification for using force or deadly force against an animal that is attacking, if the animal is not a certain type of animal. Under this condition, a person may be forced to argue that they faced a "choice of evils."   Colorado's "choice of evils" statute is a codification of the common law "doctrine of necessity."   This chapter will examine the laws that do exist relating to the use of deadly force against an animal and how your right to self-preservation can best be accomplished.

B. *"Choice of Evils"*

Because there is no specific Colorado law that allows a person to use deadly physical force against an animal in self-defense, often the best claim for legal justification a person can make in a court is one of "Choice of Evils," which is defined in Colorado Revised Statutes § 18-1-702.

> ### Definition of Choice of Evils:
> ### Colorado Revised Statutes § 18-1-702
>
> Conduct is justified when:
> - It is necessary as an emergency measure to avoid an imminent public or private injury which is about to occur by reason of a situation not caused by the actor; and
> - The emergency is of sufficient gravity that, according to ordinary standards of intelligence and morality, the desirability and urgency of avoiding injury clearly outweigh the desirability of avoiding the injury sought to be prevented by the statute designing the offence.

As this law applies to animal attacks, a person may be legally justified in using force or deadly force (such as firing their gun) against an attacking animal if a public or private injury is *imminent* and emergency action is required. Note that the "Choice of Evils" defense can only be used to justify criminal acts.

Practical Legal Tip:

Beware! Using deadly force against a dog or cat that is only digging into your flowerbed or getting into your garbage may not be justified even under the doctrine of necessity. *-Stanley*

C. *Bears, Mountain Lions, and Dogs*

Section 33-3-106 of the Colorado Revised Statutes primarily allows parks and wildlife divisions to issue permits to property owners when animals of some kind are causing excessive damage to property. These permits allow the property owner to kill a certain number of a specified animal. For self-defense purposes, the important part of this section is (3), which allows a person to kill bears, mountain lions, and dogs without a permit "to prevent them from inflicting death, damage, or injury to livestock, real property, a motor vehicle, or human life." Additionally, this provision allows for the killing of dogs "when it is necessary to prevent them from inflicting death or injury to big game and to small game, birds, and mammals." Under this statute, a person would be justified in killing an aggressive bear, mountain lion, or dog. However, in the case of any other type of animal, this section will not offer protection.

Affirmative Defense for Cruelty to Animals Statute: Colorado Revised Statutes § 18-9-202(2.5)
It shall be an affirmative defense to a charge brought under this section involving injury or death to a dog that the dog was found running, worrying, or injuring sheep, cattle, or other livestock.

D. *Dogs found "running, worrying, or injuring" livestock*
Section 35-43-126 of the Colorado Revised Statutes specifically justifies the killing of a dog if that dog is found "running, worrying, or injuring" livestock. Because of this, the cruelty to animals statute, 18-9-202(2.5), provides an affirmative defense when a dog is killed pursuant to the "worrying" statute. It is notable that this section is specifically limited to dogs harassing animals, not people.

E. *Federal law defenses*
The federal law, in a comprehensive fashion, has actually had the foresight to specifically provide that a person may kill an animal protected by federal law in self-defense, such as the regulations concerning the Mexican gray wolf in 50 CFR § 17.84(k)(3)(xii), or the grizzly bear in 50 CFR § 17.40(b)(i)(B). Unlike the Colorado statutes, this makes the Federal law clear and comprehendible. Therefore, if you are carrying a firearm in a National Park (see Chapters Nine and Ten), and you find yourself face to face with a grizzly bear, you will have a legal defense for protecting yourself.

CHAPTER SEVEN
WHEN CAN I LEGALLY USE MY GUN: PART IV
UNDERSTANDING WHEN DEADLY PHYSICAL FORCE
CAN BE USED TO PROTECT PROPERTY

I.   Overview and location of the law to protect property

Colorado law allows a person to protect, with physical force, their property from another's unlawful interference or trespass on their property or the property of another. Further, Colorado law, under certain circumstances, will also allow a person to use legally justified deadly physical force to protect property. The statutes in the Colorado Revised Statutes dealing with legally justified physical force or deadly physical force to defend property are as follows:

> 18-1-706: Use of physical force in defense of property
> 18-1-705: Use of physical force in defense of premises

Protection of property will be analyzed under the same "reasonable person" standard discussed in Chapters Four and Five.

II.   When is someone legally justified to use "physical force" but not "deadly physical force" to protect their own property?

Section 18-1-706 of the Colorado Revised Statutes governs the justified use of physical force in defense of property. This section covers the defense of one's own property and the defense of a third person's property. Importantly, this section does not expand the use of deadly physical force; rather, it says that a person who acts in defense of property may only use deadly physical force "in defense of himself or another as described in section 18-1-704." Physical force short of deadly physical force is allowed under 18-1-706 to prevent another person from committing "theft, criminal mischief, or criminal tampering involving property."

> ### Use of Physical Force in Defense of Property:
> ### Colorado Revised Statutes § 18-1-706
>
> A person is justified in using reasonable and appropriate physical force upon another person when and to the extent that he reasonably believes it necessary to prevent what he reasonably believes to be an attempt by the other person to commit theft, criminal mischief, or criminal tampering involving property, but he may use deadly physical force under these circumstances only in defense of himself or another as described in section 18-1-704

A. *What is theft?*

Theft, as defined in section 18-4-401 of the Colorado Revised Statutes, has both an action and an intent requirement. A person commits theft if he or she "knowingly obtains, retains, or exercises control over anything of value of another without authorization or by threat or deception," *and* one of the following is true:

- The person intends to permanently deprive the owner the use or benefit of the thing of value;
- The person knowingly uses, conceals, or abandons the thing of value in a way that permanently deprives the owner of its use or benefit; or
- The person demands something that he or she is not entitled to for the return of the owner's property.

To be guilty of theft, a person must both take an item without authorization and intend to permanently deprive the owner of that item or ransom the item. Do not confuse theft with its more serious cousin burglary, discussed in Chapter Five. Burglary involves entering into a dwelling or occupied structure with the intent to commit another crime within, often theft.

A person is justified in using physical force, but not deadly physical force, to prevent what they reasonably believe to be a theft. For a person to be justified in using physical force to prevent a theft, he must have a reasonable belief that a theft is occurring or about to occur, and he must use a reasonable amount of force that he reasonably believes to be necessary to prevent the theft. That is a lot of reasonableness! Ultimately, a jury will decide the reasonableness of your actions and whether the amount of force used is reasonable. Think twice before using a firearm to prevent a theft, because if the thief is killed, your actions are never justified under this statute. Even if the thief survives his wounds, a jury is likely to see the (use of a firearm) to prevent simple theft as unreasonable.

B. *What is Criminal Mischief?*
Criminal mischief is akin to vandalism. Under section 18-4-501 of the Colorado Revised Statutes, a "person commits criminal mischief when he or she knowingly damages the real or personal property of one or more other persons, including property owned by the person jointly with another person or property owned by the person in which another person has a possessory or proprietary interest, in the course of a single criminal episode." Interestingly, a person can commit criminal mischief against his own property if someone else has an interest in the same property. Just as with theft, use extreme caution when considering the use of a firearm to prevent criminal mischief, as it is unlikely to be a reasonable response.

C. *What is Criminal Tampering?*
Under the defense of property statute, physical force is justified to prevent criminal tampering when it relates to property. Second degree criminal tampering, under section 18-4-506 of the Colorado Revised Statutes, primarily deals with tampering of private property. To be guilty of second degree criminal tampering, a person must tamper "with property of another with intent to cause injury, inconvenience, or annoyance to that person or to another." Unlike with criminal mischief, criminal

tampering does not require property damage. As with theft and criminal mischief, the use of a gun to prevent criminal tampering is unlikely to be considered reasonable by a jury.

D. *Use of deadly physical force to protect property*
Colorado's defense of property statute expressly forbids the use of deadly physical force except in those situations listed in 18-1-704. There are two property-related offenses listed under 18-1-704, burglary and robbery. The use of deadly physical force to thwart a burglary or a robbery is fully covered in Chapter Five.

E. *Prevention only*
The language of the statute is clear that physical force may only be used to *prevent* a crime against property (including while the crime is ongoing). Therefore, once a theft has already been completed, a person is not justified in using physical force to retrieve the stolen item. Further, physical force in retaliation for a crime against property is never justified. *See People v. Goedecke*, 730 P.2d 900, 901 (Colo. App. 1986).

III. **Use of physical force in defense of premises**

> ### Use of Physical Force in Defense of Premises:
> ### Colorado Revised Statutes § 18-1-705
>
> A person in possession or control of any building, realty, or other premises, or a person who is licensed or privileged to be thereon, is justified in using reasonable and appropriate physical force upon another person when and to the extent that it is reasonably necessary to prevent or terminate what he reasonably believes to be the commission or attempted commission of an unlawful trespass by the other person in or upon the building, realty, or premises. However, he may use deadly force only in defense of himself or another as described in section 18-1-704, or when he reasonably believes it necessary to prevent what he reasonably believes to be an attempt by the trespasser to commit first degree arson.

Section 18-1-705 of the Colorado Revised Statutes covers the use of force in defense of premises. This differs from the defense of property statute in that it focuses on real property rather than personal property. This statute applies not only to homeowners, but also to business owners and security guards. This statute allows for the use of physical force, but not deadly physical force, to prevent a trespass. Like the defense of property statute, the use of deadly physical force is allowed under the circumstances listed in section 18-1-704. However, unlike the defense of property statute, the defense of premises statute allows for the use of deadly force when the actor reasonably believes it is necessary to prevent what he reasonably believes to be an attempt by the trespasser to commit first degree arson. What are trespass and arson?

A. *What is trespass?*

In Colorado, trespass is divided into first, second, and third degree. Unlike burglary, note that trespass does not include the use of a weapon or threats of physical force. As such, it is generally unlikely that a jury would find that the use of a firearm to shoot a trespasser was reasonable. However, remember that under Make My Day, covered in Chapter Four and Five, an occupant of a dwelling may be justified in shooting at a trespasser, if it can be shown that he reasonably believed that the trespasser intended to commit a crime in the dwelling, and he reasonably believed that the trespasser might use any degree of force against an occupant. A successful defense under Make My Day confers immunity from suit, which means that the question of reasonableness never goes before a jury. Next, let's look at the three degrees of trespass.

1. First Degree Criminal Trespass

Under section 18-4-502 of the Colorado Revised Statutes, "[a] person commits the crime of first degree criminal trespass if such person knowingly and unlawfully enters or remains in a dwelling of another or if such person enters any motor vehicle with intent to commit a crime therein." First degree criminal trespass in a dwelling differs from burglary in that the trespasser does not have the intent to commit a crime inside the dwelling and does not threaten or use force. However, to be guilty of first degree criminal trespass of a vehicle, the law does require the intent to commit a crime within the vehicle. Next, let's consider second degree criminal trespass.

2. Second Degree Criminal Trespass

Second degree criminal trespass, defined in section 18-4-503 of the Colorado Revised Statutes, has to do with unlawfully entering and remaining in the premises of another, rather than a dwelling. A person who unlawfully enters an enclosed area designed to exclude intruders or fenced in areas commits second degree criminal trespass. Also, knowingly and unlawfully entering a motor vehicle, without the intent to commit a crime within, is second degree criminal trespass. Lastly, a person who "knowingly and unlawfully enters or remains in the common areas of a hotel, motel, condominium, or apartment building" commits second degree criminal trespass. Next, let's examine third degree criminal trespass.

3. Third Degree Criminal Trespass

Third degree criminal trespass, defined in section 18-4-504 of the Colorado Revised Statutes, only has to do with unlawfully entering premises. It differs from second degree in that the premises entered is not fenced or designed to exclude intruders. Third degree criminal trespass is a petty crime. As with all actions in defense of property, consider the severity of the criminal's actions before responding with physical force. Unlike you, the jury will have the benefit of hindsight when they determine if your actions were reasonable.

B. *What is First Degree Arson?*

Section 18-1-705 allows for the use of deadly physical force against a trespasser if the person reasonably believes that the trespasser is committing or is about to commit first degree arson. First degree arson is defined in section 18-4-102 of the Colorado

Revised Statutes. "A person who knowingly sets fire to, burns, causes to be burned, or by the use of any explosive damages or destroys, or causes to be damaged or destroyed, any building or occupied structure of another without his consent commits first degree arson." If you decide to use deadly physical force against a trespasser who you believe is attempting to commit first degree arson, it will be up to the jury to decide the reasonableness of your belief. What will matter are the facts of the specific case. Did the trespasser have a gasoline can? Were explosives visible? The answers to these questions may mean the difference between a verdict of guilty and not guilty.

IV. Can I protect another person's property?

Yes. The protection of property and premises statutes function exactly the same as the self-defense statutes in that they also allow for the protection of another person's property. The use of physical force in defense of another person's property is no different under the law than an action in defense of one's own property. As such, all of the same reasonableness standards and justifications apply.

V. How can I assist law enforcement?

We would like to begin this section with a huge disclaimer. Your authors advise against using a firearm to assist law enforcement or while making a citizen's arrest. As you will see below, the Colorado Revised Statutes does allow for these types of actions. However, it is our experience as attorneys that acting in aid of police or making a citizen's arrest can have dire consequences.

When acting in aid of police, consider how you might appear to the officers at the scene or to those who arrive after you begin to assist. You are not in uniform and armed with a gun at the scene of an ongoing crime. There is a serious risk that you will be mistaken for a criminal by police and possibly shot. We advise that it is not worth the risk.

Similarly, consider how a citizen's arrest appears to an arriving police officer. It may be difficult for the officer to determine whether or not you are the aggressor in the situation. We advise that it is best to let the police handle the police work.

A. *Acting under a police officer's direction*

Almost without fail, as attorneys we are regularly asked about whether you can make a citizen's arrest, and how you can best assist law enforcement in dicey situations. Since every legal situation is unique, here we'll just provide a brief summary of the general law, as well as reference some of the statutes governing the use of citizen's arrests and how to assist authorities.

First, Colorado Revised Statutes § 16-3-202 provides that, during an arrest, a peace officer may command the assistance of any person in the vicinity. A person who is commanded this way has the same authority to arrest as the officer who commanded the assistance. This would appear to eliminate the very idea of a "citizen's arrest" in the traditional sense and looks much more like a field-commission to deputy! A person who has been commanded to help is not criminally or civilly liable for any reasonable conduct in aid of the officer or at the officer's command. Sections 18-1-707(5) and (6) of the Colorado Revised Statutes cover the use of physical force by a private citizen who has been commanded by an officer. Under this section, a person who has been commanded to assist is justified in using "reasonable and appropriate physical force when and to the extent that he reasonably believes that force to be necessary to carry out the peace officer's direction." Also, if the commanded person knows that the arrest is not authorized, then he may not use physical force. Deadly physical force may only be used by a person who has been commanded to assist an officer if the person "reasonably believes that force to be necessary to defend himself or a third person from what he reasonably believes to be the use or imminent use of deadly physical force" or he is "directed and authorized by the peace officer to use deadly physical force." Finally, if a person is directed to use deadly physical force and he knows that an officer in his position would not be allowed to use deadly physical force, then the commanded person may not use deadly physical force.

B. *Not acting under a police officer's direction*

More in the area of authorizing a "citizen's arrest" is the language found in section 16-3-201, the text of which is found in the box below, and which removes the obstacle of being in an officer's presence. Importantly, under 16-3-201 the person making a citizen's arrest must witness the crime being committed before he can make an arrest.

Arrest by a Private Person:
Colorado Revised Statutes § 16-3-201

A person who is not a peace officer may arrest another person when any crime has been or is being committed by the arrested person in the presence of the person making the arrest.

Section 18-1-707(7) also allows an ordinary person to use physical force when making an arrest under 16-3-201. A person making a citizen's arrest is justified in using "reasonable and appropriate physical force upon another person when and to the extent that he reasonably believes it necessary to effect an arrest, or to prevent the escape from custody of an arrested person." Deadly physical force can only be used during a citizen's arrest when the person "reasonably believes it necessary to defend himself or a third person from what he reasonably believes to be the use or imminent use of deadly physical force."

C. *Detaining potential thieves: "retailer's privilege"*

Section 18-4-407 of the Colorado Revised Statutes allows the employees of a store to detain and question a person who they believe has committed a theft within the store. The detainers must act in good faith, have probable cause based on a reasonable belief that the crime has been committed, and must detain and question in a reasonable manner. This is commonly called "retailer's" or "shopkeeper's privilege" or right. Common scenarios include when a loss prevention official for the store will take a person into some type of custody while they investigate whether an item was stolen from their business. A person who detains a suspect under this section is not criminally or civilly liable for "slander, false arrest, false imprisonment, malicious prosecution, or unlawful detention."

Practical Legal Tip:

If you use your firearm for defensive purposes, the first number you should call is 911. But keep your call brief: you only need to tell the operator that you have been the victim of a crime, where you are located, and some identifying information. After that, hang up! You are not required to remain on the line and doing so could cause you problems later. Remember, all 911 calls are recorded and operators are trained to gather as much information as possible. No matter how justified you are in your use of a firearm, something you say on a 911 call may become a real headache later at trial. *-Stanley*

VI. **What crimes can I be charged with when my use of deadly force is not justified?**

We've reached the end of our discussion on when you may be justified to use a weapon in defense of your person or property. Now it's time to give a brief summary of where you'll find yourself in legal trouble if you don't meet the elements of justification as we've described throughout this book. The following tables list some of the crimes involving the use of deadly physical force or a firearm and where relevant provisions may be found in Colorado law:

Crimes Involving Deadly Force or a Firearm:
1. Murder: see C.R.S. §§ 18-3-102, 18-3-103
2. Manslaughter: see C.R.S. § 18-3-104
3. Assault: see C.R.S. §§ 18-3-202, 18-3-203, 18-3-204

Practical Legal Tip:

There are plenty of clever signs and bumper stickers out there advocating the use of a firearm. "Keep honking, I'm reloading," and even "Trespassers Will Be Shot" are seen often on the bumpers of Colorado cars and the fence posts of Colorado homeowners. But these signs, despite the chuckle they may elicit from a passerby, are not a good idea. Even if meant only to prompt a laugh, if you are forced to use your firearm to defend yourself and end up in court, you can bet that the prosecutor will bring these signs up to the jury for consideration. Remember, a prosecutor will use every avenue to paint you in the worst light possible. Keep the laughs to yourself and take the signs down! -*Doug*

Crimes Against the Public Involving a Firearm:

- It is <u>menacing</u> to display a firearm or other deadly weapon in a way that knowingly places or attempts to place another person in fear of imminent serious bodily injury. *See* C.R.S. § 18-3-206(1)(a);

- It is <u>disorderly conduct</u> to display a deadly weapon in public in a manner calculated to alarm. *See* C.R.S. § 18-9-106(f);

- It is <u>felony engaging in a riot</u> to engage in a riot while employing a deadly weapon. *See* C.R.S. § 18-9-104(1);

- It is <u>endangering public transportation and utility transmission</u> to threaten an operator, crew member, attendant, or passenger on a public conveyance with a deadly weapon. *See* C.R.S. § 18-9-115(1)(c)(II);

- It is a felony to possess a loaded firearm in "any facility of public transportation." *See* C.R.S. § 18-9-118;

- It is <u>unlawfully carrying a concealed weapon</u> to carry a concealed firearm without a valid permit and outside of one's home, business, property, or vehicle. *See* C.R.S. § 18-12-105;

- It is <u>unlawfully carrying a weapon—unlawful possession of weapons—school, college, or university grounds</u> to knowingly, unlawfully, and without legal authority carry a deadly weapon onto the grounds of any school, unless the weapon is unloaded and remains inside a vehicle or the person is inside his dwelling or business. *See* C.R.S. § 18-12-105.5;

- It is a <u>prohibited use of weapons</u> to knowingly and unlawfully aim a firearm at another person, to discharge a firearm recklessly or with criminal negligence, or to possess a firearm while intoxicated. *See* C.R.S. § 18-12-106;

- It is <u>disorderly conduct</u> to discharge a firearm in a public place except when engaging in lawful target practice or hunting. *See* C. R. S. § 18-9-106(e);

- It is <u>illegal discharge of a firearm</u> to knowingly or recklessly discharge a firearm into a dwelling, building, occupied structure, or an occupied motor vehicle. *See* C.R.S. § 18-12-107.5(1);

- It is <u>reckless endangerment</u> to recklessly engage in conduct which creates a substantial risk of serious bodily injury to another person, such as firing a firearm into the air. *See* C.R.S. § 18-3-208;

- It is <u>arming rioters</u> to knowingly supply a deadly weapon for use in a riot. *See* C.R.S. § 18-9-103(1)(a).

CHAPTER EIGHT
LAW OF CONCEALED CARRY: PART I
THE PERMIT QUALIFICATIONS, REQUIREMENTS, APPEALS, AND REGULATIONS

I. Introduction to Colorado concealed carry law

Title 18, Article 12, Part 2 of the Colorado Revised Statutes contains the law on how Concealed Carry Permits are administered in Colorado. Throughout this chapter, we will discuss the requirements, the application process, as well as the rights given to permit holders for carrying a handgun in the State of Colorado. At the time of publishing, open carry of all firearms in public is generally permitted in Colorado, except for within the Denver city limits. However, local municipalities may prohibit open carry in a "building or specific area," provided that the local government posts a sign informing people of the prohibition. *See* section 29-11.7-104 of the Colorado Revised Statutes. Please refer to Chapter Two of this book for more information. A license or permit is not required to open carry a firearm in Colorado.

II. Qualifications for a Colorado Concealed Carry Permit

A. *Persons who are legally qualified to obtain a permit*

As of May 17, 2003, Colorado is a "shall issue" state. This means that, if an applicant meets all of the requirements under section 18-12-203 of the Colorado Revised Statutes, a sheriff must issue a Concealed Carry Permit to the applicant. Section 18-12-203(2) does allow the sheriff discretion under very narrow circumstances, but in the vast majority of cases, applicants who meet the following requirements are issued a permit. To be eligible for a permit in Colorado, an applicant must:

- Be at least 21 years old; and
- Be a legal resident of Colorado; or

- Be a member of the armed forces stationed in Colorado pursuant to permanent duty station orders or a member of that service person's immediate family living in Colorado.

In addition to these age and residency requirements, applicants who meet any of the following criteria are ineligible to receive a permit:

- A person who is ineligible to possess a firearm pursuant to section 18-12-108 or federal law (See Chapter Three of this book for a full explanation of this requirement); or
- A person who is subject to any kind of protection order restricting firearms use (See Chapter Three for a complete overview of protective orders);
- Anyone convicted of perjury under section 18-8-503 because of information provided or deliberately omitted while applying for a permit;
- A person who "chronically and habitually" uses alcohol "to the extent that the applicant's normal faculties are impaired," unless the applicant provides an affidavit, signed by a professional licensed counselor or addiction counselor specializing in alcohol addiction, stating that the applicant has been evaluated by the counselor and has been determined to be a recovering alcoholic who has been clean for at least three years; or
- A person who is an unlawful user of or addicted to a controlled substance as defined in section 18-18-102(5).

Lastly, an applicant must demonstrate that they have "competence with a handgun," which can be shown by submitting:

- Evidence of current military service; or
- Proof of honorable discharge from military service within the previous three years;

- Proof of honorable discharge from military service that shows that the applicant gained pistol qualifications within the previous ten years;
- A certificate showing retirement from a Colorado law enforcement agency that shows that the applicant gained pistol qualifications within the previous ten years;
- Evidence that the applicant is a certified instructor at the time the application is submitted;
- Evidence of experience with a firearm through participation in organized shooting competitions; or
- A training certificate from a handgun training class obtained within the ten years preceding submittal of the application.

Even if an applicant satisfies all of the requirements listed above and is not disqualified for any of the above reasons, the sheriff can deny the application under section 18-12-203(2) if he or she has "a reasonable belief that documented previous behavior by the applicant makes it likely the applicant will present a danger to self or others if the applicant receives a permit to carry a concealed handgun."

Whatever the reason for a denial, the applicant has the right to appeal under section 18-12-207 of the Colorado Revised Statutes, and the sheriff will have the burden to show that the denial was proper. Appeals are fully covered later in this Chapter.

Next, let's examine some of these qualifications and requirements in closer detail.

B. *Perjury as a disqualifier*
A person is disqualified from receiving a Colorado Concealed Carry Permit if they are found guilty of perjury under section 18-8-503 based on "information provided or deliberately omitted" on a permit application. Section 18-8-503 of the Colorado Revised Statutes states that "a person commits perjury in the second degree if, other than in an official proceeding, with an

intent to mislead a public servant in the performance of his duty, he makes a materially false statement, which he does not believe to be true, under an oath required or authorized by law." Not only is lying on a concealed carry permit application a class 1 misdemeanor, but the offender is also forever barred from receiving a Concealed Carry Permit. Therefore, lying on the application is simply not worth the risk.

C. *Substance abuse as a disqualifier*
As previously discussed, a person who "chronically and habitually" uses alcohol "to the extent that the [person's] normal faculties are impaired" is disqualified from obtaining a Concealed Carry Permit. To date, there has not been a case that discusses what level of alcohol abuse it takes to have one's normal faculties impaired. Without a case for guidance, we are left to look at the questions asked on the permit application. The application asks the following two questions that relate to this disqualification:

- "Have you been treated for alcoholism within the past ten years or *ever* been involuntarily committed as an alcoholic?"
- "Have you had two or more alcohol-related convictions within the past ten years?"

If the answer is yes to either one of these questions, you may be disqualified from receiving a Concealed Carry Permit. However, not all is lost. Colorado law allows a recovering alcoholic who has been clean for 3 years to provide an affidavit from his or her professional counselor or addiction counselor proving that fact. The counselor must be licensed under Colorado law for the affidavit to be accepted. *See* 18-12-203(1)(e)(II).

D. *Controlled substance abuse as a disqualifier*
Section 18-12-203(1)(f) provides that a person that is an "unlawful user of or addicted to a controlled substance as defined in section 18-18-102(5)" is disqualified from obtaining a

Concealed Carry Permit. The first question is, how is "controlled substance" defined in section 18-18-102(5)? A "controlled substance" is a "drug, substance, or immediate precursor including cocaine, marijuana, concentrate, cathinones, any synthetic cannabinoid, and salvia divinorum." Also included in the definition of "controlled substance" is any substance listed under Schedules I through V, found in sections 18-18-203 through 18-18-207. Schedule I alone lists 113 substances, all by their technical names. Rather than reproducing the lists contained on the Schedules, let's instead take a look at the question asked on the application that pertains to this disqualifier:

- "Are you an unlawful user of, or addicted to, marijuana, or any depressant, stimulant, or narcotic drug, or any other controlled substance?"

Notice that marijuana is included as a controlled substance even though it is legal for recreational use in the state of Colorado. Much like with alcohol, addiction to marijuana, even though it is legal under state law, is a disqualifier. Of course, many of the drugs listed in the Schedules are legal in some capacity, often for medical purposes, including all prescription drugs. Unlike with alcoholism, the law does not provide a way to prove that a previous addict has been rehabilitated for an allowable time.

E. *Training requirement*
The Colorado Concealed Carry Permit training requirement can be satisfied in a number of ways, but the vast majority of applicants satisfy this requirement by earning a certificate from a handgun training class. However, there are several classes of applicants that are not required to attend a handgun training class because of their demonstrated expertise with a firearm. Active military personnel and honorably discharged former military personnel within three years of discharge are deemed to have satisfied the training requirement. Honorably discharged military personnel and retired Colorado law enforcement personnel within ten years of their discharge or retirement who

can show that their service included pistol qualifications are deemed to have completed the training requirement. Lastly, those who participate in organized shooting competitions and current certified instructors satisfy the training requirement.

For the rest of us, we have to get a certificate from a handgun training class, and that class must satisfy the criteria set forth in section 18-12-202(5) of the Colorado Revised Statutes. There are three types of courses that meet the requirements of section 18-12-202(5):

- A law enforcement training firearms safety course; or
- A firearms safety course offered by a law enforcement agency, an institute of higher education, or a public or private institution or organization or firearms training school, that is open to the general public and is taught by a certified instructor; or
- A firearms safety course or class that is offered and taught by a certified instructor, as long as the class is not taught entirely online and as long as the instructor is physically present for a portion of the course.

The prohibition on training courses offered exclusively over the internet is a relatively recent change. There are internet based companies that offer online handgun training courses. These courses are accepted as valid for the purpose of getting a permit in several other states, but not in Colorado. To be acceptable, a certificate from a handgun training course must be provided in its original form or must have an original signature from the certified trainer if provided as a photocopy.

Many states have a shooting requirement included in their required training courses, however, in Colorado an applicant is not required to fire a firearm before receiving a permit! This means that there are an unknown number of permit holders in Colorado carrying a concealed firearm that they have never fired. Suffice to say they are not prepared if they ever find themselves in a situation where they must use deadly physical force to defend themselves or others from imminent harm. Although it may be allowed by law, do the right thing and practice with your weapon at a firing range. Get to know what to expect when the weapon is fired and try to improve your accuracy. The life you save because of this training may be your own.

F.   *Sheriff's discretion*
Section 18-12-203(2) allows a sheriff to deny a permit to a person, even though they meet all of the above requirements, if the sheriff has a "reasonable belief that documented previous behavior by the applicant makes it likely the applicant will present a danger to self or others if the applicant receives a permit to carry a concealed handgun." Unfortunately, there has not been a case to date that defines the limits of a sheriff's discretion under this section. It is important to note that the reasonable belief must be based on "documented previous behavior." This means that the sheriff cannot act on arbitrary grounds or based on any personal disagreements with the applicant. A situation where this type of discretion might be used is one in which the applicant is secretly under investigation for a crime that would disqualify him or her, but charges have not yet been filed. In this situation, a sheriff may be justified in exercising his discretion to deny the application.

If a sheriff denies an application or revokes a permit under this section and the decision is appealed by the applicant, the sheriff has a higher burden of proof than for any other type of denial, suspension, or revocation. *See* section 18-12-207(3). Please see the section later in this Chapter on the right to appeal a denial, suspension or revocation, for more information.

G. *Suspension, revocation, and denial of a renewal of a Colorado Concealed Carry Permit*
  1. What is the difference between suspension and revocation?

To begin, it is important to know that there *is* a difference between a suspension and a revocation of a person's Concealed Carry Permit. A suspension is only temporary, and a person's permit may be reinstated without the necessity of submitting a new application for a permit. This means that a person will not have to go through the rigors of the application process nor the training requirements again in order to regain their permit following a suspension. On the other hand, a revocation means that the acting sheriff has decided that a person's permit shall be terminated and in order for the person to ultimately regain the permit, they must reapply from step one by submitting the application with the applicable fees and the person may have to retake a training course, if it has been ten years since they received their certificate. The grounds to revoke or suspend a permit are the same. Therefore, it is up to the sheriff what course to take in each individual case.

  2. Under what circumstances can a sheriff revoke, suspend, or deny the renewal of a Colorado Concealed Carry Permit?

Section 18-12-203(3) gives a sheriff the authority to revoke, suspend, or deny the renewal of a permit if the sheriff has a "reasonable belief that a permittee no longer meets the criteria" for obtaining a permit, explained previously in this Chapter. Further, a sheriff has the authority to revoke, suspend, or deny the renewal of a permit based on his or her discretion under section 18-12-203(2), as explained previously in this Chapter.

If a sheriff decides to suspend or revoke a permit, the sheriff must notify the permittee in writing, informing the permittee of the grounds for suspension or revocation, and informing the permittee of their right to ask for a second review by the sheriff, the right to submit additional information for the record, and the right to seek judicial review. *See* 18-12-203(c). The permittee has the right to appeal these decisions, pursuant to section 18-12-207.

H. *An applicant's right to appeal a suspension, revocation, or a denial of a renewal of a Colorado Concealed Carry Permit*

Section 18-12-207 of the Colorado Revised Statutes gives a permittee the right to appeal a revocation, suspension, or denial of a renewal relating to his or her Concealed Carry Permit. Because the appeals process is a complicated court proceeding, anyone who seeks to appeal a sheriff's decision should strongly consider retaining an attorney. The following summary is by no means a complete guide to the appeals process, but it should give some insight into the extent and purpose of the proceedings.

Initially, the permittee has a right to ask the sheriff to do a second review of the application. However, this is not a required step. Instead, the permittee may immediately seek judicial review of the sheriff's decision. If the permittee does ask the sheriff for a second review, the permittee must wait to seek judicial review until the sheriff's second review is complete. *See* section 18-12-207(1).

The procedure for the appeal is specified in Colorado Rules of Civil Procedure (C.R.C.P.) 106(a)(4) and (b). The appealing party must file a complaint with the proper state district court in order to commence the appeals process. The sheriff will then file an answer to the complaint with the court. *See* C.R.C.P. 106(a)(4)(II). A motion and proposed order may be filed along with the complaint asking the court to require certification of the record that was before the sheriff when he or she made their decision. Upon receipt of the motion and proposed order, the court must order the sheriff to file the record with the court clerk along with a certificate of authenticity. *See* C.R.C.P. 106(a)(4)(III). Within 21 days after the order for certification is received by the sheriff, the sheriff may offer additional evidence not specified in the order to the record. *See* C.R.C.P. 106(a)(4)(IV).

Once all of the pertinent information has been received by the court, and each party has had the chance to file a brief setting out their positions, it will be the court's job to determine whether the sheriff abused his or her discretion, based on the evidence in the record that the decision was based on. *See* C.R.C.P. 106(a)(4)(I).

The burden of proof rests with the sheriff. Under section 18-12-207(3), the sheriff faces a different burden depending on the reason given for the denial, suspension, or revocation. If the sheriff based their decision on their belief that the applicant did not satisfy one or more of the requirements under section 18-12-203(1), then the sheriff must prove by a preponderance of the evidence that the person failed to meet a requirement. To meet this burden, the sheriff must show that it is more likely than not that the applicant or permittee did not meet one of the requirements. On the other hand, if the sheriff based their decision on sheriff's discretion under section 18-12-203(2), the sheriff must prove through "clear and convincing evidence," that there is documented evidence that shows that the person is likely to present a danger to self or others if they are granted a permit. The "clear and convincing" standard is a higher burden than "preponderance of the evidence." To satisfy this increased standard, the sheriff must show that there was a high probability, based on documented prior behavior, that the applicant or permittee presented a danger to self or others if they were allowed to obtain a Concealed Carry Permit. The court will make the final determination. If the court determines that the sheriff failed to meet the burden, then the sheriff's decision will be overturned. On the other hand, if the sheriff successfully meets the burden, then the decision will stand.

III. The Colorado Concealed Carry Permit application and process

A. *The application*

Section 18-12-205 sets out the contents of the application and the process for applying for a Colorado Concealed Carry Permit. The application asks for the following information:

- The applicant's full name, date of birth, and address; and
- The applicant's birth name, if different, and any other names the applicant may be known by; and
- The applicant's home address or addresses for the last ten years;
- Whether the applicant is a resident of Colorado as of the date of application and whether the applicant has a valid driver's license or other state-issued photo identification or military order proving residence; and
- Whether the applicant meets the criteria for obtaining a permit specified in section 18-12-203(1).

This last bullet point refers to the requirements outlined earlier in this Chapter. To determine if the requirements are met, the application will ask a series of yes/no questions. Pursuant to section 18-12-205(b), the application cannot require that the applicant disclose any privileged or confidential information, including medical records.

B. *The process*

Once the application has been completed, the applicant must submit it in person to the sheriff of the county or city and county in which the applicant resides or to the sheriff of the county or city and county in which the applicant maintains a secondary residence or owns or leases property for a business. Do not sign the completed application until the sheriff is available to witness the signature. *See* section 18-12-205(2)(a).

Be prepared to pay an application fee, which may not exceed one hundred dollars under section 18-12-205(2)(b). In addition, there will also be a fingerprint processing fee collected at the time the application is submitted. Neither of these fees are refundable in the event that the application is denied. *See* section 18-12-205(2)(b).

Along with the application, be prepared to submit the following items:

- Documents demonstrating competence with a handgun (this is the training requirement explained earlier); and
- A color photograph of the applicant's full face and hair, taken within the previous thirty days; and
- A valid Colorado driver's license or valid Colorado or military photo identification.

Some sheriff's offices will take a photo of the applicant when the application is submitted. If this occurs, then the applicant does not need to bring a photograph with them. For this reason, it makes sense to call ahead to find out what the office's policy is. *See* section 18-12-205(3)(b). After witnessing the applicant sign the application, the sheriff will compare the applicant to the picture on the applicant's driver's license or photo identification to confirm the applicant's identity. *See* section 18-12-205(4)(a).

The sheriff is then required to take two complete sets of the applicant's fingerprints. Both sets are sent to the Colorado Bureau of Investigations to facilitate a background check. *See* section 18-12-205. The Colorado Bureau of Investigations will conduct a search of the national instant criminal background check system and a search of the state integrated criminal justice information system and will notify the sheriff of the results. Also, if the applicant lives in a municipality or town, the sheriff will call the local police department or other local law enforcement agencies to gather information on the applicant's fitness for receiving a permit.

Once the sheriff has gathered all of the necessary information and has reviewed the application, the sheriff will determine whether the applicant meets all of the qualifications required under 18-12-203(1) or whether he or she will exercise their authority to deny the application under section 18-12-203(2). *See* section 18-12-205(4)(c). The sheriff has ninety days after receiving the necessary information to approve or deny the application. *See* section 18-12-206(1).

Just as with a revocation, suspension, or a denial of a renewal, if the sheriff decides to deny the application, he or she must notify the applicant in writing of the denial, and state the grounds for denial. The written notification must also inform the applicant of their right to seek a second review of the application by the sheriff, to submit additional information for the record, and to seek judicial review pursuant to section 18-12-207. *See* section 18-12-206(2).

In the event that the results of the fingerprint checks take longer than ninety days to get back to the sheriff, the sheriff will make a determination with the available evidence. If it turns out that the permit should not have been issued because of the results of the fingerprint checks, the sheriff can take action to revoke the permit pursuant to section 18-12-203(3). *See* section 18-12-206(2).

IV. **Maintenance and Renewal of a Colorado Concealed Carry Permit**

A. *Maintaining a permit*

Pursuant to section 18-12-210(1) of the Colorado Revised Statutes, if a permittee changes their address, they must notify the issuing sheriff of the change of address within 30 days. Also under that section, if a permit is lost, stolen, or destroyed, the permittee has three business days to notify the issuing sheriff. Failure to comply with either of these rules is a class 1 petty offense. *See* section 18-12-210(1).

A permit that is lost, stolen, or destroyed, is automatically invalid. The permittee may obtain a replacement by submitting a notarized statement to the issuing sheriff stating that the permit has been lost, stolen, or destroyed, and paying a fee of $15. *See* section 18-12-210(2).

B. *Permit renewals*

A Colorado Concealed Carry Permit is valid for five years after the date of issuance. *See* section 18-12-204(1)(b). Within 120 days prior to a permit's expiration, a permittee may complete and submit a renewal form to the sheriff of the county or city and county in which the permittee resides or in which the permittee maintains a secondary residence or owns or leases real property use by the permittee for business. *See* section 18-12-211(1)(a). Along with the renewal form, the permittee must submit a notarized affidavit stating that the permittee remains qualified to hold a permit based on the criteria set out in section 18-12-203(1), explained above. *See id.* Be prepared to pay a fee of up $50 for process of your renewal request. *See id.*

If the sheriff who receives the renewal request is not the issuing sheriff, the permittee must also submit a legible photocopy of the permit. *See* section 18-12-211(1)(b)(I). Also, in this case, the sheriff will contact the office of the issuing sheriff to confirm that the permit has not been revoked or suspended. *See* section 18-12-211(1)(b)(II).

In either case, the process the sheriff will follow in deciding whether to renew the permit is identical to the process used to evaluate new applications, as describe earlier in this Chapter. Further, if the renewal is denied, the permittee has all of the same appeals options as a new applicant would have. *See* section 18-12-211(1)(c).

If a renewal form is submitted after the permit's expiration date, the permittee must pay a late fee of $15 in addition to the renewal fee. *See* section 18-12-211(2). A permit that has not been renewed within six months of its expiration is deemed to have permanently expired. If a permittee's permit has permanently expired, they must submit an application again as if they never had a permit, and they must then pay the application fee, which may be up to $100. *See id.*

V. Temporary Emergency Permits

Under section 18-12-209(1) of the Colorado Revised Statutes, regardless of the requirements explained in this chapter, a sheriff "may issue a temporary emergency permit to carry a concealed handgun to a person whom the sheriff has reason to believe may be immediate danger." In order to be eligible for a temporary emergency permit, an applicant must submit all of the materials required under section 18-12-205, just as any other applicant must, as explained earlier in this Chapter, except that they do not have to fulfill the training requirement, and they can be as young as 18 years old. Further, instead of the typical application fee, an applicant for a temporary emergency permit must pay a smaller fee, not to exceed $25, when they submit the application materials. See *id.* The sheriff still must check to make sure that the applicant meets all of the other criteria under section 18-12-203, except for the age and training requirements, after receiving the results of the criminal background check. *See id.*

Temporary emergency permits are only valid for 90 days after the date of issuance. See section 18-12-209(2)(b)(I). A permittee may apply for renewal prior to or within ten days after expiration of the permit, in the same way a regular permit is renewed, as described earlier. *See id.* Just as with typical permits, if the renewing sheriff is not the same sheriff who originally issued the temporary emergency permit, the permittee must submit a legible photocopy of the permit with the renewal materials and the sheriff must contact the issuing sheriff's office to make sure that the permit has not been revoked or suspended. *See* section 18-12-209(2)(b)(II). If the permittee is 21 or older, the sheriff may only renew the permit once, making the maximum duration of such a permit 180 days. *See id.* However, if the permittee is younger than 21, the sheriff may renew the temporary emergency permit for subsequent 90 day periods until the permittee reaches 21. *See id.*

Temporary emergency permits confer all of same rights as Colorado Concealed Carry Permits. What exactly are those rights? Chapter Nine will fill in all of the blanks.

CHAPTER NINE
LAW OF CONCEALED CARRY: PART II
WHAT, HOW, AND WHERE YOU CAN
LEGALLY CARRY WITH A COLORADO CONCEALED
CARRY PERMIT

I. <u>Colorado Concealed Carry Permits only cover concealed handguns!</u>

First, it is obvious that any law that is particular to what is allowed with a Colorado Concealed Carry Permit only applies to handguns that are actually concealed. In fact, as was briefly discussed in Chapter Eight, with the exception of Denver, it is perfectly legal to carry a firearm openly throughout Colorado without a permit of any kind.

A. *Carrying a concealed weapon without a permit is a crime*

The default rule in Colorado is that it is a crime to carry a concealed weapon "on or about" one's person. Section 18-12-105(1)(b) of the Colorado Revised Statutes makes it a class 2 misdemeanor for a person to "knowingly and unlawfully" carry a "firearm concealed on or about his or her person." However, there are some exceptions where carrying a concealed weapon is permissible under the law.

The most obvious exception is for persons who hold a valid Concealed Carry Permit. It is important to note that this exception only holds for as long as the permit holder stays within the authority granted by the permit under section 18-12-214, explained later in this Chapter.

The remaining exceptions are for those who do not have permits. Even without a permit, a person is permitted to carry a concealed firearm "in his or her own dwelling or place of business or on property owned or under his or her control at the time of the act of carrying." *See* section 18-12-105(2)(a). Also, even without a permit, a person may carry a firearm concealed while "in a private automobile or private means of conveyance" for the purpose of lawful protection of their own or someone else's property. *See* section 18-12-105(2)(b); 18-12-204(3)(a)(I). Further, if a person is in possession of a handgun while legally engaged in hunting activities within the state, the gun is not considered concealed. *See* section 18-12-204(3)(a)(II). Lastly, peace officers, probation officers, and United States pretrial services officers who are on duty are exempted from the concealed carry statute. *See* section 18-12-105(2)(d), (f).

1. What does it mean for a firearm to be "concealed?"

Under Colorado law, a firearm is concealed when it is "placed out of sight so as not to be discernible or apparent by ordinary observation." *See People ex rel. O.R.*, 220 P.3d 949, 952 (Colo. App. 2008). A partially concealed firearm, like a handgun in a holster, is not concealed as it is meant in section 18-12-105. *See id.*

2. What does it mean for a firearm to be "on or about one's person?"

There probably isn't any confusion when it comes to a weapon that is on one's person, but what about weapons that are "about" one's person? For the purposes of this statute, the Colorado Court of Appeals has ruled that a firearm that was "tucked under the edge of the seat on which [the defendant] was sitting, where it was within his easy reach," was concealed on or about his person. *See People in Interest of R. J. A.*, 556 P.2d 491, 493 (Colo. App. 1976). In that case, what mattered to the court was that the firearm was "sufficiently close to the person to be readily accessible for immediate use." *See id* at 494.

II. Where can a Colorado Concealed Carry Permit holder legally carry a concealed handgun?

A person in possession of a Colorado Concealed Carry Permit may legally carry their handgun concealed any place where it is not illegal for them to possess a concealed handgun under either state or federal law. *See* section 18-12-214(1)(a), (2). Locations where all firearms are prohibited, concealed or not, under Colorado law, are covered in Chapter Ten of this book. The places where Colorado law prohibits permit holders specifically from carrying a concealed weapon are covered in the following sections.

A. *Prohibited places for Colorado Concealed Carry Permit holders*
1. Schools and school grounds

Under section 18-12-214(3) a permittee may not carry a concealed handgun onto "the real property, or into any improvements erected thereon, of a public elementary, middle, junior high, or high school." However, there are three exceptions to this rule.

First, a permittee may have a concealed handgun in their possession while on the real property of a public school so long as they remain in their vehicle. If the permittee leaves the vehicle, the handgun must remain in a compartment of the vehicle, like the trunk or glove compartment, and the vehicle must be locked while it remains on school grounds. *See* 18-12-214(3)(a).

Second, if the permittee is contracted by the school district or charter school as a school security officer, the permittee may carry a concealed handgun while on duty. *See* section 18-12-214(3)(b).

Third, a permittee may carry a concealed handgun on land owned by a school district if that land is undeveloped and is used for hunting or other shooting sports. *See* section 18-12-214(3)(c).

2. Secure public buildings

Under section 18-12-214(4) of the Colorado Revised Statutes, a permittee is prohibited from carrying a concealed handgun into a public building if all of the following are true:

- Security personnel and electronic weapons screening devices are permanently in place at each entrance to the building;
- Security personnel electronically screen each person who enters the building to determine whether the person is carrying a weapon of any kind; and
- Security personnel require each person who is carrying a weapon of any kind to leave the weapon in possession of security personnel while the person is in the building.

B. *Federal Property*

A Colorado Concealed Carry Permit and its rights are a product of state law and convey no rights to the permit holder that have been recognized under federal law. However, in certain instances, the federal government recognizes these state rights on certain federal property.

1. Federal buildings: firearms are prohibited

Firearms Prohibited in Federal Facilities: 18 U.S.C. § 930(a)
...whoever knowingly possesses or causes to be present a firearm or other dangerous weapon in a Federal facility (other than a Federal court facility), or attempts to do so, shall be fined under this title or imprisoned not more than one year, or both.

Under this statute, a "federal facility" refers to any building or part of a building that is owned or leased by the federal government and is a place where federal employees are regularly present for the purpose of performing their official duties. *See* 18 U.S.C. § 930(g)(1). However, this statute does not apply to "the lawful performance of official duties by an officer, agent, or employee of the United States, a State, or a political subdivision thereof, who is authorized by law to engage in or supervise the prevention, detection, investigation, or prosecution of any violation of law," nor does it apply to federal officials or members of the armed forces who are permitted to possess such a firearm by law, or the lawful carrying of a firearm incident to hunting or "other lawful purposes." 18 U.S.C. § 930(d). This statute does not govern the possession of a firearm in a federal court facility.

2. National parks

Colorado Concealed Carry Permit holders are permitted to concealed carry in Colorado National Parks but not inside buildings within the park, such as ranger stations, because these are federal buildings. Generally, the Park Service posts signs at these buildings warning that firearms are not allowed. Under federal law, for firearms purposes, all federal parks are subject to the state law of the state in which the park is located. *See* 16 U.S.C. § 1a-7b. A permit holder may, therefore, carry a handgun concealed in a federal park, but not in federal buildings in the park.

3. VA Hospitals: firearms prohibited

Firearms Prohibited at Veterans Affairs Hospitals: 38 CFR § 1.218(a)(13)
No person while on property shall carry firearms, other dangerous or deadly weapons, or explosives, either openly or concealed, except for official purposes.

One place where many law-abiding permit holders fall victim is at the VA Hospital. The VA Hospital system is governed by federal law which prohibits the carrying of any firearm while on VA property. This includes the parking lot, sidewalk, and any other area which is the property of the VA.

Under federal law, 38 CFR § 1.218(a)(13) states that "no person while on property shall carry firearms, other dangerous or deadly weapons, or explosives, either openly or concealed, except for official purposes." The "official purposes" specified refer specifically to the VA Hospital Police. The area where this specific law gets good people in trouble is that the Department of Veterans Affairs has its own set of laws and guidelines and is not controlled strictly by the Gun Control Act and the general provisions regarding the prohibition of firearms on federal property. The VA law is much more restrictive, and many veterans have found themselves in trouble when they valet-park their vehicle and the valet discovers a concealed handgun in the console or concealed in the door storage area. How rigidly this law is enforced is determined by the individual hospital administrators as described in 38 CFR § 1.218(a), however, regardless of how strictly the law is enforced firearms are still prohibited under the law and the VA police are very aggressive in enforcing them.

4. United States Post Offices: firearms prohibited

Firearms Prohibited at Post Offices: 39 CFR § 232.1(l)
Notwithstanding the provisions of any other law, rule or regulation, no person while on postal property may carry firearms, other dangerous or deadly weapons, or explosives, either openly or concealed, or store the same on postal property, except for official purposes.

Under this regulation, firearms or other deadly weapons are prohibited on *postal property* which includes not only the building, but all property surrounding the building where a post office is located. This includes the parking lot (*e.g.,* a person's vehicle where a firearm may be stored), as well as the sidewalks and walkways. Parking lots, sidewalks and walkways, and other related areas are generally not included when discussing the premises of a location where the carrying of a weapon is prohibited by law. Like the VA Hospital, United States Post Offices are another exception to the rule.

Recently, there was a decision by the 10th Circuit Court of Appeals addressing this issue in Colorado, *Bonidy v. U.S. Postal Serv.*, 790 F.3d 1121 (10th Cir. 2015). The plaintiff in that case, Mr. Bonidy, is a Colorado Concealed Carry Permit holder who challenged the prohibition against the possession of firearms on USPS property, both inside the building and in the parking lot, as a violation of his Second Amendment right to carry a firearm for self-defense. *See id* at 1122-23. The court ruled unequivocally that *concealed carry* was prohibited anywhere on USPS property, including in the parking lot, because the Second Amendment does not guarantee the right to carry a concealed firearm. *See id.* at 1124 (citing *Peterson v. Martinez*, 707 F.3d 1197, 1209 (10th Cir. 2013)). Although it pertains more to the discussion in Chapter Ten, the court also ruled that the USPS's prohibition on open carry on USPS property did not violate the Second Amendment and was valid. *See id.* at 1125.

5. <u>Military bases and installations: firearms generally prohibited</u>

Military bases and installations are treated much like the VA Hospital and US Post Offices in that they have, and are governed by, a separate set of rules and regulations with respect to firearms on the premises of an installation or base and are generally prohibited. Military installations are governed by the federal law under Title 32 of the Code of Federal Regulations. Moreover, the sections covering the laws governing and relating to military bases and installations are exceedingly numerous.

C. *Can municipalities restrict firearms rights?*

1. <u>Can cities or other governmental agencies enact firearms laws or regulations regarding the carrying of a concealed handgun by Colorado Concealed Carry Permit holders that are more restrictive than state laws?</u>

No, because Section 18-12-214 of the Colorado Revised Statutes authorizes the permittee to "carry a concealed handgun in all areas of the state, except as specifically limited in" section 18-12-214. Since section 18-12-214 does not limit a permit holder's rights based on local ordinances, municipalities do not have the right to limit those rights. This is consistent with the general assembly's declaration in section 18-12-201(1) that the state has the sole power to regulate the bearing of concealed handguns because "the issuance of a concealed handgun permit is based on a person's constitutional right of self-protection and there is a prevailing state interest in ensuring that no citizen is arbitrarily denied" that right.

D. *How big of a handgun can a CHP holder legally carry?*

As we mentioned in Chapter Two, federal law dictates that any firearm which has any barrel with a bore of more than one-half inch in diameter (.50 caliber) is a "destructive device" and is subject to the National Firearms Act (except for certain shotguns). Possession of any such firearm without the proper paperwork associated with NFA firearms is illegal whether a person is a Colorado Concealed Carry Permit holder or not. For more information on destructive devices and the NFA, see Chapter Fourteen.

III. Colorado Concealed Carry Permit holders dealing with law enforcement

A. *Do I legally have to present my CHP to a police officer if they ask for my identification and I am carrying my gun?*

Yes, and failure to carry or produce a permit on demand while in possession of a concealed handgun is a class 1 petty offense under section 18-12-204(2)(a) of the Colorado Revised Statutes. However, if a permittee is charged under this section, the permittee may provide the court with a valid permit and a valid photo identification "at or before the permittee's scheduled court appearance." If the permittee does this, and both the permit and the identification were valid on the date of the citation, then the charges "shall be dismissed by the court." *See* 18-12-204(2)(a).

B. *Can a police officer legally take a Colorado Concealed Carry Permit holder's handgun away?*

Yes, police are allowed to disarm permit holders in the interest of officer safety. Colorado Revised Statutes § 18-12-214(1)(b) states that a "peace officer may temporarily disarm a permittee, incident to a lawful stop of the permittee. If the permittee is discharged from the scene without arrest, the peace officer must return the handgun at that time. *See id.*

C. *What are passengers with a Colorado Concealed Carry Permit in a vehicle legally obligated to do when the driver is stopped by law enforcement?*

If a person is a passenger in a vehicle and is a permit holder carrying a concealed handgun on their person when law enforcement stops the driver, the passenger is only required to present their permit if they are asked to identify themselves. Sometimes, police will ask passengers in the vehicle for identification to run a check for outstanding warrants. Passengers who are asked for identification are required to present their permit and may be disarmed by police in the interest of safety as described earlier.

Practical Legal Tip:

Having a Concealed Carry Permit can make you feel safer as you are out and about. But remember, it is a permit to protect against trouble—not to go looking for it! *-Doug*

IV. Reciprocity

A. *Can I carry a concealed handgun in other states if I have a Colorado Concealed Carry Permit?*

Yes, as of the date of this book, the following states recognize a Colorado Concealed Carry Permit:

Alabama	Alaska	Arizona	Arkansas	Delaware
Florida	Georgia	Idaho	Indiana	Iowa
Kansas	Kentucky	Louisiana	Michigan	Mississippi
Missouri	Montana	Nebraska	New Hampshire	New Mexico
North Carolina	North Dakota	Ohio	Oklahoma	Pennsylvania
South Dakota	Tennessee	Texas	Utah	Vermont*
West Virginia	Wisconsin	Wyoming		

No permit is required in Vermont to carry a concealed handgun

Reciprocity either exists between Colorado and these states or they have unilaterally decided to recognize Colorado Concealed Carry Permits. Every state has the authority to determine whether or not their state will recognize a carry license or permit issued by another state. Reciprocity is where states enter into an agreement with each other, in this case, to recognize each other's carry permits. However, states are not required to have reciprocity with one another nor are they required to recognize another state's carry permit.

There are many states that issue their own permits, but refuse to recognize a carry permit from another state. Conversely, there are states that choose to recognize some or all other states' carry permits. Colorado only recognizes permits from states that recognize Colorado's permits under section 18-12-213(1) of the Colorado Revised Statutes. As of the date of writing, a Colorado Concealed Carry Permit is recognized by 32 other states, and Vermont does not require a permit to carry a concealed handgun.

B. *What out-of-state handgun permits/licenses does Colorado recognize?*

Colorado Revised Statutes section 18-12-213 governs which other State's permits Colorado law will recognize. Colorado only recognizes permits from States which recognize Colorado permits and only if the permit holder is 21 or older. *See* section 18-12-213(1). Also, because only residents of Colorado can be issued Colorado Concealed Carry Permits, Colorado law only recognizes out-of-state permits if the holder is a resident of the issuing state. *See* section 18-12-213(1)(b)(I). Lastly, if a holder of a permit from another state becomes a Colorado resident, the out-of-state permit is only valid for 90 days after the date a Colorado identification is issued to that person. With these guidelines in mind, Colorado recognizes concealed carry permits/licenses issued by the following states:

Alabama	Alaska	Arizona	Arkansas	Delaware
Florida	Georgia	Idaho	Indiana	Iowa
Kansas	Kentucky	Louisiana	Michigan	Mississippi
Missouri	Montana	Nebraska	New Hampshire	New Mexico
North Carolina	North Dakota	Ohio	Oklahoma	Pennsylvania
South Dakota	Tennessee	Texas	Utah	West Virginia
Wisconsin	Wyoming			

Out-of-state permits from these accepted states confer the same rights to the holder as a Colorado Concealed Carry Permit would, but they do not confer any rights that are not conferred by a Colorado Concealed Carry Permit. This is because an out-of-state concealed carry permit holder must follow Colorado law while in Colorado just like a Colorado Concealed Carry Permit holder must follow the laws of the state he or she is located in when traveling. For example, a Florida Concealed Weapons or Firearms License will allow a person to carry a concealed handgun, knife, electric weapon, billy club, and tear-gas gun while in Florida. However, a person with a Florida license will only be allowed to carry a concealed handgun in Colorado and not be legally allowed to carry other forms of concealed weapons pursuant to Florida's license.

C. *What state's laws apply to me when using my Colorado Concealed Carry Permit in another state?*

Anytime a Colorado Concealed Carry Permit holder is in another state, even if that state recognizes a Colorado permit, the law of the state where the person is currently located will be the law which governs that person's firearms possession and use. If a person is traveling to another state, they must abide by that state's laws; just like a non-Coloradan visiting Colorado must follow Colorado law. The most common laws Coloradans should be aware of are the requirements to present a license and the places that are off-limits to permit holders, as most of the time they vary from state to state.

D. *Can persons who are not Colorado residents obtain a Colorado Concealed Carry Permit?*

No. Colorado Revised Statutes § 18-12-203(1)(a) limits eligible persons to legal Colorado residents, which does include members of the armed forces stationed pursuant to a permanent duty station order at a military installation in Colorado, and members of that service person's immediate family living in Colorado. Legal residents of other states are not permitted to obtain a Colorado Concealed Carry Permit.

CHAPTER TEN
POSSESSING, CARRYING, AND TRANSPORTING FIREARMS WITHOUT A PERMIT

This chapter deals with when and where a person may possess, carry, or transport a firearm regardless as to whether they hold a recognized permit or not. Unlike many other states, it is generally legal under Colorado law to carry any kind of firearm openly, even without a permit. This Chapter explains the situations where that is not the case.

I. Where are firearms (long guns or handguns) prohibited under Colorado law?

Under Colorado law, there are certain places where all firearms, including long guns and handguns, are prohibited, concealed or not, and with or without a Colorado Concealed Carry Permit.

A. *The Colorado General Assembly*

Under section 18-12-105(1)(c) of the Colorado Revised Statutes, is a class 2 misdemeanor for a person to "knowingly and unlawfully" and "without legal authority," carry a firearm or bomb into any location affiliated with the general assembly or any of the members of the general assembly.

There are exceptions to this law, found in section 18-12-105(2) of the Colorado Revised Statutes. As usual, a person does not violate this law if they are in their own dwelling, place of business, or on property owned or under his or her control. *See* section 18-12-105(2)(a). Also, a person does not break this law if they are in a private vehicle or other means of conveyance and carrying a firearm for lawful self-defense. *See* section 18-12-105(2)(b). Peace officers and U.S. probation and pretrial services officers are also exempt under this law. *See* section 18-12-105(2)(d) and (f).

Lastly, under section 18-12-105(2)(c), Colorado Concealed Carry Permit holders are exempt from this law, *unless* their action violates the provisions of section 18-12-214, explained in Chapter Nine. Remember that one of the restrictions under section 18-12-214 is that permit holders cannot carry into a public building that has security personnel and metal detectors at each entrance to the building. Oftentimes, this restriction will be relevant when carrying a firearm into any location affiliated with the general assembly or any of the members of the general assembly.

B. *School, college, and university grounds*

> ### Unlawful Possession of Weapons—School, College, or University Grounds
> ### Colorado Revised Statutes § 18-12-105.5(1)
>
> (1) A person commits a class 6 felony if such person knowingly and unlawfully and without legal authority carries, brings, or has in such person's possession a deadly weapon as defined in section 18-1-901(3)(e) in or on the real estate and all improvements erected thereon of any public or private elementary, middle, junior high, high, or vocational school or any public or private college, university, or seminary, except for the purpose of presenting an authorized public demonstration or exhibition pursuant to instruction in conjunction with an organized school or class, for the purpose of carrying out the necessary duties and functions of an employee of an educational institution that require the use of a deadly weapon, or for the purpose of participation in an authorized extracurricular activity or on an athletic team.

In Colorado, under section 18-12-105.5(1) of the Colorado Revised Statutes, it is a class 6 felony to "knowingly and unlawfully" carry, bring, or possess a deadly weapon, as defined in section 18-1-901(3)(e), onto the grounds of any school, public or private, primary, secondary or vocational.

"Deadly weapon" is defined in section 18-1-901(3)(e) of the Colorado Revised Statutes as a "firearm, whether loaded or unloaded" or a "knife, bludgeon, or any other weapon, device, instrument, material, or substance, whether animate or inanimate, that in the manner it is used or intended to be used, is capable of producing death or serious bodily injury." It is important to notice that an unloaded firearm is still considered a deadly weapon under this section.

There are many exceptions to this law. This first three exceptions are right in section 18-12-105.5(1) itself. If the deadly weapon is brought onto school grounds for the purpose of instruction in a class, it is allowed under this section for that purpose. Also, employees of a school are allowed to carry deadly weapons on that school's grounds if their necessary duties require the use of a deadly weapon. (For example, an ISD Police Officer.) Lastly, deadly weapons that are used during an authorized extracurricular activity or for an athletic team are allowed under this section.

The remaining exceptions are covered in section 18-12-105.5(3). It is not a violation of the law if:

- The weapon is unloaded and remains inside a motor vehicle while upon the real estate of any public or private college, university, or seminary; or
- The person is in that person's own dwelling or place of business or on property owned or under that person's control at the time of the act of carrying; or
- The person is in a private automobile or other private means of conveyance and is carrying a weapon for lawful protection of his or her or another's person or property while traveling; or
- The weapon involved is a handgun and the person held a valid permit to carry a concealed handgun or a temporary emergency permit (as explained in Chapter Eight of this book), except that it shall be an offense under this section

if the person was carrying a concealed handgun in violation of section 18-12-214(3); or

- The person is a school resource officer, as defined in section 22-32-109.1(1)(g.5), or a peace officer, as described in section 16-2.5-101, when carrying a weapon in conformance with the policy of the employing agency as provided in section 16-2.5-101(2); or

- The person has possession of the weapon for use in an educational program approved by the school which includes any course designed for the repair or maintenance of weapons.

Let's examine these exceptions in greater detail. As we have seen throughout this book, Colorado law protects the right of individuals to defend themselves with a handgun inside of their own vehicles. To that end, a person is allowed to carry a weapon while inside any vehicle on school grounds, and that person may leave the weapon unloaded in the vehicle while it is parked on school grounds. Similarly, Colorado law protects the right of individuals to defend themselves on their own property and the same is true under this law.

Colorado Concealed Carry Permit and temporary emergency permit holders may carry a handgun concealed onto school property. However, permit holders must abide by the provisions of section 18-12-214(3), explained fully in Chapter Nine of this book. In brief, section 18-12-214(3) prohibits permit holders from carrying a concealed handgun onto the real property or the buildings of a public elementary, middle, junior high, or high school. There are some exceptions to section 18-12-214(3). Please refer to Chapter Nine of this book for a full explanation.

School resource officers and peace officers are exempt if they are carrying a weapon in conformance with the policy of the employing agency. "School resource officer" is defined by section 22-32-109.1 of the Colorado Revised Statutes as a "peace officer who has specialized training to work with school staff and students and who is assigned to a public school or charter school for the purpose of creating a safe learning environment and responding to threats that may impact the school." A "peace officer" is defined in section 16-2.5-101 as a person who meets all standards imposed by law on peace officers and has the authority to enforce all laws of the state of Colorado. In short, peace officers are law enforcement officers (i.e., the police). *See* 16-2.5-101(3). Section 16-2.5-101 simply states that peace officers have the authority to carry firearms at all time, concealed or not, subject only to the written policy of the agency employing the officer. Therefore, peace officers are allowed to carry firearms on school grounds under section 18-12-105.5(3)(e) as long as they follow the written rules of their employing agency.

The final exception relates to students who may be required to bring a firearm to a course that included the repair or maintenance of weapons as part of the curriculum.

C. *Possession of a loaded rifle or shotgun in a motor vehicle*

In Colorado, under section 33-6-123 of the Colorado Revised Statutes, it is a crime to possess a loaded firearm, other than a pistol or revolver, while inside a motor vehicle. If a peace officer asks to inspect a rifle or a shotgun under a person's possession or control inside a motor vehicle, that person must allow the officer to make the inspection. Muzzle-loaded firearms are only considered loaded if they are "primed," which means that they have a percussion cap on the nipple or flint in the striker and powder in the flash pan.

D. *Possession of a firearm while under the influence*

Section 18-12-106 of the Colorado Revised Statutes makes it a class 2 misdemeanor to possess a firearm while a person is "under the influence of intoxicating alcohol" or a controlled substance. There is no definition for "under the influence" and our experience has been that police officers provide purely subjective opinions in this area. We have seen officers attempt to use DUI tests to confirm intoxication on clients; however, the vast majority simply state that the subject was intoxicated or appeared to be under the influence. A "controlled substance" is defined here the same way as it is defined for the purpose of the Colorado Concealed Carry Permit application, discussed in Chapter Eight of this book. Beware, possession of a Colorado Concealed Carry Permit or a temporary emergency permit is no defense to this law.

E. *Possession of a defaced firearm*

Before getting into the law against possessing a defaced firearm, it is important to understand what defacing is. Under section 18-12-104 of the Colorado Revised Statutes, it is a class 1 misdemeanor if a person "knowingly removes, defaces, covers, alters, or destroys the manufacturer's serial number or any other distinguishing number or identification mark of a firearm."

Possessing a firearm that has been defaced in the way described in section 18-12-104 is also a class 1 misdemeanor under section 18-12-103 of the Colorado Revised Statutes. It is important to note that it is not a violation under this section if the firearm becomes defaced through normal wear and tear.

Following a conviction under either of the defaced firearms statutes 18-12-103 or 18-12-104, any defaced firearms on which the conviction was based are "deemed to be contraband," and are placed in the hands of law enforcement to be destroyed or made permanently inoperable. *See* section 18-12-103.5.

II. "Large-capacity magazines"

As of July 1, 2013, it is a class 2 misdemeanor if a person "sells, transfers, or possesses a large-capacity magazine" in Colorado under section 18-12-302(1) of the Colorado Revised Statutes. To fully understand this law, we must first define "large-capacity magazine." Under section 18-12-301(2)(a) of the Colorado Revised Statutes, all of the following are considered "large-capacity magazines":

- A fixed or detachable magazine, box, drum, feed strip, or similar device capable of accepting, or that is designed to be readily converted to accept, more than fifteen rounds of ammunition;
- A fixed, tubular shotgun magazine that holds more than twenty-eight inches of shotgun shells, including any extension device that is attached to the magazine and holds additional shotgun shells; or
- A nontubular, detachable magazine, box, drum, feed strip, or similar device that is capable of accepting more than eight shotgun shells when combined with a fixed magazine.

Section 18-12-301(2)(b) expressly states that the following three things are not considered "large-capacity magazines":

- A feeding device that has been permanently altered so that it cannot accommodate more than fifteen rounds of ammunition;
- An attached tubular device designed to accept, and capable of operating only with, .22 caliber rimfire ammunition; or
- A tubular magazine that is contained in a lever-action firearm.

There are two exemptions to this law. Under section 18-12-302(2)(a) of the Colorado Revised Statutes, a person may continue to possess any large-capacity magazines that they owned on the date this law came into effect, July 1, 2013. Note that this exception only allows the continued possession of qualifying large-capacity magazines. This exemption does not allow for the sale or transfer of these grandfathered magazines. In fact, in order for this exemption to apply, the person must maintain "continuous possession of the large-capacity magazine." *See* section 18-12-302(2)(a)(II). In the event that a possessor of a large-capacity magazine covered by this exception is accused of violating the law against possessing such magazines, if the person claims this exception, the burden of proof is on the prosecution to show that the exception doesn't apply. *See* section 18-12-302(2)(b).

The second exception is for businesses that deal with large-capacity magazines that operate in Colorado and is found in section 18-12-302(3) of the Colorado Revised Statutes. Under this exception, manufacturers of large-capacity magazines and licensed gun dealers are exempt if they exclusively sell to:

- Any branch of the United States military;
- Any department, agency, or political subdivision of Colorado or of any other state;
- Any department, agency, or political subdivision of the federal government;
- Any employee of the above three previously listed types agencies who bears a firearm in the course of his or her official duties;
- A firearms retailer for the purpose of firearm sales outside Colorado;
- A foreign national government with the approval of the federal government;
- An out-of-state customer who may legally possess such a magazine; or
- A person who possesses the magazine for the sole purpose of transporting the magazine to an out-of-state entity on behalf of a Colorado based manufacturer of large-capacity magazines (like a truck driver).

The severity of the penalty for violating the ban on the sale, transfer, or possession of a large-capacity magazine varies based on the circumstances. The first violation of this law is a class 2 misdemeanor. *See* section 18-12-302(1)(a). If a person is convicted a second time under this law, they are guilty of a class 1 misdemeanor. *See* section 18-12-302(1)(b). Lastly, if a person possesses a large-capacity magazine while committing a felony or any crime of violence, they are guilty of a class 6 felony. *See* section 18-12-302(1)(c).

Under section 18-12-303(1) of the Colorado Revised Statutes, any large-capacity magazine manufactured in Colorado after July 1, 2013 must "include a permanent stamp or marking indicating that the large-capacity magazine was manufactured or assembled after July 1, 2013. Failure to follow the labelling requirement under this section is a class 2 misdemeanor. *See* section 18-12-303(3).

III. Traveling across state lines with firearms

Many people vacation and travel outside of Colorado. Naturally, no Coloradan wants to travel unarmed if they can help it, but, unfortunately, not every state shares the same views on gun ownership and gun rights as we do in Colorado. This is especially true in the northeast corner and west coast of the United States. How then does a person pass through states that have restrictive firearms laws or those different from Colorado? For example, how does a person legally pass through a state that prohibits the possession of a handgun without a license from that state? The answer: safe-passage legislation.

A. *Federal law: qualifying for firearms "Safe Passage"*

Traveling across state lines with a firearm means that a person may need to use the provisions of the federal law known as the "Safe Passage" provision. Federal law allows individuals who are legally in possession of firearms in their state (the starting point of traveling) to travel through states that are not as friendly. This protection is only available under federal law to transport such firearms across state lines for lawful purposes, as long as they comply with the requirements of the Firearm Owners Protection Act, 18 U.S.C. § 926A, nicknamed the "Safe Passage" provision. The first requirement to qualify for the Federal "Safe Passage" provision is that throughout the duration of the trip through the anti-firearm-state, the firearm must be unloaded and locked in the trunk, or locked in a container that is out of reach or not readily accessible from the passenger compartment. The ammunition also must be locked in the trunk or a container. Note that for the storage of both firearms and ammunition, the glove box and center console compartment are specifically not allowed under the statute.

B. *"Safe Passage" requires legal start to legal finish*
To get protection under federal law, a gun owner's journey must start and end in states where the traveler's possession of the firearm is legal; for instance, a person traveling with their Glock 17 starting in Colorado and ending in Vermont. Even though a person must drive through New York or Massachusetts to get to Vermont, as long as the person qualifies under the "Safe Passage" provision then they may legally pass through. However, if the start point was Colorado and the end point was New York (a place where the handgun would be illegal), there is no protection under the federal law. Safe-passage requires legal start and legal finish.

Although traveling across state lines naturally invokes federal law, it is important to remember that whenever a person finally completes their journey and reaches their destination state, the laws of that state control the possession, carrying, and use of the firearm. Federal law does not make it legal or provide any protection for possession of a firearm that is illegal under the laws of the destination state (i.e., the end state of your travels).

C. *What is the definition of "traveling" for "Safe Passage" provisions?*
The final requirement for protection under the federal law is that individuals MUST be "traveling" while in the firearm hostile state. The legal definition of "traveling" is both murky and narrow. The "Safe Passage" provision protection has been held in courts to be limited to situations that strictly relate to traveling and nothing more. Traveling is a term that is not defined in the federal statute; however, it has received treatment in the courts that is indicative of what one can expect. Generally speaking, if a person stops somewhere for too long they cease to be "traveling" and,

therefore, lose their protection under the "Safe Passage" provision. How long this time limit is has not been determined either statutorily or by case law with any definitiveness.

While stopping for gas or restroom breaks may not disqualify a person from the "traveling" protection, any stop for an activity not directly related to traveling could be considered a destination and thus you would lose the legal protection. For example, in Chicago anyone in the city for more than 24 hours is not considered to be traveling under local policy. The moral of the story is to travel through these gun-unfriendly states as fast as you can (without breaking the speed limit, of course)!

D. *Protection under federal law does not mean protection from prosecution in unfriendly states*

To make matters even worse for firearms travelers, even if a person qualifies for protection under the federal "Safe Passage" provision, New Jersey and New York seem quite proud to treat this protection as an affirmative defense. This means that someone can be arrested even though he or she met all of the requirements of the federal statute. Then, they would have to go to court to assert this defense. In other words, while a person could beat the rap, they will not beat the ride! This becomes even more troublesome in the instance of someone who is legally flying with their firearm, and then due to flight complications, must land in New Jersey or New York, as travelers in this position have been arrested or threatened with arrest.

Once again, the "Safe Passage" provision only applies while a person is traveling; as soon as they arrive at their destination and cease their travels, the laws of that state control a person's actions. Remember: check all applicable state firearms laws before you leave for your destination!

IV. Air travel with a firearm

A. *How do I legally travel with a firearm as a passenger on a commercial airline?*

It is legal to travel with firearms on commercial airlines so long as the firearms transported are unloaded and in a locked, hard-sided container as checked baggage. Under federal law, the container must be completely inaccessible to passengers. Further, under U.S. Homeland Security rules, firearms, ammunition and firearm parts, including firearm frames, receivers, clips, and magazines, are prohibited in carry-on baggage. The Transportation Safety Administration (TSA) also requires that "realistic replicas of firearms are also prohibited in carry-on bags and must be packed in checked baggage. Rifle scopes are permitted in carry-on and checked bags."

1. Firearms must be inaccessible

Federal law makes it a crime subject to fine, imprisonment for up to ten years, or both, if a person "when on, or attempting to get on, an aircraft in, or intended for operation in, air transportation or intrastate air transportation, has on or about the individual or the property of the individual a concealed dangerous weapon that is or would be accessible to the individual in flight." 49 U.S.C. § 46505(b). Additionally, under 49 U.S.C. § 46303(a) "[a]n individual who, when on, or attempting to board, an aircraft in, or intended for operation in, air transportation or intrastate air transportation, has on or about the individual or the property of the individual a concealed dangerous weapon that is or would be accessible to the individual in flight is liable to the United States Government for a civil penalty of not more than $10,000 for each violation."

2. Firearms must be checked in baggage

The following guidelines are put out by the TSA for traveling with firearms on airlines:

"To avoid issues that could impact your travel and/or result in law enforcement action, here are some guidelines to assist you in packing your firearms and ammunition:

- All firearms must be declared to the airline during the ticket counter check-in process;
- The term firearm includes: (Please see, for instance, United States Code, Title 18, Part 1, Chapter 44 for information about firearm definitions.);
  - Any weapon (including a starter gun) which will, or is designed to, or may readily be converted to expel a projectile by the action of an explosive;
  - The frame or receiver of any such weapon;
  - Any firearm muffler or firearm silencer; or
  - Any destructive device.
- The firearm must be unloaded:
  - As defined by 49 CFR § 1540.5, 'A loaded firearm means a firearm that has a live round of ammunition, or any component thereof, in the chamber or cylinder or in a magazine inserted in the firearm.'
- The firearm must be in a hard-sided container that is locked. A locked container is defined as one that completely secures the firearm from being accessed. Locked cases that can be pulled open with little effort cannot be brought aboard the aircraft;
- If firearms are not properly declared or packaged, TSA will provide the checked bag to law enforcement for resolution with the airline. If the issue is resolved, law enforcement will release the bag to TSA so screening may be completed;
- TSA must resolve all alarms in checked baggage. If a locked container containing a firearm alarms, TSA will contact the airline, who will make a reasonable attempt to contact the owner and advise the passenger to go to the screening location. If contact is not made, the container will not be placed on the aircraft;

- If a locked container alarms during screening and is not marked as containing a declared firearm, TSA will cut the lock in order to resolve the alarm;
- Travelers should remain in the area designated by the aircraft operator or TSA representative to take the key back after the container is cleared for transportation;
- Travelers must securely pack any ammunition in fiber (such as cardboard), wood or metal boxes or other packaging specifically designed to carry small amounts of ammunition;
- Firearm magazines and ammunition clips, whether loaded or empty, must be securely boxed or included within a hard-sided case containing an unloaded firearm;
- Small arms ammunition, including ammunition not exceeding .75 caliber for a rifle or pistol and shotgun shells of any gauge, may be carried in the same hard-sided case as the firearm, as long as it follows the packing guidelines described above;
- TSA prohibits black powder or percussion caps used with black-powder;
- Rifle scopes are not prohibited in carry-on bags and do not need to be in the hard-sided, locked checked bag."

See www.tsa.gov.

B. *May I have a firearm while operating or as a passenger in a private aircraft flying just in Colorado?*
Generally, yes. For purposes of Colorado state law, a private aircraft is treated like any other motorized vehicle.

C. *May I have a firearm in a private aircraft that takes off from Colorado and lands in another state?*
In situations where a private aircraft is taking off from one state and landing in another, the law will simply view this as traveling interstate with firearms. Where no other statutes apply to the person's flight, the person will be subject to the provisions of 18 U.S.C. § 926A regarding the interstate transportation of a firearm: "any person who is not otherwise prohibited by this chapter from transporting, shipping, or receiving a firearm shall be entitled to

transport a firearm for any lawful purpose from any place where he may lawfully possess and carry such firearm to any other place where he may lawfully possess and carry such firearm if, during such transportation the firearm is unloaded, and neither the firearm nor any ammunition being transported is readily accessible or is directly accessible from the passenger compartment of such transporting vehicle."

This statute allows a person to transport firearms between states subject to the following conditions: that the person can lawfully possess the firearm at his or her points of departure and arrival, and that the firearm remain unloaded and inaccessible during the trip.

For operations of private aircraft within one state, a person will only be subject to the laws of the state within which he or she is operating. The person will need to review their state's statutes to determine whether they impose any restrictions on possession of firearms within non-secure areas of airports. The person will also need to be familiar with the airports he or she will be visiting to determine whether each airport has any restrictions.

V.   Understanding gun-free school zone laws

The discussion of gun-free school zones is one that covers many different areas of the law and affects both persons who hold a Colorado Concealed Carry Permit as well as persons who do not. That is because the "Gun Free School Zone" law and its meaning cause a lot of confusion. Signs warning about being in a "gun free school zone" are common around schools, but what does this mean to people lawfully in possession of firearms? There is not a Colorado law titled "Gun Free Zone Law;" that is a federal statute. As was explained earlier in this Chapter, in many circumstances firearms are prohibited on school grounds, but they are not prohibited in all circumstances. However, as always, gun owners have to follow both state and federal law when carrying a firearm. With that in mind, let's take a look at federal gun-free school zone law.

A. *Federal "Gun Free School Zone" law: 18 U.S.C.§ 922(q)*
The text of the federal "Gun Free School Zone" law is found in 18 U.S.C. § 922(q), and creates its own independent criminal offense. This law states that it is a federal crime for a person to possess a firearm that has moved through interstate commerce (this includes virtually all firearms), on the grounds of or within 1,000 feet of a public, parochial, or private school. As surprising as it may seem, under this federal law, the mere possession of a firearm by the occupant of a motor vehicle while driving past a school or dropping off a child, is a federal crime.

However, federal law provides seven exceptions:
1. *Exception one*: if the possession is on private property which is not part of the school grounds. This means that a person living within 1,000 feet of a school can keep a firearm in their house.
2. *Exception two*: if the individual possessing the firearm is licensed to do so by the state in which the school zone is located or a political subdivision of the state, and the law of the state or political subdivision requires that, before an individual obtains such a license, the law enforcement authorities of the state or political subdivision verify that the individual is qualified under law to receive the license. This means that a Colorado Concealed Carry Permit holder may legally carry a concealed firearm into a "gun free school zone." However, there is one important note about the statute: a person can only lawfully carry in a school zone located in the state that issued the firearms license. Therefore, if a person has a Colorado permit they can only carry through Colorado school zones. If that Colorado permit holder is traveling through another state, the exception under federal law does not apply to them, and they are in violation of this law. It also means that a Colorado resident, who holds a non-Colorado concealed carry license or permit, does not benefit from this exception and is in violation of the law if they take a firearm into a school zone.

3. *Exception three*: if the firearm is not loaded, and is in a locked container, or a locked firearms rack that is on a motor vehicle. This means that if a firearm is unloaded and carried in a locked case, or other type of locked container, such as a glove box or trunk, there is no violation of the federal law.

4. *Exception four*: if the firearm is carried by an individual for use in a program approved by a school in the school zone. This exception covers school-sponsored shooting activities, such as an ROTC program.

5. *Exception five*: if the firearm is carried by an individual in accordance with a contract entered into between a school in the school zone and the individual or an employer of the individual. This means that school security guards can carry firearms while on the job.

6. *Exception six*: if the firearm is carried by a law enforcement officer acting in his or her official capacity. This exception covers police officers while on-duty only. It does not appear to cover them while they are off-duty, even if they are required by state law to carry while off-duty.

7. *Exception seven*: if the firearm is unloaded and is in the possession of an individual while traversing school property for the purpose of gaining access to public or private lands open to hunting, if the entry on school premises is authorized by school authorities. This means that if a hunter must cross school property to get to a lawful hunting ground, they must have the permission of the school, and the firearm must be unloaded.

B. *Reconciling Colorado and federal laws on gun-free school zones*

The law puts a vast number of unknowing and unsuspecting people in conflict with federal law while being in full compliance with state law. As a result, it is likely that this law is unknowingly violated thousands of times a day. However, while this has been federal law since 1996 and its predecessor was the law since

1990, there does not appear to be a wave of federal prosecutions for the mere possession of a firearm by a person who is only driving through a school zone or picking up or dropping off their child.

CHAPTER ELEVEN
RESTORATION OF FIREARMS RIGHTS:
THE LAW OF PARDONS AND EXPUNGEMENTS

I. Is it possible to restore a person's right to bear arms?

What happens after a person has been convicted of a crime, is it possible to later clear their name and/or criminal record? If possible, then what is the process for removing a conviction and restoring a person's right to purchase and possess firearms? This chapter will explain how a person under very limited circumstances can have arrest records, criminal charges, and even criminal convictions removed or nullified. But words of caution, success in this arena may be rare and there are many publications and internet sites that purport to have the winning formula to provide you relief. ***Be very cautious and always consult with an attorney***. Further, each state has different rules concerning these issues as well as a completely different set of rules under federal law. Before we begin a meaningful discussion, it is important to explain two terms and concepts: clemency and expungement.

A. *What is clemency?*

Clemency is the action the government, usually the chief executive (*e.g.*, the President on the federal level or a governor on the state level), takes in forgiving or pardoning a crime or canceling the penalty of a crime, either wholly, or in part. Clemency can include full pardons after a conviction, full pardons after completion of deferred adjudication community supervision, conditional pardons, pardons based on innocence, commutations of a sentence, emergency medical reprieves, and family medical reprieves. Clemency can be granted at both the federal and state level.

B. *What is expungement?*

Expungement is the physical act of destroying or purging government criminal records, unlike sealing which is simply hiding the records from the public. Under certain circumstances, a person may have their criminal record either expunged or sealed.

Practical Legal Tip:

While our intention is to provide you with as much information as possible as to how you can have your firearms rights restored if you are convicted of a crime, it's also important to make sure you are aware of how rarely pardons, expungements, and restorations of firearms rights are granted. While it's certainly worth the effort to apply for a pardon, be careful not to get your hopes up, because they are seldom granted.
-*Stanley*

II. **Federal law**

A. *Presidential pardon*

Under Article II, Section 2, of the United States Constitution, the President of the United States has the power "to grant reprieves and pardons for offenses against the United States, except in cases of impeachment." The President's power to pardon offenses has also been interpreted to include the power to grant conditional pardons, commutations of sentence, conditional commutations of sentence, remission of fines and forfeitures, respites, and amnesties. However, the President's clemency authority only extends to federal offenses; the President cannot grant clemency for a state crime.

1. How does a person petition for federal clemency or a pardon?

Under federal law, a person requesting executive clemency must petition the President of the United States and submit the petition to the Office of the Pardon Attorney in the Department of Justice. The Office of the Pardon Attorney can provide petitions and other required forms necessary to complete the application for clemency. *See* 28 CFR § 1.1. Petition forms for commutation of sentence may also be obtained from the wardens of federal penal institutions. In addition, a petitioner applying for executive clemency with respect to military offenses should submit his or her petition directly to the Secretary of the military branch that had original jurisdiction over the court-martial trial and conviction of the petitioner.

The Code of Federal Regulations requires an applicant to wait five years after the date of the release of the petitioner from confinement, or in a case where no prison sentence was imposed, an applicant is required to wait five years after the date of conviction prior to submitting a petition for clemency. The regulation further states that "generally, no petition should be submitted by a person who is on probation, parole, or supervised release." 28 CFR § 1.2. With that in mind, the President can grant clemency at any time, whether an individual has made a formal petition or not. For example, President Gerald Ford granted a full and unconditional pardon to former President Richard Nixon prior to any indictment or charges being filed related to his involvement in Watergate.

2. What should a petition for clemency include?

Petitions for executive clemency should include the information required in the form prescribed by the United States Attorney General. This includes information:

- that the person requesting clemency must state specifically the purpose for which clemency is sought, as well as attach any and all relevant documentary evidence that will support how clemency will support that purpose;
- that discloses any arrests or convictions subsequent to the federal crime for which clemency is sought;
- that discloses all delinquent credit obligations (whether disputed or not), all civil lawsuits to which the applicant is a party (whether plaintiff or defendant), and all unpaid tax obligations (whether local, state, or federal);
- that includes three character affidavits from persons not related to the applicant by blood or marriage.

In addition, acceptance of a Presidential pardon generally carries with it an admission of guilt. For that reason, a petitioner should include in his or her petition a statement of the petitioner's acceptance of responsibility, an expression of remorse, and atonement for the offense. All of the requirements are contained in 28 CFR §§ 1.1-1.11.

3. <u>What happens after a petition for executive clemency is submitted?</u>

All petitions for federal clemency are reviewed by the Office of the Pardon Attorney in the Department of Justice. A non-binding recommendation on an application is made to the President. Federal regulations also provide for guidelines and requirements to notify victims of the crimes, if any, for which clemency is sought. The President will either grant or deny a pardon. There are no hearings held on the petition, and there is no appeal of the President's decision.

4. <u>What is the effect of a Presidential pardon?</u>

A pardon is the forgiveness of a crime and the cancellation of the penalty associated with that crime. While a Presidential pardon will restore various rights lost as a result of the pardoned offense, it will not expunge the record of your conviction. This means that even if a person is granted a pardon, the person must still disclose their conviction on any form where such information is required, although the person may also disclose the fact that the offense for which they were convicted was pardoned.

B. *Expungement of federal convictions*

    1. No law exists for general federal expungement

Congress has not provided federal legislation that offers any comprehensive authority or procedure for expunging criminal offenses. There exist only statutes that allow expungement in certain cases for possession of small amounts of controlled substances (see below) and interestingly, a procedure to expunge DNA samples of certain members of the military wrongfully convicted. Because there is no statutory guidance, federal courts have literally made up the rules and procedures themselves, often coming to different conclusions. Some federal court circuits have stated they have <u>no</u> power to expunge records. However, other federal courts have indicated that they do have the power to expunge. The federal Tenth Circuit, which covers Colorado, has held that a federal district court may expunge arrest records only in "the unusual and extreme case," and that this power is quite "narrow." *U.S. v. Friesen*, 853 F.2d 816, 818 (10th Cir. 1988). In any case, "mere acquittal of the subsequent charge is an insufficient reason to grant expunction." *See id.* The Supreme Court has passed on hearing cases that would have resolved the split between the circuits. This issue remains legally murky.

    2. Possible procedure for federal expungement

There are no statutory guidelines for how to seek an expungement under federal law, however, the place to start would be to file a motion with the federal court that issued the conviction that a person wants to be expunged. However, federal judges very rarely grant these types of motions. In the Tenth Circuit, a federal court may, "in extreme cases," grant expungement "when a conviction is somehow invalidated, such as by a finding that it was unconstitutional, illegal, or obtained through government misconduct." *U.S. v. Pinto*, 1 F.3d 1069,

1070 (10th Cir. 1993). Unless there exists compelling reasons, a federal judge is highly unlikely to grant expungement.

3. Expungement for drug possession: statutory authority

Under a federal law entitled "special probation and expungement procedures for drug possessors," certain persons are allowed to request a federal court to issue an expungement order from all public records. 18 U.S.C. § 3607. Congress intended this order to restore the person to the status he or she "occupied before such arrest or institution of criminal proceedings." 18 U.S.C. § 3607(c).

In order to qualify for the expungement, you must have been under the age of 21 when you were convicted, you must have no prior drug offenses, and your conviction must have been for simple possession of a small amount of a controlled substance.

4. How does a person have firearms rights restored under federal law?

Under the Gun Control Act of 1968, a person who has received a Presidential pardon is not considered convicted of a crime preventing the purchase and possession of firearms subject to all other federal laws. *See* 18 U.S.C. §§ 921(a)(20) and (a)(33). In addition, persons who had a conviction expunged or set aside, or who have had their civil rights restored are not considered to have been convicted for purposes of the GCA "unless the pardon, expungement, or restoration of civil rights expressly provides the person may not ship, transport, possess, or receive firearms." 18 U.S.C. §§ 921(a)(20) and (a)(33).

The GCA also provides the United States Attorney General with the authority to grant relief from firearms disabilities where the Attorney General determines that the person is not likely to act in a manner dangerous to the public safety and where granting relief would not be contrary to the public interest. 18 U.S.C. § 925(c). The Attorney General has delegated this authority to the ATF. Unfortunately, the ATF reports that it has been prohibited from spending any funds in order to investigate or act upon applications from individuals seeking relief from federal firearms disabilities. This means that until the ATF's prohibition has been lifted, a person's best—and most likely—option to have their firearms rights restored is through a Presidential pardon. *See* www.atf.gov.

III. Colorado law

A. *Clemency by the Governor and the Executive Clemency Advisory Board*

The Governor of Colorado possesses the authority to grant a pardon under Article IV, § 7 of the Colorado Constitution. However, the governor cannot exercise this power to pardon treason or in the case of impeachment. A pardon, also known as executive clemency, is an extraordinary measure that is rarely granted.

Note that the governor also has the authority to commute a sentence. That is, the governor can reduce the length of a sentence post-conviction. However, a commutation cannot restore firearms rights to an offender, so it will not be discussed further in this book.

1. Who is eligible for executive clemency in Colorado?

Executive clemency can be granted to any person who has been convicted of a felony or misdemeanor. Felons must wait seven years after the completion of their sentence before they are eligible for a pardon. Those convicted of a misdemeanor must wait three years after the completion of their sentence. See the "Executive Clemency Application," which is linked at https://www.colorado.gov/pacific/cdoc/clemency-requests.

2. How does a person seek executive clemency in Colorado?

A person seeking executive clemency in Colorado is required to complete an application which is available from the Colorado Department of Corrections. In addition, under section 16-17-102 of the Colorado Revised Statutes, all applications for executive clemency must be accompanied by a certificate from the superintendent of the relevant correctional facility, which shows the conduct of the applicant during his or her confinement. Further, the applicant has the opportunity to provide any other evidence of the applicant's former good character along with the application. Once properly submitted, the file of any applicant eligible for clemency may be reviewed by the Executive Clemency Advisory Board.

By executive order, dated October 19, 2012, the Board must include the Executive Director of the Colorado Department of Corrections and the Executive Director of the Department of Public Safety along with five other members appointed by the governor to three year terms. At least one of the five appointed members must be either a crime victim or a representative of victims of crime. The Board does not have to review an application, unless specifically directed by the Governor. During a review, the Board may consider any factors it wishes before making a recommendation to the Governor.

Before making a decision on a recommended application, under section 16-17-102 of the Colorado Revised Statutes, the Governor must submit the application to the current district attorney of the district in which the applicant was convicted, to the judge who sentenced the applicant, and to the attorney who prosecuted the applicant, if available, to elicit their comments on the merits of the application. The governor shall give these parties at least 14 days to comment on the application before coming to a decision. Once these comments have been received by the governor, or the 14 days have passed without comment, the governor has the sole discretion in weighing the information and making a decision on clemency. For more information on the executive clemency process, please visit https://www.colorado.gov/pacific/cdoc/clemency-requests.

3. What is the effect of executive clemency in Colorado?
Section 16-17-103(1) of the Colorado Revised Statutes provides that a governor's pardon waives "all collateral consequences"

associated with the conviction, unless the pardon specifically limits the scope of the pardon. The loss of firearm privileges is included in these "collateral consequences," as defined in section 16-17-103(3). Therefore, unless a pardon specifically states that the pardoned person's firearm rights are not restored, those rights are automatically restored by a pardon.

Similar to federal clemency, unless the person receiving clemency has their records expunged, the records of the original conviction continue to exist. A person granted clemency must still disclose the conviction on any relevant form seeking such information, however, the person may also state the nature of the clemency received.

CHAPTER TWELVE
I'M BEING SUED FOR WHAT?
CIVIL LIABILITY IF YOU HAVE USED YOUR GUN

I. What does it mean to be sued?

The term "lawsuit" refers to one party's assertion in a written filing with a court that another party has violated a civil law. In the context of firearms, typically the party suing has been injured and wants a ruling or judgment from the court which most likely will entitle the person suing to receive money.

A. *What is a civil claim or lawsuit?*

A civil "lawsuit" or "suit" refers to the actual filing of written paperwork with a court (1) asserting that another party violated the law, and (2) seeking some type of redress. A "claim" can exist without the filing of a lawsuit. A claim is simply the belief or assertion that another party has violated the law. Many parties have claims they never assert, or sometimes parties informally assert the claim in hopes of resolving the disputes without the filing of a lawsuit. Also, another term commonly used is "tort" or "tort claim." A tort is a civil claim arising out of a wrongful act, not including a breach of contract or trust, which results in injury to another's person, property, reputation, or the like. The claims described below are all tort claims.

B. *Difference between "civil claims" and "criminal charges"*

To start with the basics, there are two different aspects of the legal system that gun owners may face after the use of a firearm: criminal and civil. There are several names and descriptive terms used for each (*e.g.*, civil lawsuit, criminal actions, civil claims, criminal proceedings, etc.), but regardless of the terms, the same breakdown applies; most cases are either criminal or civil. There is another subgroup of proceedings called administrative actions. Those actions are not covered by this chapter but can sometimes impact Colorado Concealed Carry Permit holders. For example, appealing the denial of a Permit is an administrative act. *See* Chapters Eight and Nine for more information.

With that said, the three primary differences between a criminal action and a civil proceeding are: (1) who or what is bringing the action or lawsuit, (2) what are they seeking, and (3) what is the burden of proof? These differences are fairly straightforward:

1. State versus individual bringing claims
In a criminal case, the party bringing the action is the "sovereign," (meaning the United States, state, municipality, county, *etc.*) that believes that a person violated their laws. Even if an individual calls the police, fills out a criminal complaint, or even asks the district attorney to file charges, the party that actually brings a criminal action is the state, county, *etc.*, not the individual.

However, a civil action may be filed by any individual, business or other entity (partnership, LLC, trust, *etc.*). The entity bringing the claim is called the "plaintiff." Even governmental entities can bring civil claims; *e.g.*, if you negligently shoot a county propane tank causing a fire, the county can sue you civilly for those damages. The typical gun case, though, will involve an individual filing a lawsuit against another individual for damages caused by the firearm. If the incident occurs at a place of business, the plaintiff may also sue the business claiming that it is in some way at fault for the incident. The party being sued is typically called the "defendant."

2. Relief sought/awarded
In a criminal case, the entity prosecuting the case is usually seeking to imprison or fine you. Most crimes are punishable by "X" number or days/months/years in prison or jail, and a fine not to exceed "X" dollars.

By contrast, the plaintiff in the civil case is almost always seeking a monetary award. Several other types of relief are available (declaratory, injunctive, specific performance), but for the most part, gun cases will involve the plaintiff seeking monetary damages.

3. Burden of proof

In a criminal case, the standard is "beyond a reasonable doubt." In civil cases, however, a plaintiff must prove a person is liable for damages by a "preponderance of the evidence" standard. A preponderance of the evidence is a much lower standard than the criminal standard of beyond a reasonable doubt. It generally means that the party with the greater weight of credible evidence wins that issue. The preponderance of the evidence has been described as more than half, that is, if the evidence demonstrates that something "more likely occurred than not," this meets the burden of proof. Whereas in a criminal case, if there exists any "reasonable doubt," the burden of proof is not met. It does not mean the party with the most exhibits or greater number of witnesses will prevail. One highly credible witness can prevail over the testimony of a dozen biased, shady witnesses.

Example:

> *John mistakes a utility meter reader for a burglar due to his disheveled appearance, tool bag, and because he looks to be snooping around John's house. John fires a shot without warning and injures the meter reader.*

Possible criminal liability: The State of Colorado could bring criminal charges against John for a number of crimes (first degree assault, attempted murder, and so forth). The State would be seeking to imprison or fine John for his conduct, and it would be required to prove that John committed the crime at issue "beyond a reasonable doubt." Further, the State would have to prove beyond a reasonable doubt that John did not reasonably act in self-defense. In this case, that would mean that the State would have to prove that John did not have a reasonable belief that the meter reader was about to use physical force against an occupant of a dwelling while committing or attempting to commit burglary.

Please refer to Chapters Four through Seven for a full explanation of Colorado's self-defense laws.

Possible civil liability: the meter reader could also file a civil lawsuit against John alleging that John was negligent or committed the tort of assault and battery. The meter reader would seek monetary damages and be required to prove his claims by a "preponderance of the evidence." Most homeowner's insurance policies do not provide coverage for this type of incident. Be sure to consult with your insurance agent to determine whether there are any gaps in your current coverage.

C. *Impact of result in one court upon the other*
    1. <u>Can a result in a criminal trial be used in a civil trial?</u>
Yes, because of the legal doctrines of *res judicata* and collateral estoppel. These two legal doctrines govern the impact of a ruling or judgment in one case, upon a separate case involving the same set of facts and circumstances. For the present discussion, if a person is found guilty of a crime in a criminal proceeding, because that court uses a higher standard of "beyond a reasonable doubt" than the civil requirement of "preponderance of the evidence," the finding of the criminal court may be used for purposes of establishing civil liability. Entire chapters in law books have been written on these topics, so, suffice to say, this section is a brief overview of these laws.

The criminal concept of *nolo contendere* or "no contest" often generates confusion in this area. In a criminal case, a plea of *nolo contendere* or no contest means that the defendant does not admit guilt. This plea can only occur with the consent of the court and is not allowed every time it is requested. The plea, however, still results in a judgment that the defendant is guilty of the crime and operates the same as a guilty plea for that criminal case. However, although this is not true in all states, in Colorado, a plea of "no contest" in a criminal case allows the defendant to deny their fault in a subsequent civil action based on the same facts. *See People v. Darlington*, 105 P.3d 230, 233 (Colo. 2005).

Example:

> *Phil and Jeremy become involved in a road rage incident, and an altercation follows. Phil shoots Jeremy, wounding him. When all is sorted out, Phil is found guilty of first degree assault and receives punishment from the court (remember, criminal trials use the "beyond a reasonable doubt" standard).*

If Jeremy later sues Phil from the injuries he received when Phil shot him, Jeremy, in his civil action, will very likely be allowed to use the finding of guilt in the criminal case (because it used the higher standard of reasonable doubt) to establish his burden in the civil case (the lower preponderance of the evidence standard) that he is owed damages or money in the civil case. This is an example of collateral estoppel; Phil will not be permitted to re-litigate his guilt in the civil case. However, if Phil was allowed by the court to plead "no contest" in the criminal case, Jeremy would be forced to prove through a preponderance of the evidence that Jeremy caused his injuries.

Collateral estoppel is based on the concept that a party to a legal proceeding should not be able to endlessly litigate issues that have already been decided by the legal system. At its most basic level, it means that a party to a legal proceeding who receives a final ruling on a particular issue, win or lose, cannot attempt to have another trial court or even the same court decide the same issue.

Note about appeals: this is a different concept than an appeal, or asking the court in the first proceeding to reconsider its ruling, or grant a new trial. An appeal is a request to a higher court to review the decision of a lower court. Likewise, in any given case, the parties will have numerous opportunities to ask the current court to reconsider its rulings, or even ask for a new trial after a trial is completed. Collateral estoppel and *res judicata* come into play after a final judgment that is no longer subject to appeal or revision by the trial court.

Example:

> *Michele is sued for accidentally shooting Nancy. Nancy wins a judgment of $350 against Michele, much less than Nancy believed she was damaged.*

In that case, Nancy can appeal the decision, or even ask that trial court for a new trial. However, Nancy cannot file another, or new, lawsuit regarding the same incident and attempt to recover more in the second case because of the doctrine of *res judicata*. In order for the doctrine to apply, the facts, circumstances and issues must be the same.

Example:

> *Justin fires his hunting rifle from his deer blind, hitting Peter with one round. Peter files a civil suit against Justin and loses at trial. The court awards Peter no damages. Peter appeals and loses the appeal also.*

Peter is legally barred from recovering in another lawsuit against Justin involving the same incident. However, Peter is not barred from filing suit against Justin for damages arising out of another set of facts and circumstances, for example, if the two are involved in a car wreck on a different day.

2. Impact of a civil case's result on a criminal case

Suppose you lose a civil suit and a judgment is entered against you arising out of a shooting incident. Can that judgment be used to establish that you committed a crime? No. The burden of proof is much higher in the criminal context than the civil case. The plaintiff proved his civil case by a "preponderance of the evidence." This does not mean that he proved his case "beyond a reasonable doubt," meaning a separate criminal trial is required to make that determination.

The one area where a civil case can impact a criminal case is the potential overlapping use of evidence and testimony. Your admission in one case can almost always be used against you in another case. Meaning, your sworn testimony in the civil case ("yes, I shot the guy") can almost always be used against you in the criminal case, and vice versa.

II. **What might you be sued for? Gun related claims in civil courts**

A. *Liability for unintentional discharge*

This section deals with accidental or unintentional discharges of your firearm. Common unintentional discharges are associated with hunting and cleaning accidents or the mishandling of a weapon. Intentional shootings are addressed in the following section.

With that said, the following are the types of civil claims that may be asserted in connection with an unintentional discharge:

1. Negligence/gross negligence

Most civil cases for damages resulting from an accidental discharge will include a negligence or gross negligence claim. What does this mean and what does a plaintiff have to prove before they can win? Under Colorado law, negligence is defined as the failure to use reasonable care, that is, failing to do that which a reasonable person of ordinary prudence would have done under the same or similar circumstances, or doing that which a reasonable person of ordinary prudence would not have done under the same or similar circumstances. If a person fails to use reasonable care, then they have acted negligently and will be liable for damages resulting from their conduct. "Reasonable care" means that degree of care that would be used by a reasonable person of ordinary prudence under the same or similar circumstances. This is an "objective standard," meaning, the test is not whether you believed you acted prudently, but whether the judge or jury believes you acted as a reasonable person of ordinary prudence would have acted. Of course, this is the definition of negligence in the civil context. There is actually a different definition of criminal negligence, which is beyond the scope of this book's discussion.

What is gross negligence and how is it different than "regular" negligence? Many gun cases will include a claim for "gross negligence" by the plaintiff. The primary reason for this is that if a plaintiff establishes gross negligence by a defendant, the plaintiff may be entitled to additional types or amounts of money that are legally unavailable if mere negligence is established. The Colorado courts consider gross negligence to be the same as "willful and wanton conduct." Colorado courts have defined this concept as an "action committed recklessly, with conscious disregard for the safety of others." *See Hamill v. Cheley Colorado Camps, Inc.*, 262 P.3d 945, 954 (Colo. App. 2011).

The defendant's state of mind is also a key difference between negligence and gross negligence. Negligence involves an objective standard—how would a reasonable person have acted? Gross negligence applies a subjective component—was this particular person actually aware of the risk involved and disregarded it?

Example:

> *Jessica has practiced her shooting at a private range on her country property for 20 years, without incident. Jessica shoots towards an area where she has never seen another person, and she believes the range of her guns cannot reach her property line. One day, a neighbor is hit by a shot as he is strolling through the woods just off of Jessica's property.*

Result: Jessica might be liable for negligence if a jury determines, for example, that a reasonably prudent person would have acted differently, tested the range of her guns, or built a different type of back stop or berm, *etc.* However, Jessica was not subjectively aware of an extreme degree of risk so there would be no evidence of gross negligence. If you change Jessica's awareness, it changes the result.

Example:

> *Jessica has received several complaints over the years about bullets leaving her property and hitting her neighbor's property. Nevertheless, Jessica ignores the complaints and continues practicing in the direction that she typically shoots. One day while practicing, her bullet leaves her property and hits her neighbor. She is later sued by the neighbor for gross negligence.*

Result: Jessica may very well be liable for gross negligence because she was subjectively aware that her shots were reaching the neighbor's property and that there were people in the same area (*i.e.*, the folks who reported the shots), and despite that knowledge, she continued to shoot without changing direction or building a backstop or berm and someone was injured as a result.

2. Negligent entrustment of a firearm

Colorado recognizes a claim for entrusting (*e.g.*, giving, lending, transferring) a firearm to another person. To prove that a person or entity negligently entrusted a firearm, the plaintiff must show that:

- The gun owner entrusted the gun to a third party;
- The gun owner had control of the gun at the time of the transfer;
- The gun owner knew or should have known that the receiving party intended to or is likely to use the gun in a way that causes an unreasonable risk of harm to others; and
- The plaintiff was harmed by the third party's use of the gun.

Example:

> *Shaun lets his adult grandson Gordon borrow a shotgun to take on a fishing trip because he knows there are water moccasins in the spot where they plan to fish. Gordon has never been in trouble with the law, has repeatedly been trained in firearms safety, and has never had an incident with a gun. However, while on the trip, Gordon accidentally shoots a fellow fishing buddy with Shaun's shotgun. The fishing buddy, now turned plaintiff, sues Gordon for negligence and Shaun for negligent entrustment of a firearm.*

Can the plaintiff win his claim for negligent entrustment? Probably not. Shaun might get sued for giving the shotgun to his grandson, but the facts described do not meet the elements necessary to establish negligent entrustment under Colorado law; and Shaun should prevail in any lawsuit. First, there are no facts that suggest Gordon had any history of violence. Further, there are no facts showing knowledge by Shaun that Gordon intended to use the gun to cause harm or that Gordon was likely to use the gun to cause harm. Thus, the negligent entrustment claim would legally fail.

3. Is negligent storage of a firearm recognized in Colorado?

A question commonly asked by gun owners is "if someone steals my gun, am I liable if they shoot someone?" In other words, if I store my gun and a criminal or another less-than-responsible person gets the gun, am I liable if they shoot someone? As of the date of this publication, there has not been a case in Colorado concerning civil liability for negligently storing a firearm. This means that there is really no way to know how the Colorado courts would handle such a claim. Several other states have criminal statutes making it a crime to negligently store a firearm in a way that allowed a child access to the firearm. Although such a statute has been considered by the legislature in Colorado, it has not been passed to date.

As a result, while no civil claim exists in Colorado today, it remains extraordinarily important to exercise care in the storage of your firearms.

3. *Intentional discharge: a person intended to shoot*
   1. Negligence/gross negligence

Just because you intend to shoot someone, or otherwise "use" your gun, does not necessarily mean that the plaintiff will not assert negligence or gross negligence claims. In other words, you may have fully intended to pull the trigger, but the plaintiff may claim that you were negligent for any number of reasons; for example, you mistook the mailman for a burglar, or the criminal was retreating and you were negligent in using deadly physical force. The negligence and gross negligence claims, as defined above, can be brought even if you intended to pull the trigger.

   2. Assault and battery

If a person has shot at or shot someone, if they are sued, it may include a claim for assault and battery. This is an intentional act, not an accident or a claim based on a deviation from a standard of care. Assault and battery are two separate civil claims that often occur at the same time. Assault occurs when a person causes another person to be placed in "apprehension" of a harmful or offensive physical contact with the intent to cause that person to be placed in "apprehension" of the offensive or harmful contact. *See Bohrer v. DeHart*, 943 P.2d 1220, 1224 (Colo. App. 1996). Notice that an assault can occur without any actual contact. Battery, on the other hand, occurs when a person causes a harmful or offensive contact with the intent that the contact be harmful or offensive. *See White v. Muniz*, 999 P.2d 814, 816 (Colo. 2000). Therefore, a battery almost always includes an assault, as long as the victim knew the offensive or harmful contact was coming, but an assault does not necessarily include battery.

Example:

> *Bill is startled while driving. Martha is standing next to his passenger window at a light screaming that he cut her off in traffic, but taking no action to indicate she intends to harm Bill or do anything besides verbally lodge her complaints. In response, Bill fires a shot at Martha to make her go away, and hits her in the leg.*

Bill has likely committed assault and battery. He intended to cause harmful contact to Martha and did so, and Martha was likely placed in apprehension of the harmful conduct when she saw the gun. Therefore, a civil jury would likely find Bill liable and award damages to Martha.

Example:

> *Bill is startled while driving. Martha is standing next to his passenger window at a light screaming that he cut her off in traffic, but taking no action to indicate she intends to harm Bill or do anything besides verbally lodge her complaints. In response, Bill points his gun at Martha and says "You're dead!" He fires his gun but misses.*

Bill has committed a civil assault. He knowingly and intentionally threatened Martha with imminent harmful contact, which placed Martha in apprehension of such contact. However, since the harmful contact did not actually occur, Bill has not committed battery.

3. <u>False imprisonment: being sued for detaining people</u>

What if a gun owner detains someone at gunpoint? If the person who was detained later decides to sue, it will likely include a claim for "false imprisonment." Colorado recognizes a civil claim for false imprisonment. This claim can arise when someone detains persons waiting for police, *e.g.* homeowners detaining burglars, *etc.* However, it can also come up commonly in shoplifting cases. The elements of false imprisonment are:

- The defendant intended to restrict the plaintiff's freedom of movement;
- The plaintiff's freedom of movement was restricted for a period of time; and
- The plaintiff was aware that their freedom of movement was restricted.

See Goodboe v. Gabriella, 663 P.2d 1051, 1056 (Colo. App. 1983). Even if these three elements are satisfied, a defendant may contend that they were legally justified. For example, a defendant could assert "shopkeeper's privilege" as a defense (see Chapter Seven). Importantly, if the person who is claiming false imprisonment is criminally convicted of the crime for which they were being detained, the person who detained the criminal may use that fact as an affirmative defense. *See Land v. Hill*, 644 P.2d 43, 45 (Colo. App. 1981).

Example:

> *Emily fears she is about to be attacked in a grocery store parking lot by Randall. Randall follows her step-by-step through the parking lot and stops right next to Emily's car. Emily draws her .380 and tells Randall to "stay right there while I call the police." Randall complies, and Emily holds him at gunpoint until the police arrive. When the police arrive, they determine that Randall was an out-of-uniform store employee tasked with rounding up the grocery*

> *carts in the parking lot and was no threat to Emily.*

If a jury determines that Emily acted without justification (*i.e.*, she was not reasonably in fear of death or bodily injury), Emily could be civilly liable for falsely imprisoning Randall and possibly owe him damages.

4. Wrongful death

If a person is in the unfortunate position that they have shot and killed another individual and a civil suit occurs because of the shooting, it likely will include a claim for wrongful death. In Colorado, all wrongful death action must be pursued using the provisions of the Colorado Wrongful Death Act, sections 13-21-201 through 13-21-204 of the Colorado Revised Statutes. In short, a person is liable for damages when death is caused by their "wrongful act, neglect, or default." *See* section 13-21-202.

A wrongful death claim can be proven by establishing that one of the other claims described in this chapter caused the death of another person. In other words, the "wrongful act, neglect, or default" needed to establish a wrongful death claim, can be established by proving that the defendant was liable for a tort such as battery or negligence and that the tort caused the death of a person.

III. **What can the plaintiff recover?**

If a person is sued in civil court and the plaintiff convinces a jury that the defendant was liable for damages, what and how much can a plaintiff get? There are scores of cases discussing the details of each category of damages that a plaintiff can recover in a civil lawsuit. The following is a brief description of two very important concepts: (1) "proximate cause," which is essential to recover damages in most circumstances, and (2) the basic types of damages that a plaintiff may typically seek in a gun case.

A. *Proximate cause*

One basic concept that is important to most civil claims, and is usually required to recover damages, is "proximate cause." Virtually every tort claim will require the plaintiff to prove that his damages were proximately caused by the defendant. "Proximate cause" is defined as cause that was a substantial factor in bringing about an event and without which the event would not have occurred. This concept has few bright-line tests.

For a gun owner, the most obvious cases of proximate cause are pulling the trigger on a firearm and hitting the person or thing at which you aimed. The law will hold that your action proximately caused whatever physical damage the bullet did to persons or property. But what about those circumstances where the use of the gun is so far removed from the damages claimed? This is where the doctrine of proximate cause will cut off liability. If the damage is too far removed from the act, then the act cannot be a proximate cause of that damage.

Example:

> *Anthony is cleaning his AR-15 one night in his apartment and is negligent in his handling of the rifle. He has an accidental discharge and the bullet goes through the wall of his apartment and strikes his neighbor, Ray, in the leg. Ray, although in massive pain, received prompt medical care from his wife, Gail, and made a speedy recovery.*

If Anthony is later sued by Ray and his wife Gail, Anthony's negligence undoubtedly "proximately caused" damages for things like Ray's medical bills, hospital stay, and perhaps even lost wages. But what if Gail claims that because of her having to treat Ray's wounds that she missed a big job interview and lost out on a big raise in pay and that she wants Anthony to pay that as a component of damages? The law would hold that Gail likely could not recover damages for her lost raise in pay because the loss would not be "proximately caused" by the act being sued for. To put it another way, it is reasonably foreseeable that the negligent discharge of a firearm will cause medical bills, *etc.* for someone struck by a bullet. Therefore, this is recoverable. However, the law would say that the loss of a possible job opportunity for the wife who treated the person who was actually shot is not a reasonably foreseeable consequence of negligently discharging a firearm and, therefore, was not proximately caused by the act of negligence. In that case, there will be no recovery for the plaintiff, Gail. Proximate cause must be established in every case, and may appear to be arbitrary legal line drawing (because it is).

As discussed later, Colorado law also recognizes a doctrine that unforeseen criminal conduct breaks the causal link between an action and a third-party's injuries.

B. *What types of damages can a plaintiff recover?*
The following is merely a brief snapshot of the types of damages recoverable in a firearms case. To recover any of the damages below, the plaintiff must first prove one of the claims above by a preponderance of the evidence. For example, if the jury determines a defendant was not negligent, a plaintiff cannot recover his or her medical costs, no matter how severe the plaintiff's injuries. Some of the damages a plaintiff can try to recover include:

- Lost Wages;
- Medical Costs;
- Disability;
- Pain & Suffering (Physical, Mental & Emotional);
- Funeral and Burial Costs;
- Disfigurement;
- Loss of Companionship;
- Loss of Household Services;
- Lost Future Wages;
- Future Medical Costs; and

- Punitive or exemplary damages (Note, the standard of proof for punitive/exemplary damages is "clear and convincing evidence," which is higher than a "preponderance of the evidence." Punitive damages are also only available in cases of intentional or reckless conduct, or gross negligence.)

Practical Legal Tip:

Most people don't know that civil courts in Colorado have no independent means of sifting through the thousands of lawsuits filed every year to determine which are frivolous and which are meritorious and should go forward. The civil justice system is "user driven," meaning that unless one side or the other asks the judge to rule on a particular issue (usually called a "motion"), no one at the courthouse, including the judge, is going to take any action to examine the merit, or lack thereof, of a lawsuit. *-Doug*

Except for the last bullet point above, these damages are called compensatory damages. In Colorado, the law differentiates between economic and non-economic compensatory damages. Non-economic damages are capped, or limited, in Colorado and the cap differs depending on the situation.

If death has not occurred, the cap on non-economic damages is governed by section 13-21-102.5 of the Colorado Revised Statutes. Because the damage cap has been adjusted for inflation, the cap is set at $468,010 for claims occurring after January 1, 2008. See section 13-21-102.5 (in the editor's notes). However, a judge may allow for a non-economic damage award of up to twice this amount, $936,030 (this is $10 more than double because of rounding), if the judge finds justification for exceeding the cap by clear and convincing evidence. *See* id.

In a case that involves a wrongful death claim, the cap on non-economic damages is set at $341,250. *See* section 13-21-102.5 (editor's notes). However, if the death is the result of a "felonious killing," the cap is removed. *See* section 13-21-203(1)(a). Section 15-11-803 of the Colorado Revised Statutes defines "felonious killing" as a killing for which the perpetrator was "convicted of, pleads guilty to, or enters a plea of nolo contendere to the crime of murder in the first or second degree or manslaughter."

A court can find the defendant 100% at fault, but award no damages because the plaintiff failed to prove damages by a preponderance of the evidence. For example, a plaintiff who seeks reimbursement for medical expenses but has no evidence that they ever went to a doctor or hospital, will very unlikely be able to recover those medical expenses.

IV. How good are Colorado civil immunity laws for gun owners?
A. *No immunity from lawsuits*
There is a common misunderstanding that there exists a law that if you are legally justified in using your gun that you can't be sued. This is just not the case. First, if a person has the filing fee, anyone can sue anyone else in the State of Colorado. There is no one stopping anyone else from filing a lawsuit. Winning a lawsuit is a different issue entirely. If someone files the lawsuit, no matter how frivolous, it still must be dealt with, and it still must be shown to the court that a defense bars this lawsuit. This process can take significant time, money, and legal energy even for the most flimsy of cases. In short, lawyers get paid and even if you beat the "rap," you still have to take the civil "ride." So, if there is no immunity to lawsuits for gun owners, what protection is there?

B. *Immunity for certain claims*

As was discussed thoroughly in Chapters Four and Five of this book, Colorado law provides for immunity from civil liability if a person meets the provisions of Colorado's "Make My Day" law, section 18-1-704.5 of the Colorado Revised Statutes. A person can assert this defense during the initial stages of the case and the judge will determine whether the immunity applies. Please refer to Chapters Four and Five for a full explanation of this law.

Colorado's "Make My Day" law: Immunity from Civil Liability
Colorado Revised Statutes § 18-1-704.5(4)

Any occupant of a dwelling using physical force, including deadly physical force, in accordance with the provisions of subsection (2) of this section shall be immune from any civil liability for injuries or death resulting from the use of such force.

C. *Justification*

A party may still assert affirmative defenses in a civil action. This means, for example, if you shoot someone in defense of yourself, others, or your property and are sued as a result, you may assert the applicable sections of the Colorado Revised Statutes as a defense to the civil claims. If the judge or jury agrees that you acted in self-defense, or properly used physical force to defend others or property, the plaintiff will be barred from recovery. *See* Chapters Four through Seven.

D. *Statute of limitations for civil claims*

The statute of limitations is a doctrine in Colorado (and almost every other jurisdiction) that requires civil claims to be brought within a certain period of time after the incident. If the claim is not brought within the statute of limitations period, it is barred. There are a number of issues relating to *when* the statute of limitations starts to run in many cases, but for the most part, limitations will start to run immediately after a shooting incident.

The statute of limitations can vary from claim to claim; most, however, are between one and four years. In Colorado, the limitations period most likely to apply to gun cases is going to be two years. Assault and battery, negligence, wrongful death, and false imprisonment claims all provide two-year limitations periods. *See* section 13-80-102.

What does this mean for gun owners? If you "use" your gun, the plaintiff must bring a civil suit against within two years of the incident in almost all cases or else the claim will be barred. Keep in mind, though, you will still have to show up to court to assert this!

E.   *Intervening or Superseding conduct*
Colorado law recognizes a doctrine that absolves someone from responsibility for conduct that might otherwise be a tort (*e.g.*, negligence) if unforeseeable intervening or superseding conduct breaks the causal connection between the tort and the injury. To determine if the intervening or superseding conduct broke the causal connection, the court will consider whether the intervening or superseding conduct could have been "reasonably foreseen by a reasonably careful person under the circumstances." *See Scharrel v. Wal-Mart Stores, Inc.*, 949 P.2d 89, 93 (Colo. App. 1997).

Example:

> *Justin allows his nephew Randall to use his handgun for protection. Justin knows Randall has been in trouble with the law repeatedly and has been accused of armed robbery. While Randall has the handgun, his apartment is burglarized, and the gun is stolen and used in a crime spree. During the crime spree, Melanie is shot and injured.*

Melanie would not be able to recover from Justin, even though Justin may have been negligent in giving his gun to Randall, because the criminal act of burglarizing Randall's apartment and subsequent crime spree were superseding causes that broke the link between Justin's actions and the resulting injuries.

F. *Comparative Negligence*

Colorado has a doctrine called known as "modified comparative negligence," found in section 13-21-111 of the Colorado Revised Statutes. If the injured party, the plaintiff, also acted negligently in a way which contributed to their own injuries, either the judge or the jury will be tasked with determining the percentage of fault of the parties involved in the incident. If, for example, the defendant is found to be 70% at fault for the injuries, then the plaintiff could only recover 70% of their damages. However, if the judge or the jury find that the plaintiff is more than 50% responsible for their own injuries, they cannot recover anything at all! See section 13-21-111(1). This can be important for the average gun owner in that a carjacker, home invader, or general troublemaker who is the overwhelming cause of an incident cannot recover just because the judge or jury finds you made a slight misstep in defending yourself or your home.

Example:

> *Richard is a young adult trick-or-treater. He uses a fake gun as a part of his costume and knocks loudly on Nancy's door at 11:30 p.m. on October 31. Nancy, having forgotten about Halloween, is frightened by the knock, the fake gun, and the late hour of Richard's arrival. She fires through the door, injuring Richard.*

In the civil suit that follows by Richard against Nancy, the jury will be permitted to consider whether Richard's negligence, if any, contributed to cause the resulting injuries. The jury could determine that Richard was 0% at fault, 100%, or anything in between. By way of example only, if the jury awarded Richard

$100,000 in damages, but found he was 30% at fault, and Nancy 70%, Richard would only be able to recover $70,000 of his damages. If the jury determined that Richard was more than 50% at fault, he would be unable to recover any damages at all.

V. Firearm Booby Traps?

Some landowners might get the idea to defend their property with some sort of booby trap, that when tripped by an unsuspecting trespasser, fires a gun at the trespasser. Under no circumstances is this a good idea.

First, apart from the topic of this Chapter, the person who set the trap would be criminally liable for their actions. Even if the trap was set up inside one's home, Colorado's "Make My Day" law would be no defense. This is because in order to claim that defense, the person must have a reasonable belief that the intruder plans to or has committed a crime other than trespass and that the intruder might use any physical force against an occupant of the home. When the homeowner set up the trap he could not have known what the intruder's intention would be, or even whether the victim of the trap would be an intruder at all.

In addition to potential criminal charges, a person who injures even a trespasser with a booby trap will be civilly liable for any damages caused. The legal theory that governs injuries caused to visitors on a person's land is known as "premises liability," and is found in section 13-21-115 of the Colorado Revised Statutes. Under this section, even a trespasser may recover for damages that are "willfully or deliberately caused by the landowner." *See* section 13-21-115(3)(a). Certainly, the setting of a booby trap satisfies this standard and would entitle the injured party to damages, depending on the results of a comparative negligence analysis, as discussed earlier in this Chapter.

VI. **Will insurance cover it if I shoot someone?**

A. *Homeowners' insurance*

With few exceptions, almost every homeowner's insurance policy excludes coverage for intentional acts. The act of using your firearm in self-defense is almost always an intentional act. You intended to stop the threat. Plaintiffs' attorneys will very likely assert a negligence claim against a homeowner in an attempt to fall within the coverage, but at the end of the day, if the only evidence is that you intentionally shot the plaintiff because you intended to stop a threat, it is likely that any policy with an intentional act exclusion will not provide coverage for any damages awarded.

B. *Auto insurance*

Scores of cases around the country exist where the parties allege that a gun incident is covered by automobile insurance merely because the use of the firearm occurs in the auto or involves an auto. Almost universally, courts have held that these incidents are not covered merely because the discharge occurs in a car or involves a car.

In Colorado, an injury would be covered by automobile insurance if the accident occurs "on account of the use of a motor vehicle." See *Kohl v. Union Ins. Co.*, 731 P.2d 134, 135 (Colo. 1986). To satisfy this standard, the injury claimed must be "causally related to a conceivable use of the insured vehicle that is not foreign to its inherent purpose," such that the "accident would not have occurred but for the vehicle's use." See *id.* Because of this, an injury involving a gun that simply occurs inside or around a vehicle will not be covered by automobile insurance.

Example:

> Justin is cleaning his 9mm handgun in the car. It accidentally discharges, causing his passenger Edwin severe injuries.

This event will almost certainly not be covered by auto insurance.

Example:
> *Justin discharges his 9mm handgun in the car at Edwin during an attempted carjacking, causing Edwin severe injuries and also hitting a bystander.*

This event will almost certainly not be covered by auto insurance.

Colorado recognizes one minor exception. The Colorado Supreme Court has held that an injury that occurs while a hunter removes a gun from a fixed gun rack on a four-wheel-drive vehicle while on a hunting trip is covered by automobile insurance because the "transportation of hunters and their weapons to areas where they can pursue their sport is undeniably a conceivable use of a four-wheel-drive vehicle." See *id.* at 136-37. Despite this case, it is quite rare that an accident involving a gun will be covered by automobile insurance.

VII. What civil liability does a person face if their children access their firearms?

A. *Parents are not responsible for minor children's actions merely because they are parents!*

As a general rule, minors are civilly liable for their own torts (that is, their wrongful actions such as negligence, gross negligence, assault, *etc.*). The mere fact of paternity or maternity does not make a parent liable to third parties for the torts of his or her minor children. Under this general rule, parents are not responsible for their minor children's tortious actions when the minor child commits a tort and the parent had no direct relationship to the child's action, such as providing a firearm in a negligent manner, failing to supervise the child, or allowing the child to engage in behavior the parent knows is dangerous or risky.

B. *Parents who fail to "parent" may become responsible for minor children's actions*

While a parent who has no direct relationship to a minor child's tortious actions is generally not liable for that child's actions, if the "child has a known propensity to commit a potentially harmful act, the parent has a duty to use reasonable care to prevent the child from causing such harm if the parent knows or should know of the propensity and has the ability and opportunity to control the child." See *Hall v. McBryde By and Through McBryde*, 919 P.2d 910, 913 (Colo. App. 1996).

Example:

> *Your 17-year-old son, Jon, has been hunting since he was 11 and has taken several firearms training courses.*

If you take Jon hunting, and for some reason Jon accidentally discharges his shotgun, injuring another person, it is highly unlikely that you, the parent, will be civilly liable for an accident that occurs while hunting.

Example:

> *Your 12-year-old son, Gordon, has never handled a gun or taken a firearms training course. You decide to take him to the range for the first time, but you are both asked to leave the range after Gordon repeatedly fires into the ceiling and the floor. Fed up, you take Gordon to another range with no additional instruction or training.*

If Gordon shoots and injures someone at the second range, it is likely that you will be liable, because you allowed him to act in a manner likely to harm another, and you did not restrain him despite his dangerous conduct.

C. *Parents have a duty to control and discipline children*

In addition to the situations described in the preceding section where parents may become liable for a minor child's actions when the parent's own actions (or lack, thereof) played a role, Colorado has a statute that also provides limited parental liability for destruction or bodily injury caused by minors. Section 13-21-107 of the Colorado Revised Statutes allows an injured party to recover up to $3,500 in damages from the parents of a minor under the age of 18, who lives with such parents, for damages caused by the minor's malicious or willful damage or destruction of property or damages caused if the minor knowingly causes bodily injury. Although the cap on damages is set at $3,500 the actual cost of such a lawsuit is much higher because section 13-21-107 forces the defendant to pay the plaintiff's court fees and attorney's fees if the plaintiff wins the case.

Example:

> Bobby, a 14-year-old boy, does not like his neighbor. One day, he retrieves the family 12-gauge shotgun and decides to shoot the neighbor's fence. Bobby's parents know nothing about this behavior and Bobby has never had trouble with a firearm in the past. As a result of the shooting, a number of pickets from the fence were destroyed, three windows were broken, and numerous pockmarks were left in the brick façade of the home.

Under section 13-21-107(1) of the Colorado Revised Statutes, Bobby's parents would be liable for the damage Bobby caused to his neighbor's property up to $3,500 plus court costs and reasonable attorney's fees because Bobby's actions were willful and malicious.

CHAPTER THIRTEEN
BEYOND FIREARMS:
KNIVES, CLUBS, AND TASERS

I. Introduction

In addition to Colorado's many firearms laws, there also exist state laws governing the possession and use of other weapons. This includes any object that is not a firearm, but could be used as a weapon. This chapter will briefly discuss the laws governing these other weapons, including weapons that are absolutely illegal under the law, and weapons that are illegal to carry concealed.

II. Dangerous or illegal weapons

Section 18-12-102 of the Colorado Revised Statutes makes it a crime to possess a "dangerous weapon" or an "illegal weapon." Possession of a "dangerous weapon" is a class 5 felony for a first offense or a class 4 felony for each subsequent offense. *See* section 18-12-102(1). Possession of an "illegal weapon" is a class 1 misdemeanor. See section 18-12-102(4). It is important to note that peace officers and members of the armed forces are exempt from this statute under section 18-12-102(5). Which weapons are dangerous or illegal?

A. *What is a "dangerous weapon?"*

Dangerous weapons are covered in Chapter Two and Chapter Fourteen of this book. The types of firearms that are classified as dangerous weapons, and are therefore illegal under Colorado law, are machine guns, short barreled shotguns, short barreled rifles, and ballistic knives. In addition, all types of firearm silencers are prohibited under this law. See section 18-12-102(1). See Chapter Fourteen for an explanation of how to legally possess these sorts of items.

B. *What is an "illegal weapon?"*

Under section 18-12-102(2), blackjacks, gas guns, metallic knuckles, gravity knives, and switchblade knives are illegal weapons. To fully understand what types of weapons are covered by this law, we must look at how these terms are defined under section 18-12-101 of the Colorado Revised Statutes.

1. Blackjacks

Section 18-12-101(1)(a.5) defines "blackjack" as "any billy, sand club, sandbag, or other hand-operated striking weapon consisting, at the striking end, or an encased piece of lead or other heavy substance and, at the handle end, a strap or springy shaft which increases the force of impact."

Blackjack

2. Gas Guns

Section 18-12-101(1(d) defines "gas gun" as "a device designed for projecting gas-filled projectiles which release their contents after having been projected from the device and includes projectiles designed for use in such a device." A "gas gun" would include the device used by police to deliver tear gas canisters to disperse crowds. Notice that the canisters themselves are also included in the definition. This does not prohibit pepper spray, which is perfectly legal in Colorado.

3. Metallic Knuckles

Unlike all of the other items listed in 18-12-102(2) as illegal weapons, the term "metallic knuckles" is not defined anywhere in the code. However, any item that is similar in operation to the traditional "brass knuckles" will likely be considered by a court to fall under the definition of the term "metallic knuckles." Therefore, be wary of possessing any item that has finger holes and is meant to assist in punching.

Traditional "Brass Knuckles"

4. Gravity Knives

A "gravity knife" is defined in section 18-12-101(1)(e) as "any knife that has a blade released from the handle or sheath thereof by the force of gravity or the application of centrifugal force." This type of knife differs from a typical folding knife, like a Swiss Army knife, because it can be easily opened with one hand, without the use of one's fingers.

5. Switchblades

"Switchblade knife" is defined in section 18-12-101(1)(j) as "any knife, the blade of which opens automatically by hand pressure applied to a button, spring, or other device in its handle." Like a gravity knife, the switchblade can be opened with one hand. Unlike the gravity knife, the switchblade is spring assisted.

III. Carrying a concealed knife

The same statute that prohibits the carrying of a concealed firearm, section 18-12-105, also prohibits the carrying of concealed knives. *See* section 18-12-105(1)(a). The term "knife" is defined in section 18-12-101(f) as "any dagger, dirk, knife, or stiletto with a blade over three and one-half inches in length, or any other dangerous instrument capable of inflicting cutting, stabbing, or tearing wounds, but does not include a hunting or fishing knife carried for sports use."

Interestingly, knives that are less than three and one-half inches in length are not automatically covered by the "any other dangerous instrument capable of inflicting cutting, stabbing, or tearing wounds" language found in section 18-12-101(f). In *A.P.E. v. People*, the Colorado Supreme Court held that to automatically include knives shorter than three and one-half inches long in the legal definition of knife would make the length portion of the definition pointless. *A.P.E. v. People*, 20 P.3d 1179, 1183 (Colo. 2001). Therefore, the court concluded, "the legislature must have intended to exclude small knives from the definition of a weapon unless the person carrying it intended to use it as a weapon." *Id.*

A. *Exceptions to the concealed knife law*
Since section 18-12-105 is the same section that makes it a crime to carry a concealed firearm, all of the same exceptions that apply to the carrying of a concealed firearm apply to the carrying of concealed knives, although there is no Colorado permit to carry a knife concealed. Under section 18-12-105(2) of the Colorado Revised Statutes, a person is excepted from the concealed knife law if they are:

- Inside their own dwelling or place of business or on property they own or control;
- Inside a private automobile or other private means of conveyance and carrying the weapon for lawful defense;
- A peace officer; or
- A U.S. probation officer or a U.S. pretrial services officer while on duty.

The other exception to the concealed knife law is found in the definition of "knife" in section 18-12-101(1)(f), discussed above. Under that section, a "hunting or fishing knife carried for sports use" is excluded from the definition. *See id.* If a person is charged under the concealed knife statute, that person may raise the affirmative defense that the knife was a hunting or fishing knife. This means that, while the defendant will have to show evidence of this, the burden will fall on the prosecution to prove that the knife was in fact not a hunting or fishing knife. *See id.*

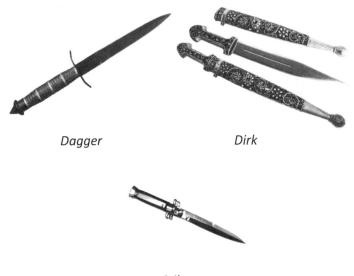

Dagger   *Dirk*

Stiletto

IV. Possession by previous offenders

Just as previous offenders are prohibited from possessing a firearm under section 18-12-108 of the Colorado Revised Statutes, covered fully in Chapter Three, section 18-12-108(1) also prohibits previous offenders from possessing "any other weapon that is subject to the provisions of this article." This prohibition covers all weapons that are discussed in this Chapter, including knives:

V. Tasers

Under Colorado law, tasers are included in the definition of "stun gun" under section 18-12-101(1)(i.5). Under that section, a "stun gun" is a "device capable of temporarily immobilizing a person by the infliction of an electrical charge." In Colorado, it is perfectly legal to purchase, possess, and use a stun gun of any kind. However, under section 18-12-106.5, it is a class 5 felony to "knowingly and unlawfully" use a stun gun while committing a crime. Because using a stun gun in this way is a felony, the punishment for using the stun gun could very well be more severe than the penalty for the underlying crime!

Handheld "Stun Gun"　　　　　Cartridge Taser

VI. Pepper Spray, Wasp Spray, and Bear Spray

The various types of sprays that people often carry for self-defense are not mentioned anywhere in the Colorado Revised Statutes, and are therefore perfectly legal to own and carry. However, this does not mean that pepper spray, wasp spray, or bear spray should be used hastily. Anything could be interpreted as a weapon by a prosecutor or jury. Reckless use of these types of sprays could still result of a disorderly conduct or assault charge. Because of this, only use a spray when you genuinely feel endangered by another person's actions.

CHAPTER FOURTEEN

SILENCERS, SHORT-BARRELED WEAPONS, AND MACHINE GUNS: THE NATIONAL FIREARMS ACT

Can an individual in Colorado legally own a silencer or suppressor, short-barreled shotgun, short-barreled rifle, or machine gun? Under Colorado law, these types of weapons are classified as "dangerous," and are illegal. However, under section 18-12-102(5) of the Colorado Revised Statutes, a private individual may own these types of weapons if they comply with the provisions of the National Firearms Act (NFA), codified in 26 U.S.C. Chapter 53. Under federal law, these firearms are illegal to purchase or possess without possessing the proper paperwork and a "tax stamp." In this chapter, we will discuss the purpose behind the NFA, what firearms are regulated by the Act, as well as the process and procedure for legally possessing weapons that are subject to the Act's provisions.

I. **What is the National Firearms Act?**

The National Firearms Act was enacted in 1934 in response to gangster crimes. Prior to the Act's passage, any person could go to the local hardware store and purchase a Thompson submachine Gun or shorten the barrel on their rifle or shotgun. President Roosevelt pushed for the passage of the NFA in an attempt to diminish a gangster's ability to possess and carry dangerous and/or easily concealable firearms, such as machine guns and short-barreled rifles and shotguns.

NFA is firearms regulation using a registration and tax requirement

The NFA requires both the registration of and tax on the manufacture and transfer of certain firearms. The law created a tax of $200 on the transfer of the following firearms: short-barreled shotguns, short-barreled rifles, machine guns, silencers, and destructive devices. The tax is only $5 for firearms that are classified as "Any Other Weapons" or AOWs. Back in 1934, a $200 tax was the approximate equivalent to about $3,500 today! Five years after the NFA's passage, the Supreme Court held in *United States v. Miller* that the right to bear arms can be subject to federal regulation. Miller brought suit against the government stating that the NFA infringed upon his Constitutional right to bear arms under the Second Amendment. While the Court agreed that the Constitution does guarantee *a right* to bear arms, it held that the right does not extend to every firearm. *See United States v. Miller*, 307 U.S. 174 (1939).

II. What firearms does the NFA regulate?
A. *Short-barreled rifles and shotguns*
In order to be legal under federal law, short-barreled shotguns and rifles must be registered, and a tax paid on the firearm. What is a short-barreled shotgun? Under both federal and Colorado law, short-barreled shotguns have one or more barrels less than 18 inches in length and the overall length of the shotgun is less than 26 inches. What is a short-barreled rifle? It is any rifle with one or more barrels less than 16 inches in length, and the overall length of the rifle is less than 26 inches. *See* 27 CFR § 478.11 and Colorado Revised Statutes § 18-12-101(1)(h) and (i).

Short-barreled shotguns and rifles may be purchased from an FFL that deals in NFA items in states where they are legal. Also, short-barreled firearms are very popular for individuals to build and/or modify on their own. This is legal under federal law if the person has properly registered the firearm to be modified into a short-barreled firearm with the ATF and paid the tax before it is modified. Under federal law, once approved, a person may alter or produce a short-barreled firearm and must engrave legally required information on the receiver of the firearm such as manufacturer, location, *etc*. *See discussion later in this chapter for detailed requirements*.

Colorado law classifies short shotguns and short rifles as "dangerous weapons," and makes it a class 5 felony to knowingly possess one. *See* section 18-12-102(1) and (3). However, there are two exceptions to this law. First, peace officers, members of the armed forces, and members of the Colorado National Guard, while lawfully discharging their duties, are allowed to carry "dangerous weapons" under this law. *See* 18-12-102(5). Second, private citizens who have complied with the provisions of the NFA and have obtained the proper paperwork and a tax stamp for possession of one of these types of weapons are also allowed to possess these "dangerous" weapons. *See id.*

All the way back in Chapter One, we mentioned that Denver's "assault weapon" ban survived court challenges and remains in effect today. This ordinance, section 38-130(e) of the Denver Revised Municipal Code, makes it illegal to "carry, store, keep, manufacture, sell or otherwise possess" "assault weapons" within the Denver city limits. Under section (1)(b) of this ordinance, "semiautomatic shotguns with a folding stock or a magazine capacity of more than six (6) rounds" are classified as "assault weapons." There are some exceptions to this ordinance. First, members of federal, state, or local government agencies are exempt from this ordinance while they are acting in their official capacities. See 38-130(e)(1). Second, "assault weapons" used as movie or television props are permitted provided the Denver police are notified in advance in writing. See 38-130(e)(2). Third, nonresidents of Denver who are in legal possession of an "assault weapon" may transport such weapons through the city. See 38-130(e)(3)(a). Lastly, anyone over 21 years old who lawfully obtained an "assault weapon" before the ban went into effect in 1989 can apply for a permit to possess the weapon. See 38-130(f). Holding such a permit is an affirmative defense to any charges under this ordinance.

B. _Machine guns_

Machine guns are illegal under federal and state law. But, under federal law, if the requirements of the NFA are satisfied, machine guns may be legally owned by individuals. However, fulfilling the requirements of the NFA does not make owning a machine gun legal under Colorado law.

First, what is a machine gun? Federal law defines a machine gun as "any weapon which shoots, is designed to shoot, or can be readily restored to shoot, automatically more than one shot, without manual reloading, by a single function of the trigger. The term shall also include the frame or receiver of any such weapon, any part designed and intended solely and exclusively, or combination of parts designed and intended, for use in converting a weapon into a machine gun, and any combination of parts from which a machine gun can be assembled if such parts are in the possession or under the control of a person." 27 CFR § 478.11. As a result of this definition, the individual metal components that make up a whole machine gun, such as a full-auto sear, individually meet the federal definition of machine gun. The parts for the machine gun do not have to be assembled.

Similarly, under Colorado law, a machine gun is defined as "any firearm, whatever its size and usual designation, that shoots automatically more than one shot, without manual reloading, by a single function of the trigger." Colorado Revised Statutes § 18-12-101(1)(g). In other words, if more than two bullets come out of a firearm with only one pull of the trigger, the firearm is a machine gun. Colorado law lists machine guns as "dangerous weapons" under section 18-12-102(1) of the Colorado Revised Statutes. Just as with short shotguns and short rifles, peace officers, members of the armed forces, and members of the Colorado National Guard, while lawfully discharging their duties, and private citizens who have complied with the NFA and have the proper paperwork and a tax stamp are allowed to carry machine guns under the "dangerous weapon" statute. _See_ section 18-12-102(5).

Practical Legal Tip:

Some of the items regulated by the NFA simply don't make as much sense as the other things it regulates. Suppressors are really nothing more than mufflers for your firearm—they aren't really firearms themselves (notwithstanding the legal definition). Thinking about the utility of the suppressor, if the firearm was invented today, you can be sure that not only would the government not prohibit them, OSHA would probably require them for safety purposes! -*Stan*

No new manufacturing of machine guns for private ownership

Because of a federal law that effectively disallows private ownership (not military, police department, etc.) of any machine guns manufactured after May 19, 1986, machine gun available for private ownership are limited to the legally registered machine guns that existed prior to May 19, 1986. Thus, the private market is very limited and prices, as a result, are very high.

C. *Firearm suppressors and silencers*

What is a suppressor? It is just a muffler for a firearm and is legal under federal law if all NFA requirements are met. In legal terms, a firearm suppressor is defined in 27 CFR § 478.11 as "any device for silencing, muffling, or diminishing the report of a portable firearm, including any combination of parts, designed or redesigned, and intended for use in assembling or fabricating a firearm silencer or firearm muffler, and any part intended only for use in such assembly or fabrication."

Colorado law does not define suppressors but does define "firearm silencer" in a way that encompasses suppressors and mufflers. Section 18-12-101(1)(c) of the Colorado Revised

Statutes defines "firearm silencer" as "any instrument, attachment, weapon, or appliance for causing the firing of any gun, revolver, pistol, or other firearm to be silent or intended to lessen or muffle the noise of the firing of any such weapon." For simplicity sake, we will use the term suppressor in this Chapter to include the Colorado definition of silencer.

Firearm suppressors are very practical instruments. They are great for hunting and recreational shooting not only because it suppresses gunshots in a way so as to not alarm other animals being hunted nearby, but also because it lessens the impact on the shooter's ears. However, firearms owners should be carefully aware that the definition of a suppressor is very broad whether under federal or Colorado law. Suppressors do not need to be items manufactured specifically for use as a suppressor. There are some ordinary, every-day items that could be easily converted into a suppressor such as a water bottle or an automotive oil filter. Possession of otherwise legal items when used or modified to be used as a suppressor is illegal.

As with other "dangerous" weapons under Colorado law, peace officers, members of the armed forces, and members of the Colorado National Guard, while lawfully discharging their duties, and private citizens who have complied with the NFA and have the proper paperwork and tax stamp are allowed to carry suppressors under the "dangerous weapon" statute. *See* section 18-12-102(5).

D. *Destructive devices*

The term "destructive device" is a legal term given to certain firearms, objects, and munitions that are illegal under the NFA. The "destructive devices" as defined in the statute are effectively broken down into three categories: explosive devices, large caliber weapons, and parts easily convertible into a destructive device.

Destructive Devices – Part A
27 C.F.R. § 478.11

Any explosive, incendiary, or poison gas (1) bomb, (2) grenade, (3) rocket having a propellant charge of more than 4 ounces, (4) missile having an explosive or incendiary charge of more than one-quarter ounce, (5) mine, or (6) device similar to any of the devices described in the preceding paragraphs of this definition.

Destructive Devices – Part B
27 C.F.R. § 478.11

Any type of weapon (other than a shotgun or shotgun shell which the Director finds is generally recognized as particularly suitable for sporting purposes) by whatever name known which will, or which may be readily converted to, expel a projectile by the action of an explosive or other propellant, and which has any barrel with a bore of more than one-half inch in diameter.

The first portion of the definition of a destructive device deals with explosive, incendiary and poison gas munitions. The definition specifies that any explosive, incendiary, or poison gas bomb, grenade, mine or similar device is a destructive device. In addition, the definition includes a rocket having a propellant charge of more than four ounces and a missile (projectile) having an explosive or incendiary charge of more than one-quarter ounce. These topics and the regulations thereof are beyond the scope of this book's discussion.

The second section of the definition addresses large caliber weapons and states that any type of weapon that has a bore diameter of <u>more than one-half inch</u> in diameter is a destructive device with the exception of shotguns (and shotgun shells) that are suitable for sporting purposes. Thus, any caliber in a rifle or handgun more than .5 inches or fifty caliber is classified as a destructive device. Shotguns are exempt from this prohibition on size <u>unless</u> the ATF rules it is not for "sporting purposes." How do you know if a shotgun is suitable for sporting purposes? The ATF keeps a list, and has issued rulings classifying specific shotguns as destructive devices because they are not considered to be particularly "suitable for sporting purposes" including the USAS-12, Striker-12, Streetsweeper, and 37/38mm Beanbags. The ATF does not provide any specific definition of what constitutes being "suitable for sporting purposes" nor does it specify the methodology in which it determines what makes a particular shotgun suitable for sporting purposes. Ultimately, one will have to check with the ATF lists to see whether a particular shotgun with a larger bore-diameter is classified as a destructive device or not.

Destructive Devices – Part C
27 C.F.R. § 478.11

Any combination of parts either designed or intended for use in converting any destructive device described in [part] (A) and (B) of this section and from which a destructive device may be readily assembled.

Finally, a destructive device does not need to be a completed and assembled product to fall under the federal definition and regulation under the NFA. Much like machine guns, if a person possesses parts that can be readily assembled into a destructive device, then whether or not the device has actually been constructed is irrelevant—by law it's already a destructive device.

Although these firearms, munitions, and devices are prohibited by the law on its face pursuant to the National Firearms Act, a person may nevertheless receive permission to possess them so long as they possess the correct legal authorization. Colorado law makes no mention of large caliber firearms.

E. *"Any Other Weapons" or AOWs*

The AOW category under the NFA pertains to firearms and weapons that may not fit the traditional definition of some of the firearms discussed elsewhere in this book due to the way in which they are manufactured or modified. Under federal law, an AOW is "any weapon or device capable of being concealed on the person from which a shot can be discharged through the energy of an explosive, a pistol or revolver having a barrel with a smooth bore designed or redesigned to fire a fixed shotgun shell, weapons with combination shotgun and rifle barrels 12 inches or more, less than 18 inches in length, from which only a single discharge can be made from either barrel without manual reloading, and shall include any such weapon which may be readily restored to fire. Such term shall not include a pistol or a revolver having a rifled bore, or rifled bores, or weapons designed, made, or intended to be fired from the shoulder and not capable of firing fixed ammunition." 26 U.S.C. § 5845(e).

1. Concealable weapons and devices

Weapons which are capable of being concealed from which one shot can be discharged are AOWs. This includes such weapons as a pengun, knife gun, or umbrella gun. Colorado law does not use the term AOW, nor does it regulate these kinds of weapons.

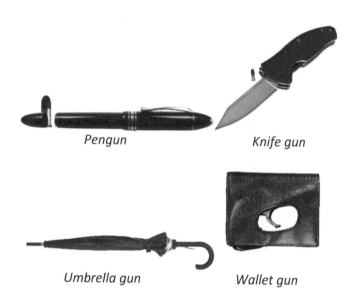

Pengun   *Knife gun*

Umbrella gun   *Wallet gun*

2. <u>Pistols and revolvers having a smooth-bore barrel for firing shotgun shells</u>

Pistols and revolvers that have a smooth bore (no rifling) that are designed to shoot shotgun ammunition are defined as an AOW. The ATF cites firearms such as the H&R Handy Gun or the Ithaca Auto & Burglar Gun as firearms which fall under the AOW category. *Note:* handguns with partially rifled barrels such as The Judge do not fall under this category due to the rifling of the barrel.

H&R Handy Gun   *Ithaca Auto & Burglar Gun*

3. <u>Weapons with barrels 12 inches or longer and lengths 18 inches or shorter</u>

The definition of Any Other Weapon also includes any weapon which has a shotgun or rifle barrel of 12 inches or more but is 18 inches or less in overall length from which only a single discharge can be made from either barrel without manual reloading. The ATF identifies the "Marble Game Getter" as the firearm most commonly associated with this definition (excluding the model with an 18" barrel and folding shoulder stock).

4. Pistols and revolvers with vertical handgrips

If a pistol is modified with a vertical grip on the front, it will now be legally classified as an AOW and require registration and a paid tax. Note, vertical grips are readily available and are legal to own as long as they are not placed on a handgun. The definition of a handgun is a weapon which is intended to be fired by one hand, the addition of the vertical foregrip makes it so the weapon now is intended to be used with two hands to fire. This modification changes the weapon from a handgun to what is known as an "AOW" and is now a prohibited weapon without the proper documentation.

F. *Antique firearms*

Firearms that are defined by the NFA as "antique firearms" are not regulated by the NFA. The NFA definition of antique firearm is found in 26 U.S.C.§ 5845(g) as "any firearm not designed or redesigned for using rim fire or conventional center fire ignition with fixed ammunition and manufactured in or before 1898 (including any matchlock, flintlock, percussion cap, or similar type of ignition system or replica thereof, whether actually manufactured before or after the year 1898) and also any firearm using fixed ammunition manufactured in or before 1898, for which ammunition is no longer manufactured in the United States and is not readily available in the ordinary channels of commercial trade." Under this statute and for NFA purposes, the only firearms that are antiques are firearms which were both actually manufactured in or before 1898 and ones for which fixed ammunition is no longer manufactured in the United States and is not readily available in the ordinary channels of commercial trade.

With this in mind, the ATF states in its NFA guidebook that "it is important to note that a specific type of fixed ammunition that has been out of production for many years may again become available due to increasing interest in older firearms. Therefore, the classification of a specific NFA firearm as an antique can change if ammunition for the weapon becomes readily available in the ordinary channels of commerce."

G.   *NFA curio firearms and relics*

Under federal law, curios or relics are defined in 27 CFR § 478.11 as "firearms which are of special interest to collectors by reason of some quality other than is associated with firearms intended for sporting use or as offensive or defensive weapons." Persons that collect curios or relics may do so with a special collector's license although one is not required. The impact of an NFA item being classified as a curio or relic, however, is that it allows the item to be transferred interstate to persons possessing a collector's license. The collector's license does not allow the individual to deal in curios or relics, nor does it allow the collector to obtain other firearms interstate as those transactions still require an FFL.

To be classified as a curio or relic, federal law states that the firearm must fall into one of the following three categories:
1. Firearms which were manufactured at least 50 years prior to the current date, but not including replicas thereof;
2. Firearms which are certified by the curator of a municipal, State, or Federal museum which exhibits firearms to be curios or relics of museum interest; or

3. Any other firearms which derive a substantial part of their monetary value from the fact that they are novel, rare, bizarre, or because of their association with some historical figure, period, or event.

See 27 CFR § 478.11.

The ATF maintains a list of firearms that are classified as curios or relics.

H. *How can some after-market gun parts make your firearm illegal?*

A number of companies manufacture and sell gun products or parts that alter the appearance or utility of a firearm (*i.e.* shoulder stocks, forward hand grips, *etc.*). However, some of these after-market products can actually change the firearm you possess from one type of a weapon to another type of weapon for legal purposes whether you realize it or not. As a result, many individuals make the modifications to their firearms thinking that because there was no special process for purchasing the accessory, any modification would be in compliance with the law. Unfortunately, this is not always the case. Consider the example of short-barreled uppers for AR-15s: selling, buying, or possessing AR-15 "uppers" with barrels less than 16 inches is legal. However, it is illegal to put the upper on a receiver of an AR-15 because this would be the act of manufacturing a short-barreled rifle and is legally prohibited. This is equally true of vertical forward grips on a handgun. Vertical foregrips are legal to buy or possess, however, if you actually install one on a handgun, you have manufactured an AOW, and it is illegal, unless registered and a tax paid. *Note:* there are other types of braces that are permissible in their proper application and illegal in any application or adaptation that would alter the classification of the weapon. For example, the Sig Arm Brace is legal to attach to an AR Pistol when used as an arm brace, but illegal when used as a shoulder stock.

III. Process and procedure for obtaining NFA firearms

A. *Who can own and possess an NFA firearm?*

Any person may own and possess an NFA firearm as long as they are legally not disqualified to own or possess firearms and live in a state that allows possession of NFA items. *See* Chapters Two and Three. The ATF also allows for a non-person legal entity to own these items, such as corporations, partnerships, and trusts, etc.

B. *What are the usual steps for buying or manufacturing NFA items?*

Whether a person is buying or making (manufacturing) an NFA firearm, there are several steps in the process. The transfer or manufacture of an NFA firearm requires the filing of an appropriate transfer form with the ATF, payment of any federally-mandated transfer tax, approval of the transfer by the ATF, and registration of the firearm to the transferee. Only after these steps have occurred may a buyer legally take possession of the NFA item, or may a person legally assemble or manufacture the NFA item. In this section, we will walk through the process, step-by-step, of (1) purchasing an NFA item that already exists, and (2) manufacturing an NFA firearm.

Steps for buying an existing NFA item (for example, a suppressor)

1. Select and purchase the item (suppressor) from a dealer;
2. Assemble appropriate paperwork (ATF Form 4, see Appendix B) and tax ($200.00);
   a. If the buyer is an individual, the individual must secure Chief Law Enforcement Officer signature on ATF Form 4, a photograph, and fingerprints (though after July 13th, 2016, only CLEO notification is required, not certification);
   b. If the buyer is a corporation/trust, no Chief Law Enforcement Officer signature, photograph, or fingerprints are required. Note that this step changes due to ATF Rule 41f, effective July 13th, 2016. Once effective, the ATF will require that for each application, all

"responsible persons" of the trust submit fingerprints and photographs as well as notify their CLEO (though no certification or approval is required).

c. After July 13th, 2016, all applicants will also have to complete and send in a copy of ATF Form 5320.23 for each responsible person. Form 5320.23 requires certain identifying information for each responsible person. This information will allow the ATF to conduct background checks on each responsible person.

3. Submit paperwork, fingerprints, and tax to the ATF → ATF review and approval;

4. ATF sends approval (tax stamp affixed to Form 4) to the dealer;

5. Pick up suppressor from the dealer.

Steps for manufacturing an NFA item (such as a short-barreled rifle)

1. Select the item to manufacture or modify, *i.e.*, short-barreled AR-15;

2. Assemble appropriate paperwork (ATF Form 1, see Appendix B) and tax ($200.00);

    a. If the buyer is an individual, the individual must secure Chief Law Enforcement Officer signature on ATF Form 1, a photograph, and fingerprints (though after July 13th, 2016, only CLEO notification is required, not certification);

    b. If the buyer is a corporation/trust, no Chief Law Enforcement Officer signature, photograph, or fingerprints are required. Note that this step changes due to ATF Rule 41f, effective July 13th, 2016. Once effective, the ATF will require that for each application, all "responsible persons" of the trust submit fingerprints and photographs as well as notify their CLEO (though no certification or approval is required).

    c. After July 13th, 2016, all applicants will also have to complete and send in a copy of ATF Form 5320.23 for each responsible person. Form 5320.23 requires certain identifying information for each responsible person. This information will allow the ATF to conduct background checks on each responsible person.

3. Submit paperwork and tax to the ATF → ATF review and approval;
4. ATF sends you the approval (tax stamp affixed to Form 1);
5. You may then legally assemble the AR-15, *i.e.*, put upper with a barrel length of less than 16 inches on a lower receiver, *etc.* The item must now be engraved and identified, see below.

When purchasing an NFA firearm from a dealer, the dealer is required to have the purchaser fill out ATF Form 4473 when the purchaser goes to pick up the item from the dealer.

C. *Who is a "responsible person" under the new ATF rule?*
The ATF defines a "responsible person" as "anyone with the power or authority to direct the management of the trust to receive, possess, ship, transport, deliver, transfer, or dispose of the NFA firearm."

In other words, pretty much everybody in a trust, except for the beneficiaries (unless they also have the power listed above), or anyone who is allowed to possess the items in a corporation.

D. *Do I have to send photographs and fingerprints for every single item I purchase?*
According to the ATF's rule, for applications submitted after July 13th, 2016, while you will have to provide this information for each responsible person, if nothing has changed since a previous purchase within the past two years where you provided this information, you can send a certification that there have been no changes instead of having to send along the photographs and fingerprints.

E. *How must an NFA item be engraved and identified if I make it myself?*
Once you receive ATF approval to manufacture your own NFA item (such as the short-barreled AR-15 in the previous section),

federal law requires that you engrave, cast, stamp, or otherwise conspicuously place or cause to be engraved, cast, stamped, or placed on the frame, receiver, or barrel of the NFA item the following information:

1. The item's serial number;
2. The item's model (if so designated);
3. Caliber or gauge;
4. The name of the owner whether individual, corporation, or trust; and
5. The city and state where the item was made.

This information must be placed on the item with a minimum depth of .003 inch and in a print size no smaller than 1/16 inch. *See* 27 CFR § 479.102.

F. *Which way should I own my NFA item? Paperwork requirements for individuals, trusts, or business entities to own NFA items*

Form 4 and Form 1

The appropriate paperwork that must be assembled and submitted to the ATF under the NFA varies depending on whether an individual, or a legal entity such as a trust, corporation, or partnership is purchasing or manufacturing the NFA item. The paperwork generally starts either with an ATF Form 4 (used for purchasing an existing item), or an ATF Form 1 which is used if a person wishes to manufacture a new NFA item. All relevant portions of the Form must be completed. Both Form 4 and Form 1 have a requirement that a Chief Law Enforcement Officer for the applicant must sign the ATF Form. However, this requirement only applies to living, breathing individuals; it does not apply to applicants who are legal entities like trusts, corporations, *etc*. Therefore, a Chief Law Enforcement Officer signature is not necessary. The signature of the Chief Law Enforcement Officer may be difficult or impossible to obtain for an individual in Colorado. There is no law that says the Chief Law Enforcement Officer must sign off on the Form 1 or Form 4.

Note that this is the law until ATF Rule 41f goes into effect, July 13th, 2016. After July 13th, 2016, the ATF will require that for each application, all "responsible persons" of the trust submit fingerprints and photographs, as well as notify their CLEO by sending a copy of the Form 1 or 4 respectively, or a copy of the 5320.23 (though no certification or approval is required). Under the ATF's new rule, all applicants will also have to complete and send in a copy of ATF Form 5320.23 for each responsible person. Form 5320.23 requires certain identifying information for each responsible person. This information will allow the ATF to conduct background checks on each responsible person.

Who may sign a Form 4 or Form 1 as a Chief Law Enforcement Officer?
For the purposes of Form 4, "the chief law enforcement officer is considered to be the Chief of Police for the transferee's city or town of residence, the Sheriff for the transferee's county of residence; the Head of the State Police for the transferee's State of residence; a State or local district attorney or prosecutor having jurisdiction in the transferee's area of residence; or another person whose certification is acceptable to the Director, Bureau of Alcohol, Tobacco and Firearms." ATF Form 1, *Instructions*. Keep in mind, this step will no longer be required for applications submitted after July 13th, 2016.

Photograph and fingerprints only required for individual applicants
In addition, if an individual is purchasing or manufacturing an NFA item, the applicant must submit an appropriate photograph and their fingerprints. Neither fingerprints nor photographs are required if the applicant is not an individual. Conversely, an entity such as a trust or corporation must submit the appropriate documents showing its existence, such as the trust or corporate formation documents. Note that this only applies to applications submitted prior to the July 13th, 2016; for trusts and corporations that attempt to purchase items after July 13, 2016, both

photographs and fingerprint cards are necessary for every responsible person in a trust or corporation.

G. *Does the new ATF rule, Rule 41f, grandfather in existing items or submitted applications?*

If you have a tax stamp prior to the new rule, or have already submitted your paperwork, the ATF will grandfather in all such applicants. However, any application submitted after the effective date of 41f, July 13th, 2016, even if the trust already existed, you will have to comply with the regulations of rule 41f.

Why are trusts so popular to own NFA items?

There are four major reasons trusts are very popular to own NFA items: turnaround time, paperwork, control, and ease of ownership. A trust is a legal entity that can hold property.

The turnaround time for NFA approvals with the ATF varies. For example in 2014, we were seeing wait times on Form 4 approval for individuals as long as 10 months or longer. In 2014, we were seeing wait times on Form 1 approval for individuals as long as 5 months or longer. In the first quarter of 2015, we saw these times reduced quite a bit. However, one important aspect to note is that the wait time for Form 1 or Form 4 approvals for trusts are reduced by several months when compared to approval times for individuals.

On the paperwork side, trusts are beneficial because they, as of the time of writing, do not require the signature of the Chief Law Enforcement Officer on Form 1 or Form 4. In addition, unlike individuals seeking ownership of an NFA item, no fingerprints or photographs are required (though after July 13th, 2016, fingerprints and photographs will be required for every responsible person in a trust). The only paperwork required to own an NFA item under a trust is the trust agreement and the appropriate ATF form or forms.

A third major reason for having a trust own an NFA item is that it makes owning and using the NFA item easier if more than one person wishes to use the item. If an individual owns the item, then only the individual can ever "possess" it. On the other hand, if the item is owned by a trust, all trustees, including co-trustees, are able to possess and use the items contained in the trust. Therefore, co-trustees may be added or removed. [Note non-trustees and non-owners may still use a properly registered NFA firearm, but only when in "the presence" of the owner.]

Third, unlike other entities such as corporations, LLCs, etc., a trust requires no filings with a government to create, which saves expenses and even preserves privacy. Further, these expense savings continue because there are no continuing government fees or compliance requirements. Thus, trusts are one of the best ways currently to own an NFA item.

H. *The Tax Stamp*

Once the ATF has an applicant's materials in hand, they will be reviewed and checked by NFA researchers and an examiner. The application will then either be approved or denied. A denial will be accompanied by an explanation of why the application was denied and how to remedy it, if possible. If the application is approved, the examiner will affix a tax stamp on one of the submitted Form 1 or Form 4 and send the newly-stamped Form to the applicant.

This tax stamp on the appropriate form is a person's evidence of compliance with the NFA's requirements and is a very important document. A copy should always be kept with the NFA item. *See below.*

I. *What documents should I have with me when I am in actual possession of my suppressor, short-barreled firearm, or other NFA item?*

If you have an NFA item, always have the proper documentation with you to prove that you legally possess the item. Again, if you are in possession of your suppressor, short-barreled firearm, destructive device, or if you are lucky enough, your machine gun—always have your paperwork showing you are legal, or it may be a long day with law enforcement. To show you are legal, always keep a copy of your ATF Form 4 or Form 1 (whichever is applicable) with the tax stamp affixed for every NFA item in your possession, personal identification, and if the item is held in a trust or corporation, a copy of the trust or articles of incorporation, and the authorization for possession. Care should be given to make sure these documents name the individual so as to show legal ownership, *i.e.*, trust and/or amendments showing the person is a co-trustee or an officer of the corporation.

Practically, individuals should not carry around the original documents as they could be destroyed by wear and tear, rain, or be misplaced, effectively destroying the required evidence of compliance. Photocopies of the stamp and any other pertinent documents are generally enough to satisfy inquisitive law enforcement officials. The more technologically advanced may take pictures on their phone or other mobile device, or even upload them to a cloud database. Keep in mind that if the phone dies or the cloud cannot be reached, and you have no way to access the documents, your proof is gone and you may have a very bad day ahead of you! We recommend keeping photocopies of the ATF form with the tax stamp affixed and appropriate documents to avoid any problems with technology.

J. *Why is the paperwork necessary?*

According to Colorado Revised Statutes § 18-12-102(1), machine guns, short-barreled firearms, and firearm suppressors are illegal to possess. However, Colorado Revised Statutes § 18-12-102(5) states that possession of a "valid permit and license" for the weapon is an affirmative defense. An affirmative defense is a defense which, if proven, defeats or mitigates the legal consequences of otherwise unlawful conduct. In other words, even though you meet the elements of committing a crime (possessing the listed items), the law provides a defense you can prove to defeat the criminal charges (proving possession pursuant to the NFA). In theory, law enforcement officers could arrest individuals, who would then be forced to show up to court to prove this affirmative defense; practically, however, simply showing the proper paperwork to the law enforcement officer is likely sufficient to avoid any further entanglement in the legal system.

APPENDICES

APPENDIX A: SELECTED COLORADO STATUTES

**Colorado Revised Statutes, Title 12, Article 26.1, Part 1
BACKGROUND CHECKS -- GUN SHOWS**

<u>Colorado Revised Statutes § 12-26.1-101</u>
BACKGROUND CHECKS AT GUN SHOWS -- PENALTY

(1) Before a gun show vendor transfers or attempts to transfer a firearm at a gun show, he or she shall:

    (a) require that a background check, in accordance with section 24-33.5-424, C.R.S., be conducted of the prospective transferee; and

    (b) obtain approval of a transfer from the Colorado Bureau of Investigation after a background check has been requested by a licensed gun dealer, in accordance with section 24-33.5-424, C.R.S.

(2) A gun show promoter shall arrange for the services of one or more licensed gun dealers on the premises of the gun show to obtain the background checks required by this article.

(3) If any part of a firearm transaction takes place at a gun show, no firearm shall be transferred unless a background check has been obtained by a licensed gun dealer.

(4) Any person violating the provisions of this section commits a class 1 misdemeanor and shall be punished as provided in section 18-1.3-501, C.R.S.

Colorado Revised Statutes § 12-26.1-101
EXEMPTION

The provisions of this article shall not apply to the transfer of an antique firearm, as defined in 18 U.S.C. sec. 921(a)(16), as amended, or a curio or relic, as defined in 27 CFR sec. 178.11, as amended.

Colorado Revised Statutes, Title 13, Article 14, Part 1
CIVIL PROTECTION ORDERS

Colorado Revised Statutes § 13-14-104.5
PROCEDURE FOR TEMPORARY CIVIL PROTECTION ORDER

(1)

(a) Any municipal court of record, if authorized by the municipal governing body; any county court; and any district, probate, or juvenile court shall have original concurrent jurisdiction to issue a temporary or permanent civil protection order against an adult or against a juvenile who is ten years of age or older for any of the following purposes:

(I) To prevent assaults and threatened bodily harm;

(II) To prevent domestic abuse;

(III) To prevent emotional abuse of the elderly or of an at-risk adult;

(IV) To prevent sexual assault or abuse; and

(V) To prevent stalking.

(b) To be eligible for a protection order, the petitioner does not need to show that he or she has reported the act that is the subject of the complaint to law enforcement, that charges have been filed, or that the petitioner is participating in the prosecution of a criminal matter.

(2) Any civil protection order issued pursuant to this section shall be issued using the standardized set of forms developed by the state court administrator pursuant to section 13-1-136.

(3) Venue for filing a motion or complaint pursuant to this section is proper in any county where the acts that are the subject of the motion or complaint occur, in any county where one of the parties resides, or in any county where one of the parties is employed. This requirement for venue does not prohibit the change of venue to any other county appropriate under applicable law.

(4) A motion for a temporary civil protection order shall be set for hearing at the earliest possible time, which hearing may be ex parte, and shall take precedence over all matters, except those matters of the same character that have been on the court docket for a longer period of time. The court shall hear all such motions as expeditiously as possible.

(5) Any district court, in an action commenced under the "Uniform Dissolution of Marriage Act", Article 10 of title 14, C.R.S., shall have authority to issue temporary and permanent protection orders pursuant to the provisions of subsection (1) of this section. Such protection order may be as a part of a motion for a protection order accompanied by an affidavit filed in an action brought under Article 10 of title 14, C.R.S. Either party may request the court to issue a protection order consistent with any other provision of this article.

(6) At the time a protection order is requested pursuant to this section, the court shall inquire about, and the requesting party and such party's attorney shall have an independent duty to disclose, knowledge such party and such party's attorney may have concerning the existence of any prior protection or restraining order of any court addressing in whole or in part the subject matter of the requested protection order. In the event there are conflicting restraining or protection orders, the court

shall consider, as its first priority, issues of public safety. An order that prevents assaults, threats of assault, or other harm shall be given precedence over an order that deals with the disposition of property or other tangible assets. Every effort shall be made by judicial officers to clarify conflicting orders.

(7)

(a) A temporary civil protection order may be issued if the issuing judge or magistrate finds that an imminent danger exists to the person or persons seeking protection under the civil protection order. In determining whether an imminent danger exists to the life or health of one or more persons, the court shall consider all relevant evidence concerning the safety and protection of the persons seeking the protection order. The court shall not deny a petitioner the relief requested because of the length of time between an act of abuse or threat of harm and the filing of the petition for a protection order.

(b) If the judge or magistrate finds that an imminent danger exists to the employees of a business entity, he or she may issue a civil protection order in the name of the business for the protection of the employees. An employer is not be liable for failing to obtain a civil protection order in the name of the business for the protection of the employees and patrons.

(8) Upon the filing of a complaint duly verified, alleging that the respondent has committed acts that would constitute grounds for a civil protection order, any judge or magistrate, after hearing the evidence and being fully satisfied therein that sufficient cause exists, may issue a temporary civil protection order to prevent the actions complained of and a citation directed to the respondent commanding the respondent to appear before the court at a specific time and date and to show cause, if any, why said temporary civil protection order should not be made permanent. In addition, the court may order any other relief that the court deems appropriate. Complaints may be filed by persons seeking

protection for themselves or for others as provided in section 26-3.1-102(1)(b) and (1)(c), C.R.S.

(9) A copy of the complaint, a copy of the temporary civil protection order, and a copy of the citation must be served upon the respondent and upon the person to be protected, if the complaint was filed by another person, in accordance with the rules for service of process as provided in rule 304 of the rules of county court civil procedure or rule 4 of the Colorado rules of civil procedure. The citation must inform the respondent that, if the respondent fails to appear in court in accordance with the terms of the citation, a bench warrant may be issued for the arrest of the respondent, and the temporary protection order previously entered by the court made permanent without further notice or service upon the respondent.

(10) The return date of the citation must be set not more than fourteen days after the issuance of the temporary civil protection order and citation. If the petitioner is unable to serve the respondent in that period, the court shall extend the temporary protection order previously issued, continue the show of cause hearing, and issue an alias citation stating the date and time to which the hearing is continued. The petitioner may thereafter request, and the court may grant, additional continuances as needed if the petitioner has still been unable to serve the respondent.

(11)

(a) Any person against whom a temporary protection order is issued pursuant to this section, which temporary protection order excludes the person from a shared residence, is permitted to return to the shared residence one time to obtain sufficient undisputed personal effects as are necessary for the person to maintain a normal standard of living during any period prior to a hearing concerning the order. The person against whom a temporary protection order is issued is permitted to return to the shared residence only if the person is accompanied at all times by a peace officer while the person is at or in the shared residence.

(b) When any person is served with a temporary protection order issued against the person excluding the person from a shared residence, the temporary protection order must contain a notification in writing to the person of the person's ability to return to the shared residence pursuant to paragraph (a) of this subsection (11). The written notification shall be in bold print and conspicuously placed in the temporary protection order. A judge, magistrate, or other judicial officer shall not issue a temporary protection order that does not comply with this section.

(c) Any person against whom a temporary protection order is issued pursuant to this section, which temporary protection order excludes the person from a shared residence, may avail himself or herself of the forcible entry and detainer remedies available pursuant to article 40 of this title. However, such person is not entitled to return to the residence until such time as a valid writ of restitution is executed and filed with the court issuing the protection order and, if necessary, the protection order is modified accordingly. A landlord whose lessee has been excluded from a residence pursuant to the terms of a protection order may also avail himself or herself of the remedies available pursuant to article 40 of this title.

Colorado Revised Statutes § 13-14-105.5
CIVIL PROTECTION ORDERS -- PROHIBITION ON POSSESSING OR PURCHASING A FIREARM

(1) If the court subjects a person to a civil protection order pursuant to a provision of this article and the protection order qualifies as an order described in 18 U.S.C. sec. 922(d)(8) or (g)(8), the court, as part of such order:

(a) Shall order the person to:

(I) Refrain from possessing or purchasing any firearm or ammunition for the duration of the order; and

(II) Relinquish, for the duration of the order, any firearm or ammunition in the respondent's immediate possession or control or subject to the respondent's immediate possession or control; and

(b) May require that before the person is released from custody on bond, the person shall relinquish, for the duration of the order, any firearm or ammunition in the person's immediate possession or control or subject to the person's immediate possession or control.

(2)

(a) Except as described in paragraph (b) of this subsection (2), upon issuance of an order pursuant to subsection (1) of this section, the respondent shall relinquish any firearm or ammunition:

(I) Not more than 24 hours after being served with the order in open court; or

(II) Not more than forty-eight hours after being served with the order outside of the court.

(b) A court may allow a respondent up to 72 hours to relinquish a firearm or up to five days to relinquish ammunition pursuant to paragraph (a) of this subsection (2) if the respondent demonstrates to the satisfaction of the court that he or she is unable to comply within the time frame set forth in said subsection (2).

(c) To satisfy the requirement in paragraph (a) of this subsection (2), the respondent may:

(I) Sell or transfer possession of the firearm or ammunition to a federally licensed firearms dealer described in 18 U.S.C. sec. 923, as amended; except that this provision shall not be interpreted to require any federally licensed firearms dealer to purchase or accept possession of any firearm or ammunition;

(II) Arrange for the storage of the firearm or ammunition by a law enforcement agency; except that this provision shall not be interpreted to require any law enforcement agency to provide storage of firearms or ammunition for any person; or

(III) Sell or otherwise transfer the firearm or ammunition to a private party who may legally possess the firearm or ammunition; except that a person who sells or transfers a firearm pursuant to this subparagraph (III) shall satisfy all of the provisions of section 18-12-112, C.R.S., concerning private firearms transfers, including but not limited to the performance of a criminal background check of the transferee.

(3) If a respondent is unable to satisfy the provisions of subsection (2) of this section because he or she is incarcerated or otherwise held in the custody of a law enforcement agency, the court shall require the respondent to satisfy such provisions not more than 24 hours after his or her release from incarceration or custody or be held in contempt of court. Notwithstanding any provision of this subsection (3), the court may, in its discretion, require the respondent to relinquish any firearm or ammunition in the respondent's immediate possession or control or subject to the respondent's immediate possession or control before the end of the respondent's incarceration. In such a case, a respondent's failure to relinquish a firearm or ammunition as required shall constitute contempt of court.

(4) A federally licensed firearms dealer who takes possession of a firearm or ammunition pursuant to this section shall issue a receipt to the respondent at the time of relinquishment. The federally licensed firearms dealer shall not return the firearm or ammunition to the respondent unless the dealer:

(a) Contacts the bureau to request that a background check of the respondent be performed; and

(b) Obtains approval of the transfer from the bureau after the performance of the background check.

(5) A local law enforcement agency may elect to store firearms or ammunition for persons pursuant to this section. If an agency so elects:

(a) The agency may charge a fee for such storage, the amount of which shall not exceed the direct and indirect costs incurred by the agency in providing such storage;

(b) The agency may establish policies for disposal of abandoned or stolen firearms or ammunition; and

(c) The agency shall issue a receipt to each respondent at the time the respondent relinquishes possession of a firearm or ammunition.

(6) If a local law enforcement agency elects to store firearms or ammunition for a person pursuant to this section, the law enforcement agency shall not return the firearm or ammunition to the respondent unless the agency:

(a) Contacts the bureau to request that a background check of the respondent be performed; and

(b) Obtains approval of the transfer from the bureau after the performance of the background check.

(7)

(a) A law enforcement agency that elects to store a firearm or ammunition for a person pursuant to this section may elect to cease storing the firearm or ammunition. A law enforcement agency that elects to cease storing a firearm or ammunition for a person shall notify the person of such decision and request that the person immediately make arrangements for the transfer of the possession of the firearm or ammunition to the person or, if the person is prohibited from possessing a firearm, to another person who is legally permitted to possess a firearm.

(b) If a law enforcement agency elects to cease storing a firearm or ammunition for a person and notifies the person as described in paragraph (a) of this subsection (7), the law enforcement agency may dispose of the firearm or ammunition if the person fails to make arrangements for the transfer of the firearm or ammunition and complete said transfer within ninety days of receiving such notification.

(8) If a respondent sells or otherwise transfers a firearm or ammunition to a private party who may legally possess the firearm or ammunition, as described in subparagraph (III) of paragraph (c) of subsection (2) of this section, the respondent shall acquire:

(a) From the transferee, a written receipt acknowledging the transfer, which receipt shall be dated and signed by the respondent and the transferee; and

(b) From the licensed gun dealer who requests from the bureau a background check of the transferee, as described in section 18-12-112, C.R.S., a written statement of the results of the background check.

(9)

> (a) Not more than three business days after the relinquishment, the respondent shall file a copy of the receipt issued pursuant to subsection (4), (5), or (8) of this section, and, if applicable, the written statement of the results of a background check performed on the respondent, as described in paragraph (b) of subsection (8) of this section, with the court as proof of the relinquishment. If a respondent fails to timely file a receipt or written statement as described in this subsection (9):
>
>> (I) The failure constitutes a violation of the protection order pursuant to section 18-6-803.5(1)(c), C.R.S.; and
>>
>> (II) The court shall issue a warrant for the respondent's arrest.
>
> (b) In any subsequent prosecution for a violation of a protection order described in this subsection (9), the court shall take judicial notice of the defendant's failure to file a receipt or written statement, which will constitute prima facie evidence of a violation of the protection order pursuant to section 18-6-803.5(1)(c), C.R.S., and testimony of the clerk of the court or his or her deputy is not required.

(10) Nothing in this section shall be construed to limit a respondent's right to petition the court for dismissal of a protection order.

(11) A person subject to a civil protection order issued pursuant to section 13-14-104.5(1)(a) who possesses or attempts to purchase or receive a firearm or ammunition while the protection order is in effect violates the order pursuant to section 18-6-803.5(1)(c), C.R.S.

(12)

(a) A law enforcement agency that elects in good faith to not store a firearm or ammunition for a person pursuant to subparagraph (II) of paragraph (c) of subsection (2) of this section shall not be held criminally or civilly liable for such election not to act.

(b) A law enforcement agency that returns possession of a firearm or ammunition to a person in good faith as permitted by subsection (6) of this section shall not be held criminally or civilly liable for such action.

Colorado Revised Statutes, Title 13, Article 21, Part 1
GENERAL PROVISIONS

Colorado Revised Statutes § 13-21-102.5
LIMITATIONS ON DAMAGES FOR NONECONOMIC LOSS OR INJURY

(1) The general assembly finds, determines, and declares that awards in civil actions for noneconomic losses or injuries often unduly burden the economic, commercial, and personal welfare of persons in this state; therefore, for the protection of the public peace, health, and welfare, the general assembly enacts this section placing monetary limitations on such damages for noneconomic losses or injuries.

(2) As used in this section:

(a) "Derivative noneconomic loss or injury" means nonpecuniary harm or emotional stress to persons other than the person suffering the direct or primary loss or injury.

(b) "Noneconomic loss or injury" means nonpecuniary harm for which damages are recoverable by the person suffering the direct or primary loss or injury, including pain and suffering, inconvenience, emotional stress, and impairment of the quality of life. "Noneconomic loss or injury" includes a damage recovery for nonpecuniary harm for actions brought under section 13-21-201 or 13-21-202.

(3)

(a) In any civil action other than medical malpractice actions in which damages for noneconomic loss or injury may be awarded, the total of such damages shall not exceed the sum of two hundred fifty thousand dollars, unless the court finds justification by clear and convincing evidence therefor. In no case shall the amount of noneconomic loss or injury damages exceed five hundred thousand dollars. The damages for noneconomic loss or injury in a medical malpractice action shall not exceed the limitations on noneconomic loss or injury specified in section 13-64-302.

(b) In any civil action, no damages for derivative noneconomic loss or injury may be awarded unless the court finds justification by clear and convincing evidence therefor. In no case shall the amount of such damages exceed two hundred fifty thousand dollars.

(c)

(I) The limitations on damages set forth in paragraphs (a) and (b) of this subsection (3) shall be adjusted for inflation as of January 1, 1998, and January 1, 2008. The adjustments made on January 1, 1998, and January 1, 2008, shall be based on the cumulative annual adjustment for inflation for each year since the effective date of the damages limitations in paragraphs (a) and (b) of this subsection (3). The adjustments made pursuant to this subparagraph (I) shall be rounded upward or downward to the nearest ten-dollar increment.

(II) As used in this paragraph (c), "inflation" means the annual percentage change in the United States department of labor, bureau of labor statistics, consumer price index for Denver-Boulder, all items, all urban consumers, or its successor index.

(III) The secretary of state shall certify[1] the adjusted limitation on damages within fourteen days after the appropriate information is available, and:

(A) The adjusted limitation on damages shall be the limitation applicable to all claims for relief that accrue on or after January 1, 1998, and before January 1, 2008; and

(B) The adjusted limitation on damages as of January 1, 2008, shall be the limitation applicable to all claims for relief that accrue on and after January 1, 2008.

(IV) Nothing in this subsection (3) shall change the limitations on damages set forth in section 13-64-302, or the limitation on damages set forth in section 33-44-113, C.R.S.

(4) The limitations specified in subsection (3) of this section shall not be disclosed to a jury in any such action, but shall be imposed by the court before judgment.

(5) Nothing in this section shall be construed to limit the recovery of compensatory damages for physical impairment or disfigurement.

(6)
    (a)
        (I) In any claim for breach of contract, damages for noneconomic loss or injury or for derivative noneconomic loss or injury are recoverable only if:

(A) The recovery for such damages is specifically authorized in the contract that is the subject of the claim; or

(B) In any first-party claim brought against an insurer for breach of an insurance contract, the plaintiff demonstrates by clear and convincing evidence that the defendant committed willful and wanton breach of contract.

(II) For purposes of this paragraph (a), "willful and wanton breach of contract" means that:

(A) The defendant intended to breach the contract;

(B) The defendant breached the contract without any reasonable justification; and

(C) The contract clearly indicated that damages for noneconomic loss or injury or for derivative noneconomic damages or loss were within the contemplation or expectation of the parties.

(b) Except for the breach of contract damages that are permitted pursuant to sub-subparagraph (B) of subparagraph (I) of paragraph (a) of this subsection (6), nothing in this subsection (6) shall be construed to prohibit one or more parties from waiving the recovery of damages for noneconomic loss or injury or for derivative noneconomic loss or injury on a breach of contract claim so long as the waiver is explicit and in writing.

(c) The limitations on damages set forth in subsection (3) of this section shall apply in any civil action to the aggregate sum of any noneconomic damages awarded under this section for breach of contract including but not limited to bad faith breach of contract.

(d) In any civil action in which an award of damages for noneconomic loss or injury or for derivative noneconomic loss or injury is made on a breach of contract claim, the court shall state such award in the judgment separately from any other damages award.

(e) Except as otherwise provided in paragraph (c) of this subsection (6), nothing in this subsection (6) shall be construed to govern the recovery of noneconomic damages on a tort claim for bad faith breach of contract.

Colorado Revised Statutes § 13-21-107
DAMAGES FOR DESTRUCTION OR BODILY INJURY CAUSED BY MINORS

(1) The state or any county, city, town, school district, or other political subdivision of the state, or any person, partnership, corporation, association, or religious organization, whether incorporated or unincorporated, is entitled to recover damages in an amount not to exceed three thousand five hundred dollars in a court of competent jurisdiction from the parents of each minor under the age of 18 years, living with such parents, who maliciously or willfully damages or destroys property, real, personal, or mixed, belonging to the state, or to any such county, city, town, or other political subdivision of the state, or to any such person, partnership, corporation, association, or religious organization or who maliciously or willfully damages or destroys any such property belonging to or used by such school district. The recovery shall be the actual damages in an amount not to exceed three thousand five hundred dollars, in addition to court costs and reasonable attorney fees.

(2) Any person is entitled to recover damages in an amount not to exceed three thousand five hundred dollars in a court of competent jurisdiction from the parents of each minor under the age of 18 years, living with such parents, who knowingly causes bodily injury to that person, including bodily injury occurring on

property belonging to or used by a school district. The recovery shall be the actual damages in an amount not to exceed three thousand five hundred dollars, in addition to court costs and reasonable attorney fees.

Colorado Revised Statutes § 13-21-111
NEGLIGENCE CASES -- COMPARATIVE NEGLIGENCE AS MEASURE OF DAMAGES

(1) Contributory negligence shall not bar recovery in any action by any person or his legal representative to recover damages for negligence resulting in death or in injury to person or property, if such negligence was not as great as the negligence of the person against whom recovery is sought, but any damages allowed shall be diminished in proportion to the amount of negligence attributable to the person for whose injury, damage, or death recovery is made.

(2) In any action to which subsection (1) of this section applies, the court, in a nonjury trial, shall make findings of fact or, in a jury trial, the jury shall return a special verdict which shall state:

(a) The amount of the damages which would have been recoverable if there had been no contributory negligence; and

(b) The degree of negligence of each party, expressed as a percentage.

(3) Upon the making of the finding of fact or the return of a special verdict, as is required by subsection (2) of this section, the court shall reduce the amount of the verdict in proportion to the amount of negligence attributable to the person for whose injury, damage, or death recovery is made; but, if the said proportion is equal to or greater than the negligence of the person against whom recovery is sought, then, in such event, the court shall enter a judgment for the defendant.

Colorado Revised Statutes § 13-21-115
ACTIONS AGAINST LANDOWNERS

(1) For the purposes of this section, "landowner" includes, without limitation, an authorized agent or a person in possession of real property and a person legally responsible for the condition of real property or for the activities conducted or circumstances existing on real property.

(1.5) The general assembly hereby finds and declares:

(a) That the provisions of this section were enacted in 1986 to promote a state policy of responsibility by both landowners and those upon the land as well as to assure that the ability of an injured party to recover is correlated with his status as a trespasser, licensee, or invitee;

(b) That these objectives were characterized by the Colorado supreme court as "legitimate governmental interests" in *Gallegos v. Phipps,* No. 88 SA 141 (September 18, 1989);

(c) That the purpose of amending this section in the 1990 legislative session is to assure that the language of this section effectuates these legitimate governmental interests by imposing on landowners a higher standard of care with respect to an invitee than a licensee, and a higher standard of care with respect to a licensee than a trespasser;

(d) That the purpose of this section is also to create a legal climate which will promote private property rights and commercial enterprise and will foster the availability and affordability of insurance;

(e) That the general assembly recognizes that by amending this section it is not reinstating the common law status categories as they existed immediately prior to *Mile Hi Fence v. Radovich,* 175 Colo. 537, 489 P.2d 308 (1971) but that its purpose is to protect landowners from liability in some circumstances when they were not protected at common law and to define the instances when liability will be imposed in the manner most consistent with the policies set forth in paragraphs (a), (c), and

(d) of this subsection (1.5).

(2) In any civil action brought against a landowner by a person who alleges injury occurring while on the real property of another and by reason of the condition of such property, or activities conducted or circumstances existing on such property, the landowner shall be liable only as provided in subsection (3) of this section. Sections 13-21-111, 13-21-111.5, and 13-21-111.7 shall apply to an action to which this section applies. This subsection (2) shall not be construed to abrogate the doctrine of attractive nuisance as applied to persons under fourteen years of age. A person who is at least fourteen years of age but is less than 18 years of age shall be presumed competent for purposes of the application of this section.

(3)

(a) A trespasser may recover only for damages willfully or deliberately caused by the landowner.

(b) A licensee may recover only for damages caused:

(I) By the landowner's unreasonable failure to exercise reasonable care with respect to dangers created by the landowner of which the landowner actually knew; or

(II) By the landowner's unreasonable failure to warn of dangers not created by the landowner which are not ordinarily present on property of the type involved and of which the landowner actually knew.

(c)

(I) Except as otherwise provided in subparagraph (II) of this paragraph (c), an invitee may recover for damages caused by the landowner's unreasonable failure to exercise reasonable care to protect against dangers of which he actually knew or should have known.

(II) If the landowner's real property is classified for property tax purposes as agricultural land or vacant land, an invitee may recover for damages caused by the landowner's unreasonable failure to exercise reasonable care to protect against dangers of which he actually knew.

(3.5) It is the intent of the general assembly in enacting the provisions of subsection (3) of this section that the circumstances under which a licensee may recover include all of the circumstances under which a trespasser could recover and that the circumstances under which an invitee may recover include all of the circumstances under which a trespasser or a licensee could recover.

(4) In any action to which this section applies, the judge shall determine whether the plaintiff is a trespasser, a licensee, or an invitee, in accordance with the definitions set forth in subsection

(5) of this section. If two or more landowners are parties defendant to the action, the judge shall determine the application of this section to each such landowner. The issues of liability and damages in any such action shall be determined by the jury or, if there is no jury, by the judge.

(6) As used in this section:

(a) "Invitee" means a person who enters or remains on the land of another to transact business in which the parties are mutually interested or who enters or remains on such land in response to the landowner's express or implied representation that the public is requested, expected, or intended to enter or remain.

(b) "Licensee" means a person who enters or remains on the land of another for the licensee's own convenience or to advance his own interests, pursuant to the landowner's permission or consent. "Licensee" includes a social guest.

(c) "Trespasser" means a person who enters or remains on the land of another without the landowner's consent.

(7) If any provision of this section is found by a court of competent jurisdiction to be unconstitutional, the remaining provisions of the section shall be deemed valid.

Colorado Revised Statutes, Title 13, Article 21, Part 2
DAMAGES FOR DEATH BY NEGLIGENCE

Colorado Revised Statutes § 13-21-201
DAMAGES FOR DEATH

(1) When any person dies from any injury resulting from or occasioned by the negligence, unskillfulness, or criminal intent of any officer, agent, servant, or employee while running, conducting, or managing any locomotive, car, or train of cars, or of any driver of any coach or other conveyance operated for the purpose of carrying either freight or passengers for hire while in charge of the same as a driver, and when any passenger dies from an injury resulting from or occasioned by any defect or insufficiency in any railroad or any part thereof, or in any locomotive or car, or other conveyance operated for the purpose of carrying either freight or passengers for hire, the corporation or individuals in whose employ any such officer, agent, servant, employee, master, pilot, engineer, or driver is at the time such injury is committed, or who owns any such railroad, locomotive, car, or other conveyance operated for the purpose of carrying either freight or passengers for hire at the time any such injury is

received, and resulting from or occasioned by the defect or insufficiency above described shall forfeit and pay for every person and passenger so injured the sum of not exceeding ten thousand dollars and not less than three thousand dollars, which may be sued for and recovered:

(a) In the first year after such death:

(I) By the spouse of the deceased;

(II) Upon the written election of the spouse, by the spouse and the heir or heirs of the deceased;

(III) Upon the written election of the spouse, by the heir or heirs of the deceased; or

(IV) If there is no spouse, by the heir or heirs of the deceased or the designated beneficiary, if there is one designated pursuant to article 22 of title 15, C.R.S., with the right to bring an action pursuant to this section, and if there is no designated beneficiary, by the heir or heirs of the deceased;

(b)

(I) In the second year after such death:

(A) By the spouse of the deceased;

(B) By the heir or heirs of the deceased;

(C) By the spouse and the heir or heirs of the deceased; or

(D) By the designated beneficiary of the deceased, if there is one designated pursuant to article 22 of title 15, C.R.S., with the right to bring an action pursuant to this section, and the heir or heirs of the deceased.

(II) However, if the heir or heirs of the deceased commence an action under the provisions of sub-subparagraph (B) of subparagraph (I) of this paragraph (b), the spouse or the designated beneficiary of the deceased, if there is one designated pursuant to article 22 of title 15, C.R.S., with the right to bring an action pursuant to this section, upon motion filed within ninety days after service of written notice of the commencement of the action upon the spouse or designated beneficiary, shall be allowed to join the action as a party plaintiff.

(c)

(I) If the deceased is an unmarried minor without descendants or an unmarried adult without descendants and without a designated beneficiary pursuant to article 22 of title 15, C.R.S., by the father or mother who may join in the suit. Except as provided in subparagraphs (II) and (III) of this paragraph (c), the father and mother shall have an equal interest in the judgment, or if either of them is dead, then the surviving parent shall have an exclusive interest in the judgment.

(II) For cases in which the father and mother are divorced, separated, or living apart, a motion may be filed by either the father or the mother prior to trial requesting the court to apportion fairly any judgment awarded in the case. Where such a motion is filed, the court shall conduct a post-judgment hearing at which the father and the mother shall have the opportunity to be heard and to produce evidence regarding each parent's relationship with the deceased child.

(III) On conclusion of the post-judgment hearing conducted pursuant to subparagraph (II) of this paragraph (c), the court shall fairly determine the percentage of the judgment to be awarded to each parent. In making such a determination, the court shall consider each parent's relationship with the deceased, including custody, control, support, parental responsibility, and any other factors the court deems pertinent. The court's determination of the percentage of the judgment awarded to each parent shall not be disturbed absent an abuse of discretion.

(d) For purposes of this section, "father or mother" means a natural parent of the deceased or a parent of the deceased by adoption. "Father or mother" does not include a person whose parental rights concerning the deceased were terminated pursuant to the provisions of title 19, C.R.S.

(2) In suits instituted under this section, it is competent for the defendant for his defense to show that the defect or insufficiency named in this section was not a negligent defect or insufficiency. The judgment obtained in an action under this section shall be owned by such persons as are heirs at law of the deceased under the statutes of descent and distribution and shall be divided among such heirs at law in the same manner as real estate is divided according to said statute of descent and distribution.

Colorado Revised Statutes § 13-21-202
ACTIONS NOTWITHSTANDING DEATH

When the death of a person is caused by a wrongful act, neglect, or default of another, and the act, neglect, or default is such as would, if death had not ensued, have entitled the party injured to maintain an action and recover damages in respect thereof, then, and in every such case, the person who or the corporation which would have been liable, if death had not ensued, shall be liable in an action for damages notwithstanding the death of the party injured.

Colorado Revised Statutes § 13-21-203
LIMITATION ON DAMAGES

(1)

(a) All damages accruing under section 13-21-202 shall be sued for and recovered by the same parties and in the same manner as provided in section 13-21-201, and in every such action the jury may give such damages as they may deem fair and just, with reference to the necessary injury resulting from such death, including damages for noneconomic loss or injury as defined in section 13-21-102.5 and subject to the limitations of this section and including within noneconomic loss or injury damages for grief, loss of companionship, pain and suffering, and emotional stress, to the surviving parties who may be entitled to sue; and also having regard to the mitigating or aggravating circumstances attending any such wrongful act, neglect, or default; except that, if the decedent left neither a widow, a widower, minor children, nor a dependent father or mother, the damages recoverable in any such action shall not exceed the limitations for noneconomic loss or injury set forth in section 13-21-102.5, unless the wrongful act, neglect, or default causing death constitutes a felonious killing, as defined in section 15-11-803(1)(b), C.R.S., and as determined in the manner described in section 15-11-803(7), C.R.S., in which case there shall be no limitation on the damages for noneconomic loss or injury recoverable in such action. No action shall be brought and no recovery shall be had under both section 13-21-201 and section 13-21-202, and in all cases the plaintiff is required to elect under which section he or she will proceed. There shall be only one civil action under this part 2 for recovery of damages for the wrongful death of any one decedent. Notwithstanding anything in this section or in section 13-21-102.5 to the contrary, there shall be no recovery under this part 2 for noneconomic loss or injury in excess of two hundred fifty thousand dollars, unless the wrongful act, neglect, or default causing death constitutes a felonious killing, as defined in section 15-11-803(1)(b), C.R.S., and as determined in the manner described in section 15-11-803(7), C.R.S.

(b) The damages recoverable for noneconomic loss or injury in any medical malpractice action shall not exceed the limitations on noneconomic loss or injury set forth in section 13-64-302.

(2) This section shall apply to a cause of action based on a wrongful act, neglect, or default occurring on or after July 1, 1969. A cause of action based on a wrongful act, neglect, or default occurring prior to July 1, 1969, shall be governed by the law in force and effect at the time of such wrongful act, neglect, or default.

(3)

(a) In all actions brought under section 13-21-201 or 13-21-202 in which damages are assessed by the trier of fact, and the death complained of is attended by circumstances of fraud, malice, or willful and wanton conduct, the trier of fact, in addition to the actual damages, may award reasonable exemplary damages. The amount of such reasonable exemplary damages shall not exceed an amount that is equal to the amount of the actual damages awarded to the injured party.

(b) For purposes of this subsection (3), "willful and wanton conduct" shall have the same meaning as set forth in section 13-21-102(1)(b).

(c)

(I) A claim for exemplary damages in an action governed by this section may not be included in any initial claim for relief. A claim for exemplary damages in an action governed by this section shall be allowed by amendment to the pleadings only after the passage of sixty days following the exchange of initial disclosures pursuant to rule 26 of the Colorado rules of civil procedure and the plaintiff establishes prima facie proof of a triable issue. After the plaintiff establishes the existence of a triable issue of exemplary damages, the court may, in its discretion, allow additional discovery on the issue of exemplary damages as the court deems appropriate.

(II) A claim for exemplary damages in an action governed by this section shall not be time barred by the applicable provisions of law for the commencement of actions, so long as:

(A) The claim for exemplary damages arises, pursuant to paragraph (a) of this subsection (3), from the claim in such action that is brought under section 13-21-201 or 13-21-202; and

(B) The claim in such action that is brought under section 13-21-201 or 13-21-202 is not time barred.

(III) The assertion of a claim for exemplary damages in an action governed by this section shall not be rendered ineffective solely because the assertion was made after the applicable deadline contained in the court's case management order, so long as the plaintiff establishes that he or she did not discover, and could not have reasonably discovered prior to such deadline, the grounds for asserting the exemplary damages claim.

(4) Notwithstanding the provisions of subsection (3) of this section, the court may reduce or disallow the award of exemplary damages to the extent that:

(a) The deterrent effect of the damages has been accomplished; or

(b) The conduct that resulted in the award has ceased; or

(c) The purpose of such damages has otherwise been served.

(5) Notwithstanding the provisions of subsection (3) of this section, the court may increase any award of exemplary damages to a sum not to exceed three times the amount of actual damages, if it is shown that:

(a) The defendant has continued the behavior or repeated the action that is the subject of the claim against the defendant in a willful and wanton manner against another person or persons during the pendency of the case; or

(b) The defendant has acted in a willful and wanton manner during the pendency of the action in a manner that has further aggravated the damages of the plaintiff when the defendant knew or should have known such action would produce aggravation.

(6) The provisions of this section shall not apply to a peace officer, as described in section 16-2.5-101, C.R.S., or to any firefighter, as defined in section 18-3-201(1.5), C.R.S., for claims arising out of injuries sustained from an act or omission of the peace officer or firefighter acting in the performance of his or her duties and within the scope of his or her employment.

(7) Nothing in this section shall be construed to alter or amend the provisions of section 13-64-302.5 or the provisions of part 1 of Article 10 of title 24, C.R.S.

Colorado Revised Statutes § 13-21-204
LIMITATION OF ACTIONS

All actions provided for by this part 2 shall be brought within the time period prescribed in section 13-80-102.

Colorado Revised Statutes, Title 13, Article 80, Part 1
LIMITATIONS -- PERSONAL ACTIONS

Colorado Revised Statutes § 13-80-102
GENERAL LIMITATION OF ACTIONS -- TWO YEARS

(1) The following civil actions, regardless of the theory upon which suit is brought, or against whom suit is brought, must be commenced within two years after the cause of action accrues, and not thereafter:

(a) Tort actions, including but not limited to actions for negligence, trespass, malicious abuse of process, malicious prosecution, outrageous conduct, interference with relationships, and tortious breach of contract; except that this paragraph (a) does not apply to any tort action arising out of the use or operation of a motor vehicle as set forth in section 13-80-101(1)(n);

(b) All actions for strict liability, absolute liability, or failure to instruct or warn;

(c) All actions, regardless of the theory asserted, against any veterinarian;

(d) All actions for wrongful death, except as described in subsection (2) of this section;

(e) Repealed by Laws 1987, S.B.75, § 8, eff. July 1, 1987.

(f) All actions against any public or governmental entity or any employee of a public or governmental entity for which insurance coverage is provided pursuant to Article 14 of title 24, C.R.S.;

(g) All actions upon liability created by a federal statute where no period of limitation is provided in said federal statute;

(h) All actions against any public or governmental entity or any employee of a public or governmental entity, except as otherwise provided in this section or section 13-80-103;

(i) All other actions of every kind for which no other period of limitation is provided;

(j) All actions brought under section 42-6-204, C.R.S.;

(k) All actions brought under section 13-21-109(2).

(2) A civil action for a wrongful death against a defendant who committed vehicular homicide, as described in section 18-3-106, C.R.S., and, as part of the same criminal episode, committed the offense of leaving the scene of an accident that resulted in the death of a person, as described in section 42-4-1601(2)(c), C.R.S., regardless of the theory upon which suit is brought, or against whom suit is brought, must be commenced within four years after the cause of action accrues, and not thereafter.

Colorado Revised Statutes, Title 15, Article 11, Part 8

GENERAL PROVISIONS CONCERNING PROBATE AND NONPROBATE TRANSFERS

Colorado Revised Statutes § 15-11-803

EFFECT OF HOMICIDE ON INTESTATE SUCCESSION, WILLS, TRUSTS, JOINT ASSETS, LIFE INSURANCE, AND BENEFICIARY DESIGNATIONS

(1) **Definitions.** As used in this section, unless the context otherwise requires:

(a) "Disposition or appointment of property" includes a transfer of an item of property or any other benefit to a beneficiary designated in a governing instrument.

(b) "Felonious killing", except as provided in subsection (7) of this section, is the killing of the decedent by an individual who, as a result thereof, is convicted of, pleads guilty to, or enters a plea of nolo contendere to the crime of murder in the first or second degree or manslaughter, as said crimes are defined in sections 18-3-102 to 18-3-104, C.R.S.

(c) "Governing instrument" means a governing instrument executed by the decedent.

(d) "Killer" is any individual who has committed a felonious killing.

(e) "Revocable", with respect to a disposition, appointment, provision, or nomination, means one under which the decedent, at the time of or immediately before death, was alone empowered, by law or under the governing instrument, to cancel the designation in favor of the killer, whether or not the decedent was then empowered to designate himself or herself in place of his or her killer and or the decedent then had capacity to exercise the power.

(2) **Forfeiture of statutory benefits.** An individual who feloniously kills the decedent forfeits all benefits with respect to the decedent's estate, including an intestate share, an elective-share, an omitted spouse's or child's share, the decedent's homestead exemption under section 38-41-204, C.R.S., exempt property, and a family allowance. If the decedent died intestate, the decedent's intestate estate passes as if the killer disclaimed his or her intestate share.

(3) **Revocation of benefits under governing instruments.** The felonious killing of the decedent:

(a) Revokes any revocable (i) disposition or appointment of property made by the decedent to the killer in a governing instrument, (ii) provision in a governing instrument conferring a general or nongeneral power of appointment on the killer, and (iii) nomination of the killer in a governing instrument, nominating or appointing the killer to serve in any fiduciary or representative capacity, including a personal representative, executor, trustee, or agent; and

(b) Severs the interests of the decedent and killer in property held by them at the time of the killing as joint tenants with the right of survivorship or as community property with the right of survivorship, transforming the interests of the decedent and killer into tenancies in common.

(4) **Effect of severance.** A severance under paragraph (b) of subsection (3) of this section does not affect any third-party interest in property acquired for value and in good faith reliance on an apparent title by survivorship in the killer unless a writing declaring the severance has been noted, registered, filed, or recorded in records appropriate to the kind and location of the property which are relied upon, in the ordinary course of transactions involving such property, as evidence of ownership.

(5) **Effect of revocation.** Provisions of a governing instrument are given effect as if the killer disclaimed all provisions revoked by this section or, in the case of a revoked nomination in a fiduciary or representative capacity, as if the killer predeceased the decedent.

(6) **Wrongful acquisition of property.** A wrongful acquisition of property or interest by a killer not covered by this section shall be treated in accordance with the principle that a killer cannot profit from his or her wrong.

(7) **Felonious killing; how determined--time limitations on civil proceedings.**

(a) **Criminal proceedings.** After all right to appeal has been waived or exhausted following the entry of a judgment of conviction establishing criminal accountability for the felonious killing of the decedent, such judgment conclusively establishes the convicted individual as the decedent's killer for purposes of this section.

(b) **Civil proceedings.** Notwithstanding the status or disposition of a criminal proceeding, a court of competent jurisdiction, upon the petition of an interested person, shall determine whether, by a preponderance of evidence standard, each of the elements of felonious killing of the decedent has been established. If such elements have been so established, such determination conclusively establishes that individual as the decedent's killer for purposes of this section.

(c) **Time limitations on civil proceedings.**
(I) A petition brought under paragraph (b) of this subsection (7) may not be filed more than three years after the date of the decedent's death.

(II) Notwithstanding any provision of subparagraph (I) of this paragraph (c) to the contrary, if a criminal proceeding is commenced in a court of this state or in another jurisdiction against an individual for the felonious killing of the decedent, a petition brought under paragraph (b) of this subsection (7) may be filed so long as the petition is filed no later than one year after all right to appeal has been waived or exhausted following an entry of a judgment of conviction, or a dismissal, or an acquittal in the criminal proceeding. However, if the death and the possible culpability of the slayer for the felonious slaying of the decedent is not known to the petitioner within the three-year period of limitations established pursuant to subparagraph (I) of this paragraph (c), the accrual of the action under paragraph (b) of this subsection (7) and the possibility of the tolling of the running of the three-year period of limitation under subparagraph (I) of this paragraph (c) shall be determined according to the principles of accrual and tolling established by case law with respect to similar limitations established under section 13-80-108, C.R.S.

(d) **Judgment of conviction.** For the purposes of this subsection

(8), a "judgment of conviction" includes a judgment of conviction on a plea of guilty or nolo contendere, or a judgment of conviction on a verdict of guilty by the court or by a jury.

(9) **Protection of payors and other third parties.**

(a) A payor or other third party is not liable for having made a payment or transferred an item of property or any other benefit to a beneficiary designated in a governing instrument affected by a felonious killing, or for having taken any other action in reliance on the beneficiary's apparent entitlement under the terms of the governing instrument, before the payor or other third party has received written notice as described in paragraph (b) of this subsection (8). A payor or other third party shall have no duty or obligation to make any determination as to whether or not the decedent was the victim of a felonious killing or to seek any evidence with respect to any such felonious killing even if the circumstances of the decedent's death are suspicious or questionable as to the beneficiary's participation in any such felonious killing. A payor or other third party is only liable for actions taken two or more business days after the payor or other third party has actual receipt of such written notice. Any form or service of notice other than that described in paragraph (b) of this subsection (8) shall not be sufficient to impose liability on a payor or other third party for actions taken pursuant to the governing instrument.

(b) The written notice shall indicate the name of the decedent, the name of the person asserting an interest, the nature of the payment or item of property or other benefit, and a statement that a claim of forfeiture or revocation is being made under this section. The written notice shall be mailed to the payor's or other third party's main office or home by registered or certified mail, return receipt requested, or served upon the payor or other third party in the same manner as a summons in a civil action.

(c) Upon receipt of the written notice described in paragraph (b) of this subsection (8), a payor or other third party may pay to the court any amount owed or transfer to or deposit with the court any item of property held by it. The availability of such actions under this section shall not prevent the payor or other third party from taking any other action authorized by law or the governing instrument. The court is the court having jurisdiction of the probate proceedings relating to the decedent's estate, or if no proceedings have been commenced, the court having jurisdiction of probate proceedings relating to decedents' estates located in the county of the decedent's residence. If no probate proceedings have been commenced, the payor or other third party shall file with the court a copy of the written notice received by the payor or other third party, with the payment of funds or transfer or deposit of property. The court shall not charge a filing fee to the payor or other third party for the payment to the court of amounts owed or transfer to or deposit with the court of any item of property, even if no probate proceedings have been commenced before such payment, transfer, or deposit. Payment of amounts to the court or transfer to or deposit with the court of any item of property pursuant to this section by the payor or other third party discharges the payor or other third party from all claims under the governing instrument or applicable law for the value of amounts paid to the court or items of property transferred to or deposited with the court.

(d) The court shall hold the funds or item of property and, upon its determination under this section, shall order disbursement in accordance with the determination. A filing fee, if any, shall be charged upon disbursement either to the recipient or against the funds or property on deposit with the court, in the discretion of the court.

(e) Upon petition to the court by the beneficiary designated in a governing instrument, the court may order that all or part of the property be paid to the beneficiary in an amount and subject to conditions consistent with this section.

(10) **Protection of bona fide purchasers; personal liability of recipient.**

(a) A person who purchases property for value and without notice, or who receives a payment or other item of property in partial or full satisfaction of a legally enforceable obligation, is neither obligated under this section to return the payment, item of property, or benefit nor is liable under this section for the amount of the payment or the value of the item of property or benefit. However, a person who, not for value, receives a payment, item of property, or any other benefit to which the person is not entitled under this section is obligated to return the payment, item of property, or benefit, or is personally liable for the amount of the payment or the value of the item of property or benefit, to the person who is entitled to it under this section.

(b) If this section or any part of this section is preempted by federal law with respect to a payment, an item of property, or any other benefit covered by this section, a person who, not for value, receives the payment, item of property, or any other benefit to which the person is not entitled under this section is obligated to return the payment, item of property, or benefit, or is personally liable for the amount of the payment or the value of the item of property or benefit, to the person who would have been entitled to it were this section or part of this section not preempted.

Colorado Revised Statutes, Title 16, Article 2.5, Part 1
PEACE OFFICERS

Colorado Revised Statutes § 16-2.5-101
PEACE OFFICER - DESCRIPTION - GENERAL AUTHORITY

(1) A person who is included within the provisions of this article and who meets all standards imposed by law on a peace officer is a peace officer, and, notwithstanding any other provision of law, no person other than a person designated in this article is a peace officer. A peace officer may be certified by the peace officers standards and training board pursuant to part 3 of article 31 of title 24, C.R.S., and, at a minimum, has the authority to enforce all laws of the state of Colorado while acting within the scope of his or her authority and in the performance of his or her duties, unless otherwise limited within this part 1.

(2) A peace officer certified by the peace officers standards and training board shall have the authority to carry firearms at all times, concealed or otherwise, subject to the written firearms policy created by the agency employing the peace officer. All other peace officers shall have the authority to carry firearms, concealed or otherwise, while engaged in the performance of their duties or as otherwise authorized by the written policy of the agency employing the officer.

(3) As used in every statute, unless the context otherwise requires, "law enforcement officer" means a peace officer.

Colorado Revised Statutes, Title 16, Article 3, Part 2
AUTHORITY OF PERSON NOT A PEACE OFFICER TO MAKE AN ARREST

Colorado Revised Statutes § 16-3-201
ARREST BY A PRIVATE PERSON

A person who is not a peace officer may arrest another person when any crime has been or is being committed by the arrested person in the presence of the person making the arrest.

Colorado Revised Statutes § 16-3-202
ASSISTING PEACE OFFICER -- ARREST -- FURNISHING INFORMATION -- IMMUNITY

(1) A peace officer making an arrest may command the assistance of any person who is in the vicinity.

(2) A person commanded to assist a peace officer has the same authority to arrest as the officer who commands his assistance.

(3) A person commanded to assist a peace officer in making an arrest shall not be civilly or criminally liable for any reasonable conduct in aid of the officer or for any acts expressly directed by the officer.

(4) Private citizens, acting in good faith, shall be immune from any civil liability for reporting to any police officer or law enforcement authority the commission or suspected commission of any crime or for giving other information to aid in the prevention of any crime.

Colorado Revised Statutes, Title 16, Article 17, Part 1
COMMUTATION OF SENTENCE

Colorado Revised Statutes § 16-17-102
APPLICATION -- CHARACTER CERTIFICATE

After a conviction, all applications for commutation of sentence or pardon for crimes committed shall be accompanied by a certificate of the respective superintendent of the correctional facility, showing the conduct of an applicant during his or her confinement in the correctional facility, together with such evidences of former good character as the applicant may be able to produce. Before the governor approves such application, it shall be first submitted to the present district attorney of the district in which the applicant was convicted and to the judge who sentenced and the attorney who prosecuted at the trial of the applicant, if available, for such comment as they may deem proper concerning the merits of the application, so as to provide the governor with information upon which to base his or her action. The governor shall make reasonable efforts to locate the judge who sentenced and the attorney who prosecuted at the trial of the applicant and shall afford them a reasonable time, not less than fourteen days, to comment on such applications. The requirements of this section shall be deemed to have been met if the persons to whom the application is submitted for comment do not comment within fourteen days after their receipt of the application or within such other reasonable time in excess of fourteen days as specified by the governor, or if the sentencing judge or prosecuting attorney cannot be located, are incapacitated, or are otherwise unavailable for comment despite the good-faith efforts of the governor to obtain their comments. Good character previous to conviction, good conduct during confinement in the correctional facility, the statements of the sentencing judge and the district attorneys, if any, and any other material concerning the merits of the application shall be given such weight as to the governor may seem just and proper, in view of the circumstances of each particular case, a due regard being had to the reformation of the accused. The governor shall have sole discretion in evaluating said comments and in soliciting other comments he or she deems appropriate.

Colorado Revised Statutes § 16-17-103

EFFECT OF PARDON AND COMMUTATION OF SENTENCE -- DEFINITIONS

(1)   A pardon issued by the governor shall waive all collateral consequences associated with each conviction for which the person received a pardon unless the pardon limits the scope of the pardon regarding collateral consequences.

(2) If the governor grants a pardon or a request for commutation of sentence, the governor shall provide a copy of the pardon or commutation of sentence to the Colorado bureau of investigation, and the Colorado bureau of investigation shall note in the individual's record in the Colorado crime information center that a pardon was issued or commutation of sentence was granted.

(3) For purposes of this section, "collateral consequences" means a penalty, prohibition, bar, disadvantage, or disqualification, however denominated, imposed on an individual as a result of the individual's conviction of an offense, which penalty, prohibition, bar, or disadvantage applies by operation of law regardless of whether the penalty, prohibition, bar, or disadvantage is included in the judgment or sentence. "Collateral consequences" does not include imprisonment, probation, parole, supervised release, forfeiture, restitution, fine, assessment, or costs of prosecution.

Colorado Revised Statutes, Title 18, Article 1, Part 4
RIGHTS OF DEFENDANT

Colorado Revised Statutes § 18-1-407
AFFIRMATIVE DEFENSE

(1) "Affirmative defense" means that unless the state's evidence raises the issue involving the alleged defense, the defendant, to raise the issue, shall present some credible evidence on that issue.

(2) If the issue involved in an affirmative defense is raised, then the guilt of the defendant must be established beyond a reasonable doubt as to that issue as well as all other elements of the offense.

Colorado Revised Statutes, Title 18, Article 1, Part 7
JUSTIFICATION AND EXEMPTIONS FROM CRIMINAL
RESPONSIBILITY

Colorado Revised Statutes § 18-1-702
CHOICE OF EVILS

(1) Unless inconsistent with other provisions of sections 18-1-703 to 18-1-707, defining justifiable use of physical force, or with some other provision of law, conduct which would otherwise constitute an offense is justifiable and not criminal when it is necessary as an emergency measure to avoid an imminent public or private injury which is about to occur by reason of a situation occasioned or developed through no conduct of the actor, and which is of sufficient gravity that, according to ordinary standards of intelligence and morality, the desirability and urgency of avoiding the injury clearly outweigh the desirability of avoiding the injury sought to be prevented by the statute defining the offense in issue.

(2) The necessity and justifiability of conduct under subsection (1) of this section shall not rest upon considerations pertaining only to the morality and advisability of the statute, either in its general application or with respect to its application to a particular class of cases arising thereunder. When evidence relating to the defense of justification under this section is offered by the defendant, before it is submitted for the consideration of the jury, the court shall first rule as a matter of law whether the claimed facts and circumstances would, if established, constitute a justification

Colorado Revised Statutes § 18-1-704
USE OF PHYSICAL FORCE IN DEFENSE OF A PERSON

(1) Except as provided in subsections (2) and (3) of this section, a person is justified in using physical force upon another person in order to defend himself or a third person from what he reasonably believes to be the use or imminent use of unlawful physical force by that other person, and he may use a degree of force which he reasonably believes to be necessary for that purpose.

(2) Deadly physical force may be used only if a person reasonably believes a lesser degree of force is inadequate and:

(a) The actor has reasonable ground to believe, and does believe, that he or another person is in imminent danger of being killed or of receiving great bodily injury; or

(b) The other person is using or reasonably appears about to use physical force against an occupant of a dwelling or business establishment while committing or attempting to commit burglary as defined in sections 18-4-202 to 18-4-204; or

(c) The other person is committing or reasonably appears about to commit kidnapping as defined in section 18-3-301 or 18-3-302, robbery as defined in section 18-4-301 or 18-4-302, sexual assault as set forth in section 18-3-402, or in section

18-3-403 as it existed prior to July 1, 2000, or assault as defined in sections 18-3-202 and 18-3-203.

(3) Notwithstanding the provisions of subsection (1) of this section, a person is not justified in using physical force if:

(a) With intent to cause bodily injury or death to another person, he provokes the use of unlawful physical force by that other person; or

(b) He is the initial aggressor; except that his use of physical force upon another person under the circumstances is justifiable if he withdraws from the encounter and effectively communicates to the other person his intent to do so, but the latter nevertheless continues or threatens the use of unlawful physical force; or

(c) The physical force involved is the product of a combat by agreement not specifically authorized by law.

(4) In a case in which the defendant is not entitled to a jury instruction regarding self-defense as an affirmative defense, the court shall allow the defendant to present evidence, when relevant, that he or she was acting in self-defense. If the defendant presents evidence of self-defense, the court shall instruct the jury with a self-defense law instruction. The court shall instruct the jury that it may consider the evidence of self-defense in determining whether the defendant acted recklessly, with extreme indifference, or in a criminally negligent manner. However, the self-defense law instruction shall not be an affirmative defense instruction and the prosecuting attorney shall not have the burden of disproving self-defense. This section shall not apply to strict liability crimes.

Colorado Revised Statutes § 18-1-704.5
USE OF DEADLY PHYSICAL FORCE AGAINST AN INTRUDER

(1) The general assembly hereby recognizes that the citizens of Colorado have a right to expect absolute safety within their own homes.

(2) Notwithstanding the provisions of section 18-1-704, any occupant of a dwelling is justified in using any degree of physical force, including deadly physical force, against another person when that other person has made an unlawful entry into the dwelling, and when the occupant has a reasonable belief that such other person has committed a crime in the dwelling in addition to the uninvited entry, or is committing or intends to commit a crime against a person or property in addition to the uninvited entry, and when the occupant reasonably believes that such other person might use any physical force, no matter how slight, against any occupant.

(3) Any occupant of a dwelling using physical force, including deadly physical force, in accordance with the provisions of subsection (2) of this section shall be immune from criminal prosecution for the use of such force.
(4) Any occupant of a dwelling using physical force, including deadly physical force, in accordance with the provisions of subsection (2) of this section shall be immune from any civil liability for injuries or death resulting from the use of such force.

Colorado Revised Statutes § 18-1-705
USE OF PHYSICAL FORCE IN DEFENSE OF PREMISES

A person in possession or control of any building, realty, or other premises, or a person who is licensed or privileged to be thereon, is justified in using reasonable and appropriate physical force upon another person when and to the extent that it is reasonably necessary to prevent or terminate what he reasonably believes to be the commission or attempted commission of an unlawful trespass by the other person in or upon the building, realty, or premises. However, he may use deadly force only in defense of himself or another as described in section 18-1-704, or when he reasonably believes it necessary to prevent what he reasonably believes to be an attempt by the trespasser to commit first degree arson.

Colorado Revised Statutes § 18-1-706
USE OF PHYSICAL FORCE IN DEFENSE OF PROPERTY

A person is justified in using reasonable and appropriate physical force upon another person when and to the extent that he reasonably believes it necessary to prevent what he reasonably believes to be an attempt by the other person to commit theft, criminal mischief, or criminal tampering involving property, but he may use deadly physical force under these circumstances only in defense of himself or another as described in section 18-1-704.

Colorado Revised Statutes § 18-1-707
USE OF PHYSICAL FORCE IN MAKING AN ARREST OR IN PREVENTING AN ESCAPE

(1) Except as provided in subsection (2) of this section, a peace officer is justified in using reasonable and appropriate physical force upon another person when and to the extent that he reasonably believes it necessary:

(a) To effect an arrest or to prevent the escape from custody of an arrested person unless he knows that the arrest is unauthorized; or

(b) To defend himself or a third person from what he reasonably believes to be the use or imminent use of physical force while effecting or attempting to effect such an arrest or while preventing or attempting to prevent such an escape.

(2) A peace officer is justified in using deadly physical force upon another person for a purpose specified in subsection (1) of this section only when he reasonably believes that it is necessary:

(a) To defend himself or a third person from what he reasonably believes to be the use or imminent use of deadly physical force; or

(b) To effect an arrest, or to prevent the escape from custody, of a person whom he reasonably believes:

(I) Has committed or attempted to commit a felony involving the use or threatened use of a deadly weapon; or

(II) Is attempting to escape by the use of a deadly weapon; or

(III) Otherwise indicates, except through a motor vehicle violation, that he is likely to endanger human life or to inflict serious bodily injury to another unless apprehended without delay.

(3) Nothing in subsection (2)(b) of this section shall be deemed to constitute justification for reckless or criminally negligent conduct by a peace officer amounting to an offense against or with respect to innocent persons whom he is not seeking to arrest or retain in custody.

(4) For purposes of this section, a reasonable belief that a person has committed an offense means a reasonable belief in facts or circumstances which if true would in law constitute an offense. If the believed facts or circumstances would not in law constitute an offense, an erroneous though not unreasonable belief that the law is otherwise does not render justifiable the use of force to make an arrest or to prevent an escape from custody. A peace officer who is effecting an arrest pursuant to a warrant is justified

in using the physical force prescribed in subsections (1) and (2) of this section unless the warrant is invalid and is known by the officer to be invalid.

(5) Except as provided in subsection (6) of this section, a person who has been directed by a peace officer to assist him to effect an arrest or to prevent an escape from custody is justified in using reasonable and appropriate physical force when and to the extent that he reasonably believes that force to be necessary to carry out the peace officer's direction, unless he knows that the arrest or prospective arrest is not authorized.

(6) A person who has been directed to assist a peace officer under circumstances specified in subsection (5) of this section may use deadly physical force to effect an arrest or to prevent an escape only when:

(a) He reasonably believes that force to be necessary to defend himself or a third person from what he reasonably believes to be the use or imminent use of deadly physical force; or

(b) He is directed or authorized by the peace officer to use deadly physical force and does not know, if that happens to be the case, that the peace officer himself is not authorized to use deadly physical force under the circumstances.

(7) A private person acting on his own account is justified in using reasonable and appropriate physical force upon another person when and to the extent that he reasonably believes it necessary to effect an arrest, or to prevent the escape from custody of an arrested person who has committed an offense in his presence; but he is justified in using deadly physical force for the purpose only when he reasonably believes it necessary to defend himself or a third person from what he reasonably believes to be the use or imminent use of deadly physical force.

(8) A guard or peace officer employed in a detention facility is justified:

(a) In using deadly physical force when he reasonably believes it necessary to prevent the escape of a prisoner convicted of, charged with, or held for a felony or confined under the maximum security rules of any detention facility as such facility is defined in subsection (9) of this section;

(b) In using reasonable and appropriate physical force, but not deadly physical force, in all other circumstances when and to the extent that he reasonably believes it necessary to prevent what he reasonably believes to be the escape of a prisoner from a detention facility.

(9) "Detention facility" as used in subsection (8) of this section means any place maintained for the confinement, pursuant to law, of persons charged with or convicted of an offense, held pursuant to the "Colorado Children's Code",[1] held for extradition, or otherwise confined pursuant to an order of a court.

Colorado Revised Statutes, Title 18, Article 1, Part 9
DEFINITIONS

Colorado Revised Statutes § 18-1-901

(1) Definitions set forth in any section of this title apply wherever the same term is used in the same sense in another section of this title unless the definition is specifically limited or the context indicates that it is inapplicable.

(2) The terms defined in section 18-1-104 and in section 18-1-501, as well as the terms defined in subsection (3) of this section, are terms which appear in various articles of this code. Other terms which need definition but which are used only in a limited number of sections of this code are defined in the particular section or article in which the terms appear.

(3)

(a) "To aid" or "to assist" includes knowingly to give or lend money or extend credit to be used for, or to make possible or available, or to further the activity thus aided or assisted.

(b) "Benefit" means any gain or advantage to the beneficiary including any gain or advantage to another person pursuant to the desire or consent of the beneficiary.

(c) "Bodily injury" means physical pain, illness, or any impairment of physical or mental condition.

(d) "Deadly physical force" means force, the intended, natural, and probable consequence of which is to produce death, and which does, in fact, produce death.

(e) "Deadly weapon" means:

(I) A firearm, whether loaded or unloaded; or
(II) A knife, bludgeon, or any other weapon, device, instrument, material, or substance, whether animate or inanimate, that, in the manner it is used or intended to be used, is capable of producing death or serious bodily injury.

(III), (IV) Deleted by Laws 2013, Ch. 39, § 1, eff. March 15, 2013.

(f) "Deface" means to alter the appearance of something by removing, distorting, adding to, or covering all or a part of the thing.

(g) "Dwelling" means a building which is used, intended to be used, or usually used by a person for habitation.

(h) "Firearm" means any handgun, automatic, revolver, pistol, rifle, shotgun, or other instrument or device capable or intended to be capable of discharging bullets, cartridges, or other explosive charges.

(i) "Government" includes the United States, any state, county, municipality, or other political unit, any branch, department, agency, or subdivision of any of the foregoing, and any corporation or other entity established by law to carry out any governmental function.

(j) "Governmental function" includes any activity which a public servant is legally authorized to undertake on behalf of government.

(k) "Motor vehicle" includes any self-propelled device by which persons or property may be moved, carried, or transported from one place to another by land, water, or air, except devices operated on rails, tracks, or cables fixed to the ground or supported by pylons, towers, or other structures.

(l) Repealed by Laws 2003, Ch. 242, § 1, eff. Aug. 6, 2003.

(m) "Pecuniary benefit" means benefit in the form of money, property, commercial interests, or anything else, the primary significance of which is economic gain.

(n) "Public place" means a place to which the public or a substantial number of the public has access, and includes but is not limited to highways, transportation facilities, schools, places of amusement, parks, playgrounds, and the common areas of public and private buildings and facilities.

(o) "Public servant" means any officer or employee of government, whether elected or appointed, and any person participating as an advisor, consultant, process server, or otherwise in performing a governmental function, but the term does not include witnesses.

(o.5) "Restorative justice practices" means practices that emphasize repairing the harm caused to victims and the community by offenses. Restorative justice practices include victim-offender conferences, family group conferences, circles, community conferences, and other similar victim-centered practices. Restorative justice practices are facilitated meetings attended voluntarily by the victim or victim's representatives, the victim's supporters, the offender, and the offender's supporters and may include community members. By engaging the parties to the offense in voluntary dialogue, restorative justice practices provide an opportunity for the offender to accept responsibility for the harm caused to the victim and community, promote victim healing, and enable the participants to agree on consequences to repair the harm, to the extent possible, including but not limited to apologies, community service, reparation, restoration, and counseling. Restorative justice practices may be used in addition to any other conditions, consequences, or sentence imposed by the court.

(p) "Serious bodily injury" means bodily injury which, either at the time of the actual injury or at a later time, involves a substantial risk of death, a substantial risk of serious permanent disfigurement, a substantial risk of protracted loss or impairment of the function of any part or organ of the body, or breaks, fractures, or burns of the second or third degree.

(q) "Tamper" means to interfere with something improperly, to meddle with it, or to make unwarranted alterations in its condition.

(r) "Thing of value" includes real property, tangible and intangible personal property, contract rights, choses in action, services, confidential information, medical records information, and any rights of use or enjoyment connected therewith.

(s) "Utility" means an enterprise which provides gas, sewer, electric, steam, water, transportation, or communication services, and includes any carrier, pipeline, transmitter, or source, whether publicly or privately owned or operated.

Colorado Revised Statutes, Title 18, Article 3, Part 2
ASSAULTS

Colorado Revised Statutes § 18-3-202
ASSAULT IN THE FIRST DEGREE

(1) A person commits the crime of assault in the first degree if:

(a) With intent to cause serious bodily injury to another person, he causes serious bodily injury to any person by means of a deadly weapon; or

(b) With intent to disfigure another person seriously and permanently, or to destroy, amputate, or disable permanently a member or organ of his body, he causes such an injury to any person; or

(c) Under circumstances manifesting extreme indifference to the value of human life, he knowingly engages in conduct which creates a grave risk of death to another person, and thereby causes serious bodily injury to any person; or

(d) Repealed by Laws 1995, H.B.95-1070, § 6, eff. July 1, 1995.

(e) With intent to cause serious bodily injury upon the person of a peace officer, firefighter, or emergency medical service provider, he or she threatens with a deadly weapon a peace officer, firefighter, or emergency medical service provider engaged in the performance of his or her duties, and the offender knows or reasonably should know that the victim is a peace officer, firefighter, or emergency medical service provider acting in the performance of his or her duties; or (e.5) With intent to cause serious bodily injury upon the person of a judge of a court of competent jurisdiction or an officer of said court, he threatens with a deadly weapon a judge of a court of competent jurisdiction or an officer of said court, and the offender knows or reasonably should know that the victim is a judge of a court of competent jurisdiction or an officer of said court; or

(f) While lawfully confined or in custody as a result of being charged with or convicted of a crime or as a result of being charged as a delinquent child or adjudicated as a delinquent child and with intent to cause serious bodily injury to a person employed by or under contract with a detention facility, as defined in section 18-8-203(3), or to a person employed by the division in the department of human services responsible for youth services and who is a youth services counselor or is in the youth services worker classification series, he or she threatens with a deadly weapon such a person engaged in the performance of his or her duties and the offender knows or reasonably should know that the victim is such a person engaged in the performance of his or her duties while employed by or under contract with a detention facility or while employed by the division in the department of human services responsible for youth services. A sentence imposed pursuant to this paragraph (f) shall be served in the department of corrections and shall run consecutively with any sentences being served by the offender. A person who participates in a work release program, a furlough, or any other similar authorized supervised or unsupervised absence from a detention facility, as defined in section 18-8-203(3), and who is required to report back to the detention facility at a specified time shall be deemed to be in custody.

(2)

(a) If assault in the first degree is committed under circumstances where the act causing the injury is performed upon a sudden heat of passion, caused by a serious and highly provoking act of the intended victim, affecting the person causing the injury sufficiently to excite an irresistible passion in a reasonable person, and without an interval between the provocation and the injury sufficient for the voice of reason and humanity to be heard, it is a class 5 felony.

(b) If assault in the first degree is committed without the circumstances provided in paragraph (a) of this subsection (2), it is a class 3 felony.

(c) If a defendant is convicted of assault in the first degree pursuant to subsection (1) of this section, the court shall sentence the defendant in accordance with the provisions of section 18-1.3-406.

(3)

(a) The court shall order any adult or juvenile who is bound over for trial for an offense described in subsection (1) of this section subsequent to a preliminary hearing or after having waived the right to a preliminary hearing, or any person who is indicted for or is convicted of any such offense, to submit to a medical test for communicable diseases and to supply blood, feces, urine, saliva, or other bodily fluid required for the test if the person's blood, seminal fluid, urine, feces, saliva, mucus, or vomit came into contact with any victim of the assault, peace officer, firefighter, emergency medical care provider, or emergency medical service provider. Within ten days after receipt of the medical test results, the defendant shall report the results to the court or the court's designee, who shall then disclose the results to any victim, peace officer, firefighter, emergency medical care provider, or emergency medical service provider who came into contact with the substance and requests such disclosure. Review and disclosure of medical test results by the court must be closed and confidential, and any transaction records relating thereto are also closed and confidential. If a person subject to a medical test for communicable diseases pursuant to this paragraph (a) voluntarily submits to a medical test for communicable diseases, the fact of such person's voluntary submission is admissible in mitigation of sentence if the person is convicted of the charged offense.

(b) In addition to any other penalty provided by law, the court may order any person who is convicted of the offense described in subsection (1) of this section to meet all or any portion of the financial obligations of medical tests performed on and treatment prescribed for the victim, peace officer, firefighter, emergency medical care provider, or emergency medical service provider.

(c) Any person who receives the results of a medical test pursuant to this section shall not publicly disclose the results.

Colorado Revised Statutes § 18-3-203
ASSAULT IN THE SECOND DEGREE

(1) A person commits the crime of assault in the second degree if:

(a) Repealed by Laws 1994, H.B.94-1126, § 8, eff. July 1, 1994.

(b) With intent to cause bodily injury to another person, he or she causes such injury to any person by means of a deadly weapon; or

(c) With intent to prevent one whom he or she knows, or should know, to be a peace officer, firefighter, emergency medical care provider, or emergency medical service provider from performing a lawful duty, he or she intentionally causes bodily injury to any person; or (c.5) With intent to prevent one whom he or she knows, or should know, to be a peace officer, firefighter, or emergency medical service provider from performing a lawful duty, he or she intentionally causes serious bodily injury to any person; or

(d) He recklessly causes serious bodily injury to another person by means of a deadly weapon; or

(e) For a purpose other than lawful medical or therapeutic treatment, he intentionally causes stupor, unconsciousness, or other physical or mental impairment or injury to another person by administering to him, without his consent, a drug, substance, or preparation capable of producing the intended harm; or

(f) While lawfully confined or in custody, he or she knowingly and violently applies physical force against the person of a peace officer, firefighter, or emergency medical service provider engaged in the performance of his or her duties, or a judge of a court of competent jurisdiction, or an officer of said court, or, while lawfully confined or in custody as a result of being charged with or convicted of a crime or as a result of being charged as a delinquent child or adjudicated as a delinquent child, he or she knowingly and violently applies physical force against a person engaged in the performance of his or her duties while employed by or under contract with a detention facility, as defined in section 18-8-203(3), or while employed by the division in the department of human services responsible for youth services and who is a youth services counselor or is in the youth services worker classification series, and the person committing the offense knows or reasonably should know that the victim is a peace officer, firefighter, or emergency medical service provider engaged in the performance of his or her duties, or a judge of a court of competent jurisdiction, or an officer of said court, or a person engaged in the performance of his or her duties while employed by or under contract with a detention facility or while employed by the division in the department of human services responsible for youth services. A sentence imposed pursuant to this paragraph (f) shall be served in the department of corrections and shall run consecutively with any sentences being served by the offender; except that, if the offense is committed against a person employed by the division in the department of human services responsible for youth services, the court may grant probation or a suspended sentence in whole or in part, and the sentence may run concurrently or consecutively with any sentences being served. A person who participates in a work release program, a furlough, or any other similar authorized supervised or unsupervised absence from a detention facility, as defined in section 18-8-203(3), and who is required to report back to the detention facility at a specified time is deemed to be in custody.

(f.5)
(I) While lawfully confined in a detention facility within this state, a person with intent to infect, injure, harm, harass, annoy, threaten, or alarm a person in a detention facility whom the actor knows or reasonably should know to be an employee of a detention facility, causes such employee to come into contact with blood, seminal fluid, urine, feces, saliva, mucus, vomit, or any toxic, caustic, or hazardous material by any means, including but not limited to throwing, tossing, or expelling such fluid or material.

(II) Repealed by Laws 2015, Ch. 109, § 1, eff. July 1, 2015.

(III)
    (A) As used in this paragraph (f.5), "detention facility" means any building, structure, enclosure, vehicle, institution, or place, whether permanent or temporary, fixed or mobile, where persons are or may be lawfully held in custody or confinement

under the authority of the state of Colorado or any political subdivision of the state of Colorado.

(B) As used in this paragraph (f.5), "employee of a detention facility" includes employees of the department of corrections, employees of any agency or person operating a detention facility, law enforcement personnel, and any other persons who are present in or in the vicinity of a detention facility and are performing services for a detention facility. "Employee of a detention facility" does not include a person lawfully confined in a detention facility.

(g) With intent to cause bodily injury to another person, he or she causes serious bodily injury to that person or another; or

(h) With intent to infect, injure, or harm another person whom the actor knows or reasonably should know to be engaged in the performance of his or her duties as a peace officer, a firefighter, an emergency medical care provider, or an emergency medical service provider, he or she causes such person to come into contact with blood, seminal fluid, urine, feces, saliva, mucus, vomit, or any toxic, caustic, or hazardous material by any means, including by throwing, tossing, or expelling such fluid or material.

(2)

(a) If assault in the second degree is committed under circumstances where the act causing the injury is performed upon a sudden heat of passion, caused by a serious and highly provoking act of the intended victim, affecting the person causing the injury sufficiently to excite an irresistible passion in a reasonable person, and without an interval between the provocation and the injury sufficient for the voice of reason and humanity to be heard, it is a class 6 felony.

(b) If assault in the second degree is committed without the circumstances provided in paragraph (a) of this subsection (2), it is a class 4 felony.

(b.5) Assault in the second degree by any person under subsection (1) of this section without the circumstances provided in paragraph (a) of this subsection (2) is a class 3 felony if the person who is assaulted, other than a participant in the crime, suffered serious bodily injury during the commission or attempted commission of or flight from the commission or attempted commission of murder, robbery, arson, burglary, escape, kidnapping in the first degree, sexual assault, sexual assault in the first or second degree as such offenses existed prior to July 1, 2000, or class 3 felony sexual assault on a child.

(c)

(I) If a defendant is convicted of assault in the second degree pursuant to paragraph (b), (c.5), (d), or (g) of subsection (1) of this section or paragraph (b.5) of this subsection (2), except with respect to sexual assault or sexual assault in the first degree as it existed prior to July 1, 2000, the court shall sentence the defendant in accordance with the provisions of section 18-1.3-406. A defendant convicted of assault in the second degree pursuant to paragraph (b.5) of this subsection (2) with respect to sexual assault or sexual assault in the first degree as it existed prior to July 1, 2000, shall be sentenced in accordance with section 18-1.3-401(8)(e) or (8)(e.5).

(II) If a defendant is convicted of assault in the second degree pursuant to paragraph (c) of subsection (1) of this section, the court shall sentence the offender in accordance with section 18-1.3-406; except that, notwithstanding the provisions of section 18-1.3-406, the court is not required to sentence the defendant to the department of corrections for a mandatory term of incarceration.

(3)

(a) The court shall order any adult or juvenile who is bound over for trial for an offense described in subsection (1) of this section subsequent to a preliminary hearing or after having waived the right to a preliminary hearing, any person who is indicted for or is convicted of any such offense, or any person who is determined to have provided blood, seminal fluid, urine, feces, saliva, mucus, or vomit to a person bound over for trial for, indicted for, or convicted of such an offense to submit to a medical test for communicable diseases and to supply blood, feces, urine, saliva, or other bodily fluid required for the test if the person's blood, seminal fluid, urine, feces, saliva, mucus, or vomit came into contact with any victim of the assault, peace officer, firefighter, emergency medical care provider, or emergency medical service provider. Within ten days after receipt of the medical test results, the defendant shall report the results to the court or the court's designee, who shall then disclose the results to any victim, peace officer, firefighter, emergency medical care provider, or emergency medical service provider who came into contact with the substance and requests such disclosure. Review and disclosure of medical test results by the court must be closed and confidential, and any related transaction records are also closed and confidential. If a person subject to a medical test for communicable diseases pursuant to this paragraph (a) voluntarily submits to a medical test for communicable diseases, the fact of such person's voluntary submission is admissible in mitigation of sentence if the person is convicted of the charged offense.

(b) In addition to any other penalty provided by law, the court may order any person who is convicted of the offense described in subsection (1) of this section to meet all or any portion of the financial obligations of medical tests performed on and treatment prescribed for the victim, peace officer, firefighter, emergency medical care provider, or emergency medical service provider.

(c) Any person who receives the results of a medical test pursuant to this section shall not publicly disclose the results.

Colorado Revised Statutes § 18-3-206
MENACING

(1) A person commits the crime of menacing if, by any threat or physical action, he or she knowingly places or attempts to place another person in fear of imminent serious bodily injury. Menacing is a class 3 misdemeanor, but, it is a class 5 felony if committed:

(a) By the use of a deadly weapon or any article used or fashioned in a manner to cause a person to reasonably believe that the article is a deadly weapon; or

(b) By the person representing verbally or otherwise that he or she is armed with a deadly weapon.

Colorado Revised Statutes, Title 18, Article 3, Part 3
KIDNAPPING

Colorado Revised Statutes § 18-3-301
FIRST DEGREE KIDNAPPING

(1) Any person who does any of the following acts with the intent thereby to force the victim or any other person to make any concession or give up anything of value in order to secure a release of a person under the offender's actual or apparent control commits first degree kidnapping:

(a) Forcibly seizes and carries any person from one place to another; or

(b) Entices or persuades any person to go from one place to another; or

(c) Imprisons or forcibly secretes any person.

(2) Whoever commits first degree kidnapping is guilty of a class 1 felony if the person kidnapped shall have suffered bodily injury; but no person convicted of first degree kidnapping shall suffer the death penalty if the person kidnapped was liberated alive prior to the conviction of the kidnapper.

(3) Whoever commits first degree kidnapping commits a class 2 felony if, prior to his conviction, the person kidnapped was liberated unharmed.

Colorado Revised Statutes § 18-3-302
SECOND DEGREE KIDNAPPING

(1) Any person who knowingly seizes and carries any person from one place to another, without his consent and without lawful justification, commits second degree kidnapping.

(2) Any person who takes, entices, or decoys away any child not his own under the age of 18 years with intent to keep or conceal the child from his parent or guardian or with intent to sell, trade, or barter such child for consideration commits second degree kidnapping.

(3) Second degree kidnapping is a class 2 felony if any of the following circumstances exist:

(a) The person kidnapped is a victim of a sexual offense pursuant to part 4 of this article; or

(b) The person kidnapped is a victim of a robbery.

(4)

(a) Unless it is a class 2 felony under subsection (3) of this section, second degree kidnapping is a class 3 felony if any of the following circumstances exist:

(I) The kidnapping is accomplished with intent to sell, trade, or barter the victim for consideration; or

(II) The kidnapping is accomplished by the use of a deadly weapon or any article used or fashioned in a manner to cause a person to reasonably believe that the article is a deadly weapon; or

(III) The kidnapping is accomplished by the perpetrator representing verbally or otherwise that he or she is armed with a deadly weapon.

(b) A defendant convicted of second degree kidnapping committed under any of the circumstances set forth in this subsection (4) shall be sentenced by the court in accordance with the provisions of section 18-1.3-406.

(5) Second degree kidnapping is a class 4 felony, except as provided in subsections (3) and (4) of this section.

Colorado Revised Statutes, Title 18, Article 3, Part 4
UNLAWFUL SEXUAL BEHAVIOR

Colorado Revised Statutes § 18-3-402
SEXUAL ASSAULT

(1) Any actor who knowingly inflicts sexual intrusion or sexual penetration on a victim commits sexual assault if:

(a) The actor causes submission of the victim by means of sufficient consequence reasonably calculated to cause submission against the victim's will; or

(b) The actor knows that the victim is incapable of appraising the nature of the victim's conduct; or

(c) The actor knows that the victim submits erroneously, believing the actor to be the victim's spouse; or

(d) At the time of the commission of the act, the victim is less than fifteen years of age and the actor is at least four years older than the victim and is not the spouse of the victim; or

(e) At the time of the commission of the act, the victim is at least fifteen years of age but less than seventeen years of age and the actor is at least ten years older than the victim and is not the spouse of the victim; or

(f) The victim is in custody of law or detained in a hospital or other institution and the actor has supervisory or disciplinary authority over the victim and uses this position of authority to coerce the victim to submit, unless the act is incident to a lawful search; or

(g) The actor, while purporting to offer a medical service, engages in treatment or examination of a victim for other than a bona fide medical purpose or in a manner substantially inconsistent with reasonable medical practices; or

(h) The victim is physically helpless and the actor knows the victim is physically helpless and the victim has not consented.

(2) Sexual assault is a class 4 felony, except as provided in subsections (3), (3.5), (4), and (5) of this section.

(3) If committed under the circumstances of paragraph (e) of subsection (1) of this section, sexual assault is a class 1 misdemeanor and is an extraordinary risk crime that is subject to the modified sentencing range specified in section 18-1.3-501(3).

(3.5) Sexual assault is a class 3 felony if committed under the circumstances described in paragraph (h) of subsection (1) of this section.

(4) Sexual assault is a class 3 felony if it is attended by any one or more of the following circumstances:

(a) The actor causes submission of the victim through the actual application of physical force or physical violence; or

(b) The actor causes submission of the victim by threat of imminent death, serious bodily injury, extreme pain, or kidnapping, to be inflicted on anyone, and the victim believes that the actor has the present ability to execute these threats; or

(c) The actor causes submission of the victim by threatening to retaliate in the future against the victim, or any other person, and the victim reasonably believes that the actor will execute this threat. As used in this paragraph (c), "to retaliate" includes threats of kidnapping, death, serious bodily injury, or extreme pain; or

(d) The actor has substantially impaired the victim's power to appraise or control the victim's conduct by employing, without the victim's consent, any drug, intoxicant, or other means for the purpose of causing submission.

(5)

(a) Sexual assault is a class 2 felony if any one or more of the following circumstances exist:

(I) In the commission of the sexual assault, the actor is physically aided or abetted by one or more other persons; or

(II) The victim suffers serious bodily injury; or

(III) The actor is armed with a deadly weapon or an article used or fashioned in a manner to cause a person to reasonably believe that the article is a deadly weapon or represents verbally or otherwise that the actor is armed with a deadly weapon and uses the deadly weapon, article, or representation to cause submission of the victim.

(b)

(I) If a defendant is convicted of sexual assault pursuant to this subsection (5), the court shall sentence the defendant in accordance with section 18-1.3-401(8)(e). A person convicted solely of sexual assault pursuant to this subsection (5) shall not be sentenced under the crime of violence provisions of section 18-1.3-406(2). Any sentence for a conviction under this subsection (5) shall be consecutive to any sentence for a conviction for a crime of violence under section 18-1.3-406.

(II) The provisions of this paragraph (b) shall apply to offenses committed prior to November 1, 1998.

(6) Any person convicted of felony sexual assault committed on or after November 1, 1998, under any of the circumstances described in this section shall be sentenced in accordance with the provisions of part 10 of Article 1.3 of this title.

(7) A person who is convicted on or after July 1, 2013, of a sexual assault under this section, upon conviction, shall be advised by the court that the person has no right:

(a) To notification of the termination of parental rights and no standing to object to the termination of parental rights for a child conceived as a result of the commission of that offense;

(b) To allocation of parental responsibilities, including parenting time and decision-making responsibilities for a child conceived as a result of the commission of that offense;

(c) Of inheritance from a child conceived as a result of the commission of that offense; and

(d) To notification of or the right to object to the adoption of a child conceived as a result of the commission of that offense.

Colorado Revised Statutes, Title 18, Article 4, Part 1
ARSON

Colorado Revised Statutes § 18-4-102
FIRST DEGREE ARSON

(1) A person who knowingly sets fire to, burns, causes to be burned, or by the use of any explosive damages or destroys, or causes to be damaged or destroyed, any building or occupied structure of another without his consent commits first degree arson.

(2) First degree arson is a class 3 felony.

(3) A defendant convicted of committing first degree arson by the use of any explosive shall be sentenced by the court in accordance with the provisions of section 18-1.3-406.

Colorado Revised Statutes, Title 18, Article 4, Part 2
BURGLARY AND RELATED OFFENSES

Colorado Revised Statutes § 18-4-202
FIRST DEGREE BURGLARY

(1) A person commits first degree burglary if the person knowingly enters unlawfully, or remains unlawfully after a lawful

or unlawful entry, in a building or occupied structure with intent to commit therein a crime, other than trespass as defined in this article, against another person or property, and if in effecting entry or while in the building or occupied structure or in immediate flight therefrom, the person or another participant in the crime assaults or menaces any person, the person or another participant is armed with explosives, or the person or another participant uses a deadly weapon or possesses and threatens the use of a deadly weapon.

(2) First degree burglary is a class 3 felony.

(3) If under the circumstances stated in subsection (1) of this section the property involved is a controlled substance, as defined in section 18-18-102(5), within a pharmacy or other place having lawful possession thereof, such person commits first degree burglary of controlled substances, which is a class 2 felony.

Colorado Revised Statutes § 18-4-203
SECOND DEGREE BURGLARY

(1) A person commits second degree burglary, if the person knowingly breaks an entrance into, enters unlawfully in, or remains unlawfully after a lawful or unlawful entry in a building or occupied structure with intent to commit therein a crime against another person or property.

(2) Second degree burglary is a class 4 felony, but it is a class 3 felony if:

(a) It is a burglary of a dwelling; or

(b) It is a burglary, the objective of which is the theft of a controlled substance, as defined in section 18-18-102(5), lawfully kept within any building or occupied structure.

Colorado Revised Statutes § 18-4-204
THIRD DEGREE BURGLARY

(1) A person commits third degree burglary if with intent to commit a crime he enters or breaks into any vault, safe, cash register, coin vending machine, product dispenser, money depository, safety deposit box, coin telephone, coin box, or other apparatus or equipment whether or not coin operated.

(2) Third degree burglary is a class 5 felony, but it is a class 4 felony if it is a burglary, the objective of which is the theft of a controlled substance, as defined in section 18-18-102(5), lawfully kept in or upon the property burglarized.

Colorado Revised Statutes, Title 18, Article 4, Part 3
ROBBERY

Colorado Revised Statutes § 18-4-301
ROBBERY
(1) A person who knowingly takes anything of value from the person or presence of another by the use of force, threats, or intimidation commits robbery.

(2) Robbery is a class 4 felony.

Colorado Revised Statutes § 18-4-302
AGGRAVATED ROBBERY

(1) A person who commits robbery is guilty of aggravated robbery if during the act of robbery or immediate flight therefrom:

(a) He is armed with a deadly weapon with intent, if resisted, to kill, maim, or wound the person robbed or any other person; or

(b) He knowingly wounds or strikes the person robbed or any other person with a deadly weapon or by the use of force, threats, or intimidation with a deadly weapon knowingly puts the person robbed or any other person in reasonable fear of death or bodily injury; or

(c) He has present a confederate, aiding or abetting the perpetration of the robbery, armed with a deadly weapon, with the intent, either on the part of the defendant or confederate, if resistance is offered, to kill, maim, or wound the person robbed or any other person, or by the use of force, threats, or intimidation puts the person robbed or any other person in reasonable fear of death or bodily injury; or

(d) He possesses any article used or fashioned in a manner to lead any person who is present reasonably to believe it to be a deadly weapon or represents verbally or otherwise that he is then and there so armed.

(2) Repealed by Laws 1989, S.B.246, § 156.
(3) Aggravated robbery is a class 3 felony and is an extraordinary risk crime that is subject to the modified presumptive sentencing range specified in section 18-1.3-401(10).

(4) If a defendant is convicted of aggravated robbery pursuant to paragraph (b) of subsection (1) of this section, the court shall sentence the defendant in accordance with the provisions of section 18-1.3-406.

Colorado Revised Statutes, Title 18, Article 4, Part 4
THEFT

Colorado Revised Statutes § 18-4-401
THEFT

(1) A person commits theft when he or she knowingly obtains, retains, or exercises control over anything of value of another without authorization or by threat or deception; or receives, loans money by pawn or pledge on, or disposes of anything of

value or belonging to another that he or she knows or believes to have been stolen, and:

(a) Intends to deprive the other person permanently of the use or benefit of the thing of value;

(b) Knowingly uses, conceals, or abandons the thing of value in such manner as to deprive the other person permanently of its use or benefit;

(c) Uses, conceals, or abandons the thing of value intending that such use, concealment, or abandonment will deprive the other person permanently of its use or benefit;

(d) Demands any consideration to which he or she is not legally entitled as a condition of restoring the thing of value to the other person; or

(e) Knowingly retains the thing of value more than 72 hours after the agreed-upon time of return in any lease or hire agreement.

(1.5) For the purposes of this section, a thing of value is that of "another" if anyone other than the defendant has a possessory or proprietary interest therein.

(2) Theft is:

(a) Deleted by Laws 2007, Ch. 384, § 3, eff. July 1, 2007.

(b) A class 1 petty offense if the value of the thing involved is less than fifty dollars;

(b.5) Repealed by Laws 2013, Ch. 373, § 1, eff. June 5, 2013.

(c) A class 3 misdemeanor if the value of the thing involved is fifty dollars or more but less than three hundred dollars;

(d) A class 2 misdemeanor if the value of the thing involved is three hundred dollars or more but less than seven hundred fifty dollars;

(e) A class 1 misdemeanor if the value of the thing involved is seven hundred fifty dollars or more but less than two thousand dollars;

(f) A class 6 felony if the value of the thing involved is two thousand dollars or more but less than five thousand dollars;

(g) A class 5 felony if the value of the thing involved is five thousand dollars or more but less than twenty thousand dollars;

(h) A class 4 felony if the value of the thing involved is twenty thousand dollars or more but less than one hundred thousand dollars;

(i) A class 3 felony if the value of the thing involved is one hundred thousand dollars or more but less than one million dollars; and

(j) A class 2 felony if the value of the thing involved is one million dollars or more.

(3), (3.1) Repealed by Laws 1977, H.B.1574, § 9.

(4)

(a) When a person commits theft twice or more within a period of six months, two or more of the thefts may be aggregated and charged in a single count, in which event the thefts so aggregated and charged shall constitute a single offense, the penalty for which shall be based on the aggregate value of the things involved, pursuant to subsection (2) of this section.

(b) When a person commits theft twice or more against the same person pursuant to one scheme or course of conduct, the thefts may be aggregated and charged in a single count, in which event they shall constitute a single offense, the penalty for which shall be based on the aggregate value of the things involved, pursuant to subsection (2) of this section.

(5) Theft from the person of another by means other than the use of force, threat, or intimidation is a class 5 felony without regard to the value of the thing taken.

(6) In every indictment or information charging a violation of this section, it shall be sufficient to allege that, on or about a day certain, the defendant committed the crime of theft by unlawfully taking a thing or things of value of a person or persons named in the indictment or information. The prosecuting attorney shall at the request of the defendant provide a bill of particulars.

(7) Repealed by Laws 1993, H.B.93-1088, § 42, eff. July 1, 1993.

(8) A municipality shall have concurrent power to prohibit theft, by ordinance, where the value of the thing involved is less than one thousand dollars.

(9)

(a) If a person is convicted of or pleads guilty or nolo contendere to theft by deception and the underlying factual basis of the case involves the mortgage lending process, a minimum fine of the amount of pecuniary harm resulting from the theft shall be mandatory, in addition to any other penalty the court may impose.

(b) A court shall not accept a plea of guilty or nolo contendere to another offense from a person charged with a violation of this section that involves the mortgage lending process unless the plea agreement contains an order of restitution in accordance with part 6 of Article 1.3 of this title that compensates the victim for any costs to the victim caused by the offense.

(c) The district attorneys and the attorney general have concurrent jurisdiction to investigate and prosecute a violation of this section that involves making false statements or filing or facilitating the use of a document known to contain a false statement or material omission relied upon by another person in the mortgage lending process.

(d) Documents involved in the mortgage lending process include, but are not limited to, uniform residential loan applications or other loan applications; appraisal reports; HUD-1 settlement statements; supporting personal documentation for loan applications such as W-2 forms, verifications of income and employment, bank statements, tax returns, and payroll stubs; and any required disclosures.

(e) For the purposes of this subsection (9):

(I) "Mortgage lending process" means the process through which a person seeks or obtains a residential mortgage loan, including, without limitation, solicitation, application, or origination; negotiation of terms; third-party provider services; underwriting; signing and closing; funding of the loan; and perfecting and releasing the mortgage.

(II) "Residential mortgage loan" means a loan or agreement to extend credit, made to a person and secured by a mortgage or lien on residential real property, including, but not limited to, the refinancing or renewal of a loan secured by residential real property.

(III) "Residential real property" means real property used as a residence and containing no more than four families housed separately.

Colorado Revised Statutes § 18-4-407
QUESTIONING OF PERSON SUSPECTED OF THEFT WITHOUT LIABILITY (SHOPKEEPER'S PRIVILEGE)

If any person triggers an alarm or a theft detection device as defined in section 18-4-417(2) or conceals upon his person or otherwise carries away any unpurchased goods, wares, or merchandise held or owned by any store or mercantile establishment, the merchant or any employee thereof or any peace officer, acting in good faith and upon probable cause based upon reasonable grounds therefor, may detain and question such person, in a reasonable manner for the purpose of ascertaining whether the person is guilty of theft. Such questioning of a person by a merchant, merchant's employee, or peace or police officer does not render the merchant, merchant's employee, or peace officer civilly or criminally liable for slander, false arrest, false imprisonment, malicious prosecution, or unlawful detention.

Colorado Revised Statutes, Title 18, Article 4, Part 5
TRESPASS, TAMPERING, AND CRIMINAL MISCHIEF

Colorado Revised Statutes § 18-4-501
CRIMINAL MISCHIEF

(1)   A person commits criminal mischief when he or she knowingly damages the real or personal property of one or more other persons, including property owned by the person jointly with another person or property owned by the person in which another person has a possessory or proprietary interest, in the course of a single criminal episode.

(2) Repealed by Laws 2009, Ch. 347, § 1, eff. Aug. 5, 2009.

(3) Repealed by Laws 2009, Ch. 347, § 1, eff. Aug. 5, 2009.

(4) Criminal mischief is:

(a) A class 3 misdemeanor when the aggregate damage to the real or personal property is less than three hundred dollars;

(b) A class 2 misdemeanor when the aggregate damage to the real or personal property is three hundred dollars or more but less than seven hundred fifty dollars;

(c) A class 1 misdemeanor when the aggregate damage to the real or personal property is seven hundred fifty dollars or more but less than one thousand dollars;

(d) A class 6 felony when the aggregate damage to the real or personal property is one thousand dollars or more but less than five thousand dollars;

(e) A class 5 felony when the aggregate damage to the real or personal property is five thousand dollars or more but less than twenty thousand dollars;

(f) A class 4 felony when the aggregate damage to the real or personal property is twenty thousand dollars or more but less than one hundred thousand dollars;

(g) A class 3 felony when the aggregate damage to the real or personal property is one hundred thousand dollars or more but less than one million dollars; and

(h) A class 2 felony when the aggregate damage to the real or personal property is one million dollars or more.

Colorado Revised Statutes § 18-4-502
FIRST DEGREE CRIMINAL TRESPASS

A person commits the crime of first degree criminal trespass if such person knowingly and unlawfully enters or remains in a dwelling of another or if such person enters any motor vehicle with intent to commit a crime therein. First degree criminal trespass is a class 5 felony.

Colorado Revised Statutes § 18-4-503
SECOND DEGREE CRIMINAL TRESPASS

(1) A person commits the crime of second degree criminal trespass if such person:

(a) Unlawfully enters or remains in or upon the premises of another which are enclosed in a manner designed to exclude intruders or are fenced; or

(b) Knowingly and unlawfully enters or remains in or upon the common areas of a hotel, motel, condominium, or apartment building; or

(c) Knowingly and unlawfully enters or remains in a motor vehicle of another.

(2) Second degree criminal trespass is a class 3 misdemeanor, but:

(a) It is a class 2 misdemeanor if the premises have been classified by the county assessor for the county in which the land is situated as agricultural land pursuant to section 39-1-102(1.6), C.R.S.; and

(b) It is a class 4 felony if the person trespasses on premises so classified as agricultural land with the intent to commit a felony thereon.

(3) Whenever a person is convicted of, pleads guilty or nolo contendere to, receives a deferred judgment or sentence for, or is adjudicated a juvenile delinquent for, a violation of paragraph (c) of subsection (1) of this section, the offender's driver's license shall be revoked as provided in section 42-2-125, C.R.S.

Colorado Revised Statutes § 18-4-504
THIRD DEGREE CRIMINAL TRESPASS

(1) A person commits the crime of third degree criminal trespass if such person unlawfully enters or remains in or upon premises of another.

(2) Third degree criminal trespass is a class 1 petty offense, but:

(a) It is a class 3 misdemeanor if the premises have been classified by the county assessor for the county in which the land is situated as agricultural land pursuant to section 39-1-102(1.6), C.R.S.; and

(b) It is a class 5 felony if the person trespasses on premises so classified as agricultural land with the intent to commit a felony thereon.

Colorado Revised Statutes § 18-4-506
SECOND DEGREE CRIMINAL TAMPERING

Except as provided in sections 18-4-506.3 and 18-4-506.5, a person commits the crime of second degree criminal tampering if he tampers with property of another with intent to cause injury, inconvenience, or annoyance to that person or to another or if he knowingly makes an unauthorized connection with property of a utility. Second degree criminal tampering is a class 2 misdemeanor.

Colorado Revised Statutes, Title 18, Article 6, Part 8
DOMESTIC VIOLENCE

Colorado Revised Statutes § 18-6-800.3
DEFINITIONS

As used in this part 8, unless the context otherwise requires:

(1) "Domestic violence" means an act or threatened act of violence upon a person with whom the actor is or has been involved in an intimate relationship. "Domestic violence" also includes any other crime against a person, or against property, including an animal, or any municipal ordinance violation against a person, or against property, including an animal, when used as a method of coercion, control, punishment, intimidation, or revenge directed against a person with whom the actor is or has been involved in an intimate relationship.

(2) "Intimate relationship" means a relationship between spouses, former spouses, past or present unmarried couples, or persons who are both the parents of the same child regardless of whether the persons have been married or have lived together at any time.

Colorado Revised Statutes § 18-6-801
DOMESTIC VIOLENCE -- SENTENCING

(1)

    (a) In addition to any sentence that is imposed upon a person for violation of any criminal law under this title, any person who is convicted of any crime, the underlying factual basis of which has been found by the court on the record to include an act of domestic violence, as defined in section 18-6-800.3(1), or any crime against property, whether or not such crime is a felony, when such crime is used as a method of coercion, control, punishment, intimidation, or revenge directed against a person with whom the actor is or has been involved in an intimate relationship shall be ordered to complete a treatment program and a treatment evaluation that conform with the standards adopted by the domestic violence offender management board as required by section 16-11.8-103(4), C.R.S. If an intake evaluation conducted by an approved treatment program provider discloses that sentencing to a treatment program would be inappropriate, the person shall be referred back to the court for alternative disposition.

(b) The court may order a treatment evaluation to be conducted prior to sentencing if a treatment evaluation would assist the court in determining an appropriate sentence. The person ordered to undergo such evaluation shall be required to pay the cost of the treatment evaluation. If such treatment evaluation recommends treatment, and if the court so finds, the person shall be ordered to complete a treatment program that conforms with the standards adopted by the domestic violence offender management board as required by section 16-11.8-103(4), C.R.S.

(c) Nothing in this subsection (1) shall preclude the court from ordering domestic violence treatment in any appropriate case.

(2) Subsection (1) of this section shall not apply to persons sentenced to the department of corrections.

(3) A person charged with the commission of a crime, the underlying factual basis of which includes an act of domestic violence as defined in section 18-6-800.3(1), shall not be entitled to plead guilty or plead nolo contendere to an offense which does not include the domestic violence designation required in section 16-21-103, C.R.S., unless the prosecuting attorney makes a good faith representation on the record that such attorney would not be able to establish a prima facie case that the person and the alleged victim were currently or formerly involved in an intimate

relationship if the defendant were brought to trial on the original domestic violence offense and upon such a finding by the court. The prosecuting attorney's record and the court's findings shall specify the relationship in the alleged domestic violence case which the prosecuting attorney is not able to prove beyond a reasonable doubt and the reasons therefor. No court shall accept a plea of guilty or nolo contendere to an offense which does not include the domestic violence designation required in section 16-21-103, C.R.S., when the facts of the case indicate that the underlying factual basis includes an act of domestic violence as defined in section 18-6-800.3(1) unless there is a good faith representation by the prosecuting attorney that he or she would be unable to establish a prima facie case if the defendant were brought to trial on the original offense.

(4) No person accused or convicted of a crime, the underlying factual basis of which has been found by the court on the record to include an act of domestic violence, as defined in section 18-6-800.3(1), shall be eligible for home detention in the home of the victim pursuant to section 18-1.3-105 or 18-1.3-106. Nothing in this subsection (4) is intended to prohibit a court from ordering a deferred sentence for a person accused or convicted of a crime, the underlying factual basis of which has been found by the court on the record to include an act of domestic violence, as defined in section 18-6-800.3(1).

(5) Before granting probation, the court shall consider the safety of the victim and the victim's children if probation is granted.

(6) Nothing in this section shall preclude the ability of a municipality to enact concurrent ordinances.

(7) In the event a person is convicted in this state on or after July 1, 2000, of any offense which would otherwise be a misdemeanor, the underlying factual basis of which has been found by the court on the record to include an act of domestic violence as defined in section 18-6-800.3(1), and that person has

been three times previously convicted, upon charges separately brought and tried and arising out of separate and distinct criminal episodes, of a felony or misdemeanor or municipal ordinance violation, the underlying factual basis of which was found by the court on the record to include an act of domestic violence, the prosecuting attorney may petition the court to adjudge the person an habitual domestic violence offender, and such person shall be convicted of a class 5 felony. If the person is adjudged an habitual domestic violence offender, the court shall sentence the person pursuant to the presumptive range set forth in section 18-1.3-401 for a class 5 felony. The former convictions and judgments shall be set forth in apt words in the indictment or information.

(8)

(a) In addition to any sentence that is imposed upon a defendant for violation of any criminal law under this title, if a defendant is convicted of any crime, the underlying factual basis of which is found by the court on the record to be a misdemeanor crime of domestic violence, as defined in 18 U.S.C. sec. 921(a)(33), or that is punishable by a term of imprisonment exceeding one year and includes an act of domestic violence, as defined in section 18-6-800.3(1), the court:

(I) Shall order the defendant to:

(A) Refrain from possessing or purchasing any firearm or ammunition for the duration of the order; and

(B) Relinquish any firearm or ammunition in the defendant's immediate possession or control or subject to the defendant's immediate possession or control; and

(II) May require that before the defendant is released from custody on bond, the defendant shall relinquish, for the duration of the order, any firearm or ammunition in the defendant's immediate possession or control or subject to the defendant's immediate possession or control.

(b) Upon issuance of an order to relinquish one or more firearms or ammunition pursuant to paragraph (a) of this subsection (8), the defendant shall relinquish any firearm or ammunition not more than 24 hours after being served with the order; except that a court may allow a defendant up to 72 hours to relinquish a firearm or up to five days to relinquish ammunition pursuant to this paragraph (b) if the defendant demonstrates to the satisfaction of the court that he or she is unable to comply within 24 hours. To satisfy this requirement, the defendant may:

(I) Sell or transfer possession of the firearm or ammunition to a federally licensed firearms dealer described in 18 U.S.C. sec. 923, as amended; except that this provision shall not be interpreted to require any federally licensed firearms dealer to purchase or accept possession of any firearm or ammunition;

(II) Arrange for the storage of the firearm or ammunition by a law enforcement agency; except that this provision shall not be interpreted to require any law enforcement agency to provide storage of firearms or ammunition for any person; or

(III) Sell or otherwise transfer the firearm or ammunition to a private party who may legally possess the firearm or ammunition; except that a defendant who sells or transfers a firearm pursuant to this subparagraph (III) shall satisfy all of the provisions of section 18-12-112, concerning private firearms transfers, including but not limited to the performance of a criminal background check of the transferee.

(c) If a defendant is unable to satisfy the provisions of paragraph (b) of this subsection (8) because he or she is incarcerated or otherwise held in the custody of a law enforcement agency, the court shall require the defendant to satisfy such provisions not more than 24 hours after his or her release from incarceration or custody or be held in contempt of court. Notwithstanding any provision of this paragraph (c), the court may, in its discretion, require the defendant to relinquish any firearm or ammunition in the defendant's immediate possession or control or subject to the defendant's immediate possession or control before the end of the defendant's incarceration. In such a case, a defendant's failure to relinquish a firearm or ammunition as required shall constitute contempt of court.

(d) A federally licensed firearms dealer who takes possession of a firearm or ammunition pursuant to this subsection (8) shall issue a receipt to the defendant at the time of relinquishment. The federally licensed firearms dealer shall not return the firearm or ammunition to the defendant unless the dealer:

(I) Contacts the bureau to request that a background check of the defendant be performed; and

(II) Obtains approval of the transfer from the bureau after the performance of the background check.

(e) A local law enforcement agency may elect to store firearms or ammunition for persons pursuant to this subsection (8). If an agency so elects:

(I) The agency may charge a fee for such storage, the amount of which shall not exceed the direct and indirect costs incurred by the agency in providing such storage;

(II) The agency may establish policies for disposal of abandoned or stolen firearms or ammunition; and

(III) The agency shall issue a receipt to each defendant at the time the defendant relinquishes possession of a firearm or ammunition.

(f) If a local law enforcement agency elects to store firearms or ammunition for a defendant pursuant to this subsection (8), the law enforcement agency shall not return the firearm or ammunition to the defendant unless the agency:

(I) Contacts the bureau to request that a background check of the defendant be performed; and

(II) Obtains approval of the transfer from the bureau after the performance of the background check.

(g)

(I) A law enforcement agency that elects to store a firearm or ammunition for a defendant pursuant to this subsection (8) may elect to cease storing the firearm or ammunition. A law enforcement agency that elects to cease storing a firearm or ammunition for a defendant shall notify the defendant of such decision and request that the defendant immediately make arrangements for the transfer of the possession of the firearm or ammunition to the defendant or, if the defendant is prohibited from possessing a firearm, to another person who is legally permitted to possess a firearm.

(II) If a law enforcement agency elects to cease storing a firearm or ammunition for a defendant and notifies the defendant as described in subparagraph (I) of this paragraph (g), the law enforcement agency may dispose of the firearm or ammunition if the defendant fails to make arrangements for the transfer of the firearm or ammunition and complete said transfer within ninety days of receiving such notification.

(h) If a defendant sells or otherwise transfers a firearm or ammunition to a private party who may legally possess the firearm or ammunition, as described in subparagraph (III) of paragraph (b) of this subsection (8), the defendant shall acquire:

(I) From the transferee, a written receipt acknowledging the transfer, which receipt shall be dated and signed by the defendant and the transferee; and

(II) From the licensed gun dealer who requests from the bureau a background check of the transferee, as described in section 18-12-112, a written statement of the results of the background check.

(i)

(I) Not more than three business days after the relinquishment, the defendant shall file a copy of the receipt issued pursuant to paragraph (d), (e), or (h) of this subsection (8), and, if applicable, the written statement of the results of a background check performed on the transferee, as described in subparagraph (II) of paragraph (h) of this subsection (8), with the court as proof of the relinquishment. If a defendant fails to timely file a receipt or written statement as described in this paragraph (i):

(A) The failure constitutes a class 2 misdemeanor, and the defendant shall be punished as provided in section 18-1.3-501; and

(B) The court shall issue a warrant for the defendant's arrest.

(II) In any subsequent prosecution for a violation of this paragraph (i), the court shall take judicial notice of the defendant's failure to file a receipt or written statement, which will constitute prima facie evidence that the defendant has violated this paragraph (i), and testimony of the clerk of the court or his or her deputy is not required.

(j)

(I) A law enforcement agency that elects in good faith to not store a firearm or ammunition for a defendant pursuant to sub-subparagraph (B) of subparagraph (III) of paragraph (b) of this subsection (8) shall not be held criminally or civilly liable for such election not to act.

(II) A law enforcement agency that returns possession of a firearm or ammunition to a defendant in good faith as permitted by paragraph (f) of this subsection (8) shall not be held criminally or civilly liable for such action.

Colorado Revised Statutes, Title 18, Article 8, Part 5
PERJURY AND RELATED OFFENSES

Colorado Revised Statutes § 18-8-503
PERJURY IN THE SECOND DEGREE

(1) A person commits perjury in the second degree if, other than in an official proceeding, with an intent to mislead a public servant in the performance of his duty, he makes a materially false statement, which he does not believe to be true, under an oath required or authorized by law.

(2) Perjury in the second degree is a class 1 misdemeanor.

Colorado Revised Statutes, Title 18, Article 9, Part 2
CRUELTY TO ANIMALS

Colorado Revised Statutes § 18-9-202
CRUELTY TO ANIMALS -- AGGRAVATED CRUELTY TO ANIMALS -- CRUELTY TO A SERVICE ANIMAL -- RESTITUTION

(1)

(a) A person commits cruelty to animals if he or she knowingly, recklessly, or with criminal negligence overdrives, overloads, overworks, torments, deprives of necessary sustenance, unnecessarily or cruelly beats, allows to be housed in a manner that results in chronic or repeated serious physical harm, carries or confines in or upon any vehicles in a cruel or reckless manner, engages in a sexual act with an animal, or otherwise mistreats or neglects any animal, or causes or procures it to be done, or, having the charge or custody of any animal, fails to provide it with proper food, drink, or protection from the weather consistent with the species, breed, and type of animal involved, or abandons an animal.

(b) Any person who intentionally abandons a dog or cat commits the offense of cruelty to animals.

(1.5)

(a) A person commits cruelty to animals if he or she recklessly or with criminal negligence tortures, needlessly mutilates, or needlessly kills an animal.

(b) A person commits aggravated cruelty to animals if he or she knowingly tortures, needlessly mutilates, or needlessly kills an animal.

(c) A person commits cruelty to a service animal if he or she violates the provisions of subsection (1) of this section with respect to a service animal as defined in section 18-1.3-602(3.5), whether the service animal is on duty or not on duty.

(1.6) As used in this section, unless the context otherwise requires:

(a) "Serious physical harm" means any of the following:

(I) Any physical harm that carries a substantial risk of death;

(II) Any physical harm that causes permanent maiming or that involves some temporary, substantial maiming; or

(III) Any physical harm that causes acute pain of a duration that results in substantial suffering.

(1.8) A peace officer having authority to act under this section may take possession of and impound an animal that the peace officer has probable cause to believe is a victim of a violation of subsection (1) or (1.5) of this section or is a victim of a violation of section 18-9-204 and as a result of the violation is endangered if it remains with the owner or custodian. If, in the opinion of a licensed veterinarian, an animal impounded pursuant to this subsection (1.8) is experiencing extreme pain or suffering, or is severely injured past recovery, severely disabled past recovery, or severely diseased past recovery, the animal may be euthanized without a court order.

(2)
(a) Except as otherwise provided in paragraph (b) of this subsection (2), cruelty to animals is a class 1 misdemeanor.

(a.5)
(I) Repealed by Laws 2000, Ch. 282, § 2, eff. July 1, 2005.

(II) In addition to any other sentence imposed for a violation of this section, the court may order an offender to complete an anger management treatment program or any other appropriate treatment program.

(III) The court shall order an evaluation to be conducted prior to sentencing to assist the court in determining an appropriate sentence. The person ordered to undergo an evaluation shall be required to pay the cost of the evaluation, unless the person qualifies for a public defender, then the cost will be paid by the judicial district. If the evaluation results in a recommendation of treatment and if the court so finds, the person shall be ordered to complete an anger management treatment program or any other treatment program that the court may deem appropriate.

(IV) Upon successful completion of an anger management treatment program or any other treatment program deemed appropriate by the court, the court may suspend any fine imposed, except for a five hundred dollar mandatory minimum fine which shall be imposed at the time of sentencing.

(V) In addition to any other sentence imposed upon a person for a violation of any criminal law under this title, any person convicted of a second or subsequent conviction for any crime, the underlying factual basis of which has been found by the court to include an act of cruelty to animals, shall be required to pay a mandatory minimum fine of one thousand dollars and shall be required to complete an anger management treatment program or any other appropriate treatment program.

(VI) Nothing in this paragraph (a.5) shall preclude the court from ordering treatment in any appropriate case.

(VII) This paragraph (a.5) does not apply to the treatment of pack or draft animals by negligently overdriving, overloading, or overworking them, or the treatment of livestock and other animals used in the farm or ranch production of food, fiber, or other agricultural products when such treatment is in accordance with accepted agricultural animal husbandry practices, the treatment of animals involved in activities regulated pursuant to article 60 of title 12, C.R.S., the treatment of animals involved in research if such research facility is operating under rules set forth by the state or federal government, the treatment of animals involved in rodeos, the treatment of dogs used for legal hunting activities, wildlife nuisances, or to statutes regulating activities concerning wildlife and predator control in the state, including trapping.

(b)

(I) A second or subsequent conviction under the provisions of paragraph (a) of subsection (1) of this section is a class 6 felony. A plea of nolo contendere accepted by the court shall be considered a conviction for the purposes of this section.

(II) In any case where the court sentences a person convicted of a class 6 felony under the provisions of this paragraph (b) to probation, the court shall, in addition to any other condition of probation imposed, order that:

(A) The offender, pursuant to section 18-1.3-202(1), be committed to the county jail for ninety days; or

(B) The offender, pursuant to section 18-1.3-105(3), be subject to home detention for no fewer than ninety days.

(III) In any case where an offender is committed to the county jail or placed in home detention pursuant to subparagraph (II) of this paragraph (b), the court shall enter judgment against the offender for all costs assessed pursuant to section 18-1.3-701, including, but not limited to, the cost of care.

(c) Aggravated cruelty to animals is a class 6 felony; except that a second or subsequent conviction for the offense of aggravated cruelty to animals is a class 5 felony. A plea of nolo contendere accepted by the court shall be considered a conviction for purposes of this section.

(d) If a person is convicted of cruelty to a service animal pursuant to paragraph (c) of subsection (1.5) of this section, he or she shall be ordered to make restitution to the agency or individual owning the animal for any veterinary bills and replacement costs of the animal if it is disabled or killed as a result of the cruelty to animals incident.

(2.5) It shall be an affirmative defense to a charge brought under this section involving injury or death to a dog that the dog was found running, worrying, or injuring sheep, cattle, or other livestock.

(3) Nothing in this part 2 modifies in any manner the authority of the parks and wildlife commission, as established in title 33, C.R.S., or prohibits any conduct authorized or permitted under title 33, C.R.S.

Colorado Revised Statutes, Title 18, Article 12, Part 1
FIREARMS AND WEAPONS

Colorado Revised Statutes § 18-12-101
DEFINITIONS

(1) As used in this article, unless the context otherwise requires:

(a) "Adult" means any person 18 years of age or older.

(a.3) "Ballistic knife" means any knife that has a blade which is forcefully projected from the handle by means of a spring-loaded device or explosive charge.

(a.5) "Blackjack" includes any billy, sand club, sandbag, or other hand-operated striking weapon consisting, at the striking end, of an encased piece of lead or other heavy substance and, at the handle end, a strap or springy shaft which increases the force of impact.

(b) "Bomb" means any explosive or incendiary device or molotov cocktail as defined in section 9-7-103, C.R.S., or any chemical device which causes or can cause an explosion, which is not specifically designed for lawful and legitimate use in the hands of its possessor.

(b.5) "Bureau" means the Colorado bureau of investigation created in section 24-33.5-401, C.R.S.

(c) "Firearm silencer" means any instrument, attachment, weapon, or appliance for causing the firing of any gun, revolver, pistol, or other firearm to be silent or intended to lessen or muffle the noise of the firing of any such weapon.

(d) "Gas gun" means a device designed for projecting gas-filled projectiles which release their contents after having been projected from the device and includes projectiles designed for use in such a device.

(e) "Gravity knife" means any knife that has a blade released from the handle or sheath thereof by the force of gravity or the application of centrifugal force.

(e.5) "Handgun" means a pistol, revolver, or other firearm of any description, loaded or unloaded, from which any shot, bullet, or other missile can be discharged, the length of the barrel of which, not including any revolving, detachable, or magazine breech, does not exceed twelve inches.

(e.7) "Juvenile" means any person under the age of 18 years.

(f) "Knife" means any dagger, dirk, knife, or stiletto with a blade over three and one-half inches in length, or any other dangerous instrument capable of inflicting cutting, stabbing, or tearing wounds, but does not include a hunting or fishing knife carried for sports use. The issue that a knife is a hunting or fishing knife must be raised as an affirmative defense.

(g) "Machine gun" means any firearm, whatever its size and usual designation, that shoots automatically more than one shot, without manual reloading, by a single function of the trigger.

(h) "Short rifle" means a rifle having a barrel less than sixteen inches long or an overall length of less than twenty-six inches.

(i) "Short shotgun" means a shotgun having a barrel or barrels less than 18 inches long or an overall length of less than twenty-six inches.

(i.5) "Stun gun" means a device capable of temporarily immobilizing a person by the infliction of an electrical charge.

(j) "Switchblade knife" means any knife, the blade of which opens automatically by hand pressure applied to a button, spring, or other device in its handle.

(2) It shall be an affirmative defense to any provision of this article that the act was committed by a peace officer in the lawful discharge of his duties.

Colorado Revised Statutes § 18-12-102
POSSESSING A DANGEROUS OR ILLEGAL WEAPON -- AFFIRMATIVE DEFENSE

(1) As used in this section, the term "dangerous weapon" means a firearm silencer, machine gun, short shotgun, short rifle, or ballistic knife.

(2) As used in this section, the term "illegal weapon" means a blackjack, gas gun, metallic knuckles, gravity knife, or switchblade knife.

(3) A person who knowingly possesses a dangerous weapon commits a class 5 felony. Each subsequent violation of this subsection (3) by the same person shall be a class 4 felony.

(4) A person who knowingly possesses an illegal weapon commits a class 1 misdemeanor.

(5) It shall be an affirmative defense to the charge of possessing a dangerous weapon, or to the charge of possessing an illegal weapon, that the person so accused was a peace officer or member of the armed forces of the United States or Colorado National Guard acting in the lawful discharge of his duties, or that said person has a valid permit and license for possession of such weapon.

Colorado Revised Statutes § 18-12-103
POSSESSION OF A DEFACED FIREARM

A person commits a class 1 misdemeanor if he knowingly and unlawfully possesses a firearm, the manufacturer's serial number of which, or other distinguishing number or identification mark, has been removed, defaced, altered, or destroyed, except by normal wear and tear.

Colorado Revised Statutes § 18-12-103.5
DEFACED FIREARMS -- CONTRABAND -- DESTRUCTION

(1) After a judgment of conviction under section 18-12-103 or 18-12-104 has become final, any defaced firearm upon which the judgment was based shall be deemed to be contraband, the possession of which is contrary to the public peace, health, and safety.

(2) Defaced firearms that are deemed to be contraband shall be placed in the possession of the bureau or of a local law enforcement agency designated by the bureau and shall be destroyed or rendered permanently inoperable.

Colorado Revised Statutes § 18-12-104
DEFACING A FIREARM

A person commits a class 1 misdemeanor if such person knowingly removes, defaces, covers, alters, or destroys the manufacturer's serial number or any other distinguishing number or identification mark of a firearm.

Colorado Revised Statutes § 18-12-105
UNLAWFULLY CARRYING A CONCEALED WEAPON -- UNLAWFUL POSSESSION OF WEAPONS

(1) A person commits a class 2 misdemeanor if such person knowingly and unlawfully:

(a) Carries a knife concealed on or about his or her person; or

(b) Carries a firearm concealed on or about his or her person; or

(c) Without legal authority, carries, brings, or has in such person's possession a firearm or any explosive, incendiary, or other dangerous device on the property of or within any building in which the chambers, galleries, or offices of the general assembly, or either house thereof, are located, or in which a legislative hearing or meeting is being or is to be conducted, or in which the official office of any member, officer, or employee of the general assembly is located.

(2) It shall not be an offense if the defendant was:

(a) A person in his or her own dwelling or place of business or on property owned or under his or her control at the time of the act of carrying; or

(b) A person in a private automobile or other private means of conveyance who carries a weapon for lawful protection of such person's or another's person or property while traveling; or

(c) A person who, at the time of carrying a concealed weapon, held a valid written permit to carry a concealed weapon issued pursuant to section 18-12-105.1, as it existed prior to its repeal, or, if the weapon involved was a handgun, held a valid permit to carry a concealed handgun or a temporary emergency permit issued pursuant to part 2 of this article; except that it shall be an offense under this section if the person was carrying a concealed handgun in violation of the provisions of section 18-12-214; or

(d) A peace officer, as described in section 16-2.5-101, C.R.S., when carrying a weapon in conformance with the policy of the employing agency as provided in section 16-2.5-101(2), C.R.S.; or

(e) Deleted by Laws 2003, Ch. 242, § 46, eff. Aug. 6, 2003.

(f) A United States probation officer or a United States pretrial services officer while on duty and serving in the state of Colorado under the authority of rules and regulations promulgated by the judicial conference of the United States.

Colorado Revised Statutes § 18-12-105.5
UNLAWFULLY CARRYING A WEAPON -- UNLAWFUL POSSESSION OF WEAPONS -- SCHOOL, COLLEGE, OR UNIVERSITY GROUNDS

(1) A person commits a class 6 felony if such person knowingly and unlawfully and without legal authority carries, brings, or has in such person's possession a deadly weapon as defined in section 18-1-901(3)(e) in or on the real estate and all improvements erected thereon of any public or private elementary, middle, junior high, high, or vocational school or any public or private college, university, or seminary, except for the purpose of presenting an authorized public demonstration or exhibition pursuant to instruction in conjunction with an organized school or class, for the purpose of carrying out the necessary duties and functions of an employee of an educational institution that require the use of a deadly weapon, or for the purpose of participation in an authorized extracurricular activity or on an athletic team.

(2) Deleted by Laws 2000, Ch. 171, § 45, eff. July 1, 2000.

(3) It shall not be an offense under this section if:

(a) The weapon is unloaded and remains inside a motor vehicle while upon the real estate of any public or private college, university, or seminary; or

(b) The person is in that person's own dwelling or place of business or on property owned or under that person's control at the time of the act of carrying; or

(c) The person is in a private automobile or other private means of conveyance and is carrying a weapon for lawful protection of that person's or another's person or property while traveling; or

(d) The person, at the time of carrying a concealed weapon, held a valid written permit to carry a concealed weapon issued pursuant to section 18-12-105.1, as said section existed prior to its repeal; except that it shall be an offense under this section if the person was carrying a concealed handgun in violation of the provisions of section 18-12-214(3); or

(d.5) The weapon involved was a handgun and the person held a valid permit to carry a concealed handgun or a temporary emergency permit issued pursuant to part 2 of this article; except that it shall be an offense under this section if the person was carrying a concealed handgun in violation of the provisions of section 18-12-214(3); or

(e) The person is a school resource officer, as defined in section 22-32-109.1(1)(g.5), C.R.S., or a peace officer, as described in section 16-2.5-101, C.R.S., when carrying a weapon in conformance with the policy of the employing agency as provided in section 16-2.5-101(2), C.R.S.; or

(f) Deleted by Laws 2003, Ch. 242, § 51, eff. Aug. 6, 2003.

(g) Deleted by Laws 2003, Ch. 242, § 51, eff. Aug. 6, 2003.

(h) The person has possession of the weapon for use in an educational program approved by a school which program includes, but shall not be limited to, any course designed for the repair or maintenance of weapons.

Colorado Revised Statutes § 18-12-105.6
LIMITATION ON LOCAL ORDINANCES REGARDING FIREARMS IN PRIVATE VEHICLES

(1) The general assembly hereby finds that:

(a) A person carrying a weapon in a private automobile or other private means of conveyance for hunting or for lawful protection of such person's or another's person or property, as permitted in sections 18-12-105(2)(b) and 18-12-105.5(3)(c), may tend to travel within a county, city and county, or municipal jurisdiction or in or through different county, city and county, and municipal jurisdictions, en route to the person's destination;

(b) Inconsistent laws exist in local jurisdictions with regard to the circumstances under which weapons may be carried in automobiles and other private means of conveyance;

(c) This inconsistency creates a confusing patchwork of laws that unfairly subjects a person who lawfully travels with a weapon to criminal penalties because he or she travels within a jurisdiction or into or through another jurisdiction;

(d) This inconsistency places citizens in the position of not knowing when they may be violating local laws while traveling within a jurisdiction or in, through, or between different jurisdictions, and therefore being unable to avoid committing a crime.

(2)

(a) Based on the findings specified in subsection (1) of this section, the general assembly concludes that the carrying of weapons in private automobiles or other private means of conveyance for hunting or for lawful protection of a person's or another's person or property while traveling into, through, or within, a municipal, county, or city and county jurisdiction, regardless of the number of times the person stops in a jurisdiction, is a matter of statewide concern and is not an offense.

(b) Notwithstanding any other provision of law, no municipality, county, or city and county shall have the authority to enact or enforce any ordinance or resolution that would restrict a person's ability to travel with a weapon in a private automobile or other private means of conveyance for hunting or for lawful protection of a person's or another's person or property while traveling into, through, or within, a municipal, county, or city and county jurisdiction, regardless of the number of times the person stops in a jurisdiction.

Colorado Revised Statutes § 18-12-106
PROHIBITED USE OF WEAPONS

(1) A person commits a class 2 misdemeanor if:

(a) He knowingly and unlawfully aims a firearm at another person; or

(b) Recklessly or with criminal negligence he discharges a firearm or shoots a bow and arrow; or

(c) He knowingly sets a loaded gun, trap, or device designed to cause an explosion upon being tripped or approached, and leaves it unattended by a competent person immediately present; or

(d) The person has in his or her possession a firearm while the person is under the influence of intoxicating liquor or of a controlled substance, as defined in section 18-18-102(5). Possession of a permit issued under section 18-12-105.1, as it existed prior to its repeal, or possession of a permit or a temporary emergency permit issued pursuant to part 2 of this article is no defense to a violation of this subsection (1).

(e) He knowingly aims, swings, or throws a throwing star or nunchaku as defined in this paragraph (e) at another person, or he knowingly possesses a throwing star or nunchaku in a public place except for the purpose of presenting an authorized public demonstration or exhibition or pursuant to instruction in conjunction with an organized school or class. When transporting throwing stars or nunchaku for a public demonstration or exhibition or for a school or class, they shall be transported in a closed, nonaccessible container. For purposes of this paragraph (e), "nunchaku" means an instrument consisting of two sticks, clubs, bars, or rods to be used as handles, connected by a rope, cord, wire, or chain, which is in the design of a weapon used in connection with the practice of a system of self-defense, and "throwing star" means a disk having sharp radiating points or any disk-shaped bladed object which is hand-held and thrown and which is in the design of a weapon used in connection with the practice of a system of self-defense.

Colorado Revised Statutes § 18-12-106.5
USE OF STUN GUNS

A person commits a class 5 felony if he knowingly and unlawfully uses a stun gun in the commission of a criminal offense.

Colorado Revised Statutes § 18-12-108
POSSESSION OF WEAPONS BY PREVIOUS OFFENDERS

(1)   A person commits the crime of possession of a weapon by a previous offender if the person knowingly possesses, uses, or carries upon his or her person a firearm as described in section 18-1-901(3)(h) or any other weapon that is subject to the provisions of this article subsequent to the person's conviction for a felony, or subsequent to the person's conviction for attempt or conspiracy to commit a felony, under Colorado or any other state's law or under federal law.

(2)

    (a) Except as otherwise provided by paragraphs (b) and (c) of this subsection (2), a person commits a class 6 felony if the person violates subsection (1) of this section.

    (b) A person commits a class 5 felony, as provided by section 18-12-102, if the person violates subsection (1) of this section and the weapon is a dangerous weapon, as defined in section 18-12-102(1).

    (c) A person commits a class 5 felony if the person violates subsection (1) of this section and the person's previous conviction was for burglary, arson, or any felony involving the use of force or the use of a deadly weapon and the violation of subsection (1) of this section occurs as follows:

        (I) From the date of conviction to ten years after the date of conviction, if the person was not incarcerated; or

        (II) From the date of conviction to ten years after the date of release from confinement, if such person was incarcerated or, if subject to supervision imposed as a result of conviction, ten years after the date of release from supervision.

    (d) Any sentence imposed pursuant to this subsection (2) shall run consecutively with any prior sentences being served by the offender.

(3) A person commits the crime of possession of a weapon by a previous offender if the person knowingly possesses, uses, or carries upon his or her person a firearm as described in section 18-1-901(3)(h) or any other weapon that is subject to the provisions of this article subsequent to the person's adjudication for an act which, if committed by an adult, would constitute a felony, or subsequent to the person's adjudication for attempt or

conspiracy to commit a felony, under Colorado or any other state's law or under federal law.

(4)

(a) Except as otherwise provided by paragraphs (b) and (c) of this subsection (4), a person commits a class 6 felony if the person violates subsection (3) of this section.

(b) A person commits a class 5 felony, as provided by section 18-12-102, if the person violates subsection (3) of this section and the weapon is a dangerous weapon, as defined in section 18-12-102(1).

(c) A person commits a class 5 felony if the person commits the conduct described in subsection (3) of this section and the person's previous adjudication was based on an act that, if committed by an adult, would constitute burglary, arson, or any felony involving the use of force or the use of a deadly weapon and the violation of subsection (3) of this section occurs as follows:

(I) From the date of adjudication to ten years after the date of adjudication, if the person was not committed to the department of institutions, or on or after July 1, 1994, to the department of human services; or

(II) From the date of adjudication to ten years after the date of release from commitment, if such person was committed to the department of institutions, or on or after July 1, 1994, to the department of human services or, if subject to supervision imposed as a result of an adjudication, ten years after the date of release from supervision.

(d) Any sentence imposed pursuant to this subsection (4) shall run consecutively with any prior sentences being served by the offender.

(5) A second or subsequent offense under paragraphs (b) and (c) of subsection (2) and paragraphs (b) and (c) of subsection (4) of this section is a class 4 felony.

(6)

(a) Upon the discharge of any inmate from the custody of the department of corrections, the department shall provide a written advisement to such inmate of the prohibited acts and penalties specified in this section. The written advisement, at a minimum, shall include the written statement specified in paragraph (c) of this subsection (6).

(b) Any written stipulation for deferred judgment and sentence entered into by a defendant pursuant to section 18-1.3-102 shall contain a written advisement of the prohibited acts and penalties specified in this section. The written advisement, at a minimum, shall include the written statement specified in paragraph (c) of this subsection (6).

(c) The written statement shall provide that:

(I)

(A) A person commits the crime of possession of a weapon by a previous offender in violation of this section if the person knowingly possesses, uses, or carries upon his or her person a firearm as described in section 18-1-901(3)(h), or any other weapon that is subject to the provisions of this title subsequent to the person's conviction for a felony, or subsequent to the person's conviction for attempt or conspiracy to commit a felony, or subsequent to the person's conviction for a misdemeanor crime of domestic violence as defined in 18 U.S.C. sec. 921(a)(33)(A), or subsequent to the person's conviction for attempt or conspiracy to commit such misdemeanor crime of domestic violence; and

(B) For the purposes of this paragraph (c), "felony" means any felony under Colorado law, federal law, or the laws of any other state; and

(II) A violation of this section may result in a sentence of imprisonment or fine, or both.

(d) The act of providing the written advisement described in this subsection (6) or the failure to provide such advisement may not be used as a defense to any crime charged and may not provide any basis for collateral attack on, or for appellate relief concerning, any conviction.

Colorado Revised Statutes § 18-12-108.5
POSSESSION OF HANDGUNS BY JUVENILES -- PROHIBITED -- EXCEPTIONS -- PENALTY

(1)

(a) Except as provided in this section, it is unlawful for any person who has not attained the age of 18 years knowingly to have any handgun in such person's possession.

(b) Any person possessing any handgun in violation of paragraph (a) of this subsection (1) commits the offense of illegal possession of a handgun by a juvenile.

(c)

(I) Illegal possession of a handgun by a juvenile is a class 2 misdemeanor.

(II) For any second or subsequent offense, illegal possession of a handgun by a juvenile is a class 5 felony.

(d) Any person under the age of 18 years who is taken into custody by a law enforcement officer for an offense pursuant to this section shall be taken into temporary custody in the manner described in section 19-2-508, C.R.S.

(2) This section shall not apply to:

(a) Any person under the age of 18 years who is:

(I) In attendance at a hunter's safety course or a firearms safety course; or

(II) Engaging in practice in the use of a firearm or target shooting at an established range authorized by the governing body of the jurisdiction in which such range is located or any other area where the discharge of a firearm is not prohibited; or

(III) Engaging in an organized competition involving the use of a firearm or participating in or practicing for a performance by an organized group under 501(c)(3)[1] as determined by the federal internal revenue service which uses firearms as a part of such performance; or

(IV) Hunting or trapping pursuant to a valid license issued to such person pursuant to article 4 of title 33, C.R.S.; or

(V) Traveling with any handgun in such person's possession being unloaded to or from any activity described in subparagraph (I), (II), (III), or (IV) of this paragraph (a);

(b) Any person under the age of 18 years who is on real property under the control of such person's parent, legal guardian, or grandparent and who has the permission of such person's parent or legal guardian to possess a handgun;

(c) Any person under the age of 18 years who is at such person's residence and who, with the permission of such person's parent or legal guardian, possesses a handgun for the purpose of exercising the rights contained in section 18-1-704 or section 18-1-704.5.

(3) For the purposes of subsection (2) of this section, a handgun is "loaded" if:

(a) There is a cartridge in the chamber of the handgun; or
(b) There is a cartridge in the cylinder of the handgun, if the handgun is a revolver; or

(c) The handgun, and the ammunition for such handgun, is carried on the person of a person under the age of 18 years or is in such close proximity to such person that such person could readily gain access to the handgun and the ammunition and load the handgun.

Colorado Revised Statutes § 18-12-108.7
UNLAWFULLY PROVIDING OR PERMITTING A JUVENILE TO POSSESS A HANDGUN -- PENALTY -- UNLAWFULLY PROVIDING A FIREARM OTHER THAN A HANDGUN TO A JUVENILE -- PENALTY

(1)

(a) Any person who intentionally, knowingly, or recklessly provides a handgun with or without remuneration to any person under the age of 18 years in violation of section 18-12-108.5 or any person who knows of such juvenile's conduct which violates section 18-12-108.5 and fails to make reasonable efforts to prevent such violation commits the crime of unlawfully providing a handgun to a juvenile or permitting a juvenile to possess a handgun.

(b) Unlawfully providing a handgun to a juvenile or permitting a juvenile to possess a handgun in violation of this subsection (1) is a class 4 felony.

(2)

(a) Any person who intentionally, knowingly, or recklessly provides a handgun to a juvenile or permits a juvenile to possess a handgun, even though such person is aware of a substantial risk that such juvenile will use a handgun to commit a felony offense, or who, being aware of such substantial risk, fails to make reasonable efforts to prevent the commission of the offense, commits the crime of unlawfully providing or permitting a juvenile to possess a handgun. A person shall be deemed to have violated this paragraph (a) if such person provides a handgun to or permits the possession of a handgun by any juvenile who has been convicted of a crime of violence, as defined in section 18-1.3-406, or any juvenile who has been adjudicated a juvenile delinquent for an offense which would constitute a crime of violence, as defined in section 18-1.3-406, if such juvenile were an adult.

(b) Unlawfully providing a handgun to a juvenile or permitting a juvenile to possess a handgun in violation of this subsection (2) is a class 4 felony.

(3) With regard to firearms other than handguns, no person shall sell, rent, or transfer ownership or allow unsupervised possession of a firearm with or without remuneration to any juvenile without the consent of the juvenile's parent or legal guardian. Unlawfully providing a firearm other than a handgun to a juvenile in violation of this subsection (3) is a class 1 misdemeanor.

(4) It shall not be an offense under this section if a person believes that a juvenile will physically harm the person if the person attempts to disarm the juvenile or prevent the juvenile from committing a violation of section 18-12-108.5.

Colorado Revised Statutes § 18-12-111
UNLAWFUL PURCHASE OF FIREARMS

(1) Any person who knowingly purchases or otherwise obtains a firearm on behalf of or for transfer to a person who the transferor knows or reasonably should know is ineligible to

possess a firearm pursuant to federal or state law commits a class 4 felony.

(2)

(a) Any person who is a licensed dealer, as defined in 18 U.S.C. sec. 921(a)(11), shall post a sign displaying the provisions of subsection (1) of this section in a manner that is easily readable. The person shall post such sign in an area that is visible to the public at each location from which the person sells firearms to the general public.

(b) Any person who violates any provision of this subsection (2) commits a class 2 petty offense and, upon conviction thereof, shall be punished by a fine of two hundred fifty dollars.

Colorado Revised Statutes § 18-12-112

PRIVATE FIREARMS TRANSFERS -- BACKGROUND CHECK REQUIRED -- PENALTY – DEFINITIONS

(1)

(a) On and after July 1, 2013, except as described in subsection (6) of this section, before any person who is not a licensed gun dealer, as defined in section 12-26.1-106(6), C.R.S., transfers or attempts to transfer possession of a firearm to a transferee, he or she shall:

(I) Require that a background check, in accordance with section 24-33.5-424, C.R.S., be conducted of the prospective transferee; and

(II) Obtain approval of a transfer from the bureau after a background check has been requested by a licensed gun dealer, in accordance with section 24-33.5-424, C.R.S.

(b) As used in this section, unless the context requires otherwise, "transferee" means a person who desires to receive or acquire a firearm from a transferor. If a transferee is not a natural person, then each natural person who is authorized by the transferee to possess the firearm after the transfer shall undergo a background check, as described in paragraph (a) of this subsection (1), before taking possession of the firearm.

(2)

(a) A prospective firearm transferor who is not a licensed gun dealer shall arrange for a licensed gun dealer to obtain the background check required by this section.

(b) A licensed gun dealer who obtains a background check on a prospective transferee shall record the transfer, as provided in section 12-26-102, C.R.S., and retain the records, as provided in section 12-26-103, C.R.S., in the same manner as when conducting a sale, rental, or exchange at retail. The licensed gun dealer shall comply with all state and federal laws, including 18 U.S.C. sec. 922, as if he or she were transferring the firearm from his or her inventory to the prospective transferee.

(c) A licensed gun dealer who obtains a background check for a prospective firearm transferor pursuant to this section shall provide the firearm transferor and transferee a copy of the results of the background check, including the bureau's approval or disapproval of the transfer.

(d) A licensed gun dealer may charge a fee for services rendered pursuant to this section, which fee shall not exceed ten dollars.

(3)

(a) A prospective firearm transferee under this section shall not accept possession of the firearm unless the prospective firearm transferor has obtained approval of the transfer from the bureau after a background check has been requested by a licensed gun dealer, as described in paragraph (b) of subsection (1) of this section.

(b) A prospective firearm transferee shall not knowingly provide false information to a prospective firearm transferor or to a licensed gun dealer for the purpose of acquiring a firearm.

(4) If the bureau approves a transfer of a firearm pursuant to this section, the approval shall be valid for thirty calendar days, during which time the transferor and transferee may complete the transfer.

(5) A person who transfers a firearm in violation of the provisions of this section may be jointly and severally liable for any civil damages proximately caused by the transferee's subsequent use of the firearm.

(6) The provisions of this section do not apply to:

(a) A transfer of an antique firearm, as defined in 18 U.S.C. sec. 921(a)(16), as amended, or a curio or relic, as defined in 27 CFR 478.11, as amended;

(b) A transfer that is a bona fide gift or loan between immediate family members, which are limited to spouses, parents, children, siblings, grandparents, grandchildren, nieces, nephews, first cousins, aunts, and uncles;

(c) A transfer that occurs by operation of law or because of the death of a person for whom the prospective transferor is an executor or administrator of an estate or a trustee of a trust created in a will;

(d) A transfer that is temporary and occurs while in the home of the unlicensed transferee if:

(I) The unlicensed transferee is not prohibited from possessing firearms; and

(II) The unlicensed transferee reasonably believes that possession of the firearm is necessary to prevent imminent death or serious bodily injury to the unlicensed transferee;

(e) A temporary transfer of possession without transfer of ownership or a title to ownership, which transfer takes place:

(I) At a shooting range located in or on premises owned or occupied by a duly incorporated organization organized for conservation purposes or to foster proficiency in firearms;

(II) At a target firearm shooting competition under the auspices of, or approved by, a state agency or a nonprofit organization; or

(III) While hunting, fishing, target shooting, or trapping if:

(A) The hunting, fishing, target shooting, or trapping is legal in all places where the unlicensed transferee possesses the firearm; and

(B) The unlicensed transferee holds any license or permit that is required for such hunting, fishing, target shooting, or trapping;

(f) A transfer of a firearm that is made to facilitate the repair or maintenance of the firearm; except that this paragraph (f) does not apply unless all parties who possess the firearm as a result of the transfer may legally possess a firearm;

(g) Any temporary transfer that occurs while in the continuous presence of the owner of the firearm;

(h) A temporary transfer for not more than 72 hours. A person who transfers a firearm pursuant to this paragraph (h) may be jointly and severally liable for damages proximately caused by the transferee's subsequent unlawful use of the firearm; or

(i) A transfer of a firearm from a person serving in the armed forces of the United States who will be deployed outside of the United States within the next thirty days to any immediate family member, which is limited to a spouse, parent, child, sibling, grandparent, grandchild, niece, nephew, first cousin, aunt, and uncle of the person.

(7) For purposes of paragraph (f) of subsection (6) of this section:

(a) An owner, manager, or employee of a business that repairs or maintains firearms may rely upon a transferor's statement that he or she may legally possess a firearm unless the owner, manager, or employee has actual knowledge to the contrary and may return possession of the firearm to the transferor upon completion of the repairs or maintenance without a background check;

(b) Unless a transferor of a firearm has actual knowledge to the contrary, the transferor may rely upon the statement of an owner, manager, or employee of a business that repairs or maintains firearms that no owner, manager, or employee of the business is prohibited from possessing a firearm.

(8) Nothing in subsection (6) of this section shall be interpreted to limit or otherwise alter the applicability of section 18-12-111 concerning the unlawful purchase or transfer of firearms.

(9)

(a) A person who violates a provision of this section commits a class 1 misdemeanor and shall be punished in accordance with section 18-1.3-501. The person shall also be prohibited from possessing a firearm for two years, beginning on the date of his or her conviction.

(b) When a person is convicted of violating a provision of this section, the state court administrator shall report the conviction to the bureau and to the national instant criminal background check system created by the federal "Brady Handgun Violence Prevention Act", Pub.L. 103-159, the relevant portion of which is codified at 18 U.S.C. sec. 922(t). The report shall include information indicating that the person is prohibited from possessing a firearm for two years, beginning on the date of his or her conviction.

Colorado Revised Statutes, Title 18, Article 12, Part 2
PERMITS TO CARRY CONCEALED HANDGUNS

Colorado Revised Statutes § 18-12-201
LEGISLATIVE DECLARATION

(1) The general assembly finds that:

(a) There exists a widespread inconsistency among jurisdictions within the state with regard to the issuance of permits to carry concealed handguns and identification of areas of the state where it is lawful to carry concealed handguns;

(b) This inconsistency among jurisdictions creates public uncertainty regarding the areas of the state in which it is lawful to carry concealed handguns;

(c) Inconsistency results in the arbitrary and capricious denial of permits to carry concealed handguns based on the jurisdiction of residence rather than the qualifications for obtaining a permit;

(d) The criteria and procedures for the lawful carrying of concealed handguns historically has been regulated by state statute and should be consistent throughout the state to ensure the consistent implementation of state law; and

(e) It is necessary that the state occupy the field of regulation of the bearing of concealed handguns since the issuance of a concealed handgun permit is based on a person's constitutional right of self-protection and there is a prevailing state interest in ensuring that no citizen is arbitrarily denied a concealed handgun permit and in ensuring that the laws controlling the use of the permit are consistent throughout the state.

(2) Based on the findings specified in subsection (1) of this section, the general assembly hereby concludes that:

(a) The permitting and carrying of concealed handguns is a matter of statewide concern; and

(b) It is necessary to provide statewide uniform standards for issuing permits to carry concealed handguns for self-defense.

(3) In accordance with the findings and conclusions specified in subsections (1) and (2) of this section, the general assembly hereby instructs each sheriff to implement and administer the provisions of this part 2. The general assembly does not delegate to the sheriffs the authority to regulate or restrict the issuance of permits provided for in this part 2 beyond the provisions of this part 2. An action or rule that encumbers the permit process by placing burdens on the applicant beyond those sworn statements and specified documents detailed in this part 2 or that creates restrictions beyond those specified in this part 2 is in conflict with the intent of this part 2 and is prohibited.

Colorado Revised Statutes § 18-12-202

DEFINITIONS

As used in this part 2, unless the context otherwise requires:

(1) Repealed by Laws 2013, Ch. 47, § 7, eff. March 20, 2013.

(2) "Certified instructor" means an instructor for a firearms safety course who is certified as a firearms instructor by:

(a) A county, municipal, state, or federal law enforcement agency;

(b) The peace officers standards and training board created in section 24-31-302, C.R.S.;

(c) A federal military agency; or

(d) A national nonprofit organization that certifies firearms instructors, operates national firearms competitions, and provides training, including courses in personal protection, in small arms safety, use, and marksmanship.

(3) "Chronically and habitually uses alcoholic beverages to the extent that the applicant's normal faculties are impaired" means:

(a) The applicant has at any time been committed as an alcoholic pursuant to section 27-81-111 or 27-81-112, C.R.S.; or

(b) Within the ten-year period immediately preceding the date on which the permit application is submitted, the applicant:

(I) Has been committed as an alcoholic pursuant to section 27-81-109 or 27-81-110, C.R.S.; or

(II) Has had two or more alcohol-related convictions under section 42-4-1301(1) or (2), C.R.S., or a law of another state that has similar elements, or revocations related to misdemeanor, alcohol-related convictions under section 42-2-126, C.R.S., or a law of another state that has similar elements.

(4) "Handgun" means a handgun as defined in section 18-12-101(1)(e.5); except that the term does not include a machine gun as defined in section 18-12-101(1)(g).

(5)

(a) "Handgun training class" means:

(I) A law enforcement training firearms safety course;

(II) A firearms safety course offered by a law enforcement agency, an institution of higher education, or a public or private institution or organization or firearms training school, that is open to the general public and is taught by a certified instructor; or

(III) A firearms safety course or class that is offered and taught by a certified instructor.

(b) Notwithstanding paragraph (a) of this subsection (5), "handgun training class" does not include any firearms safety course that allows a person to complete the entire course:

(I) Via the internet or an electronic device; or

(II) In any location other than the physical location where the certified instructor offers the course.

(6) "Permit" means a permit to carry a concealed handgun issued pursuant to the provisions of this part 2; except that "permit"

does not include a temporary emergency permit issued pursuant to section 18-12-209.

(7) "Sheriff" means the sheriff of a county, or his or her designee, or the official who has the duties of a sheriff in a city and county, or his or her designee.

(8) "Training certificate" means a certificate, affidavit, or other document issued by the instructor, school, club, or organization that conducts a handgun training class that evidences an applicant's successful completion of the class requirements.

Colorado Revised Statutes § 18-12-203
CRITERIA FOR OBTAINING A PERMIT

(1) Beginning May 17, 2003, except as otherwise provided in this section, a sheriff shall issue a permit to carry a concealed handgun to an applicant who:

(a) Is a legal resident of the state of Colorado. For purposes of this part 2, a person who is a member of the armed forces and is stationed pursuant to permanent duty station orders at a military installation in this state, and a member of the person's immediate family living in Colorado, shall be deemed to be a legal resident of the state of Colorado.

(b) Is 21 years of age or older;

(c) Is not ineligible to possess a firearm pursuant to section 18-12-108 or federal law;

(d) Has not been convicted of perjury under section 18-8-503, in relation to information provided or deliberately omitted on a permit application submitted pursuant to this part 2;

(e)

    (I) Does not chronically and habitually use alcoholic beverages to the extent that the applicant's normal faculties are impaired.

    (II) The prohibition specified in this paragraph (e) shall not apply to an applicant who provides an affidavit, signed by a professional counselor or addiction counselor who is licensed pursuant to article 43 of title 12, C.R.S., and specializes in alcohol addiction, stating that the applicant has been evaluated by the counselor and has been determined to be a recovering alcoholic who has refrained from using alcohol for at least three years.

(f) Is not an unlawful user of or addicted to a controlled substance as defined in section 18-18-102(5). Whether an applicant is an unlawful user of or addicted to a controlled substance shall be determined as provided in federal law and regulations.

(g) Is not subject to:

    (I) A protection order issued pursuant to section 18-1-1001 or section 19-2-707, C.R.S., that is in effect at the time the application is submitted; or

    (II) A permanent protection order issued pursuant to Article 14 of title 13, C.R.S.; or

    (III) A temporary protection order issued pursuant to Article 14 of title 13, C.R.S., that is in effect at the time the application is submitted;

(h) Demonstrates competence with a handgun by submitting:

(I) Evidence of experience with a firearm through participation in organized shooting competitions or current military service;

(II) Evidence that, at the time the application is submitted, the applicant is a certified instructor;

(III) Proof of honorable discharge from a branch of the United States armed forces within the three years preceding submittal of the application;

(IV) Proof of honorable discharge from a branch of the United States armed forces that reflects pistol qualifications obtained within the ten years preceding submittal of the application;

(V) A certificate showing retirement from a Colorado law enforcement agency that reflects pistol qualifications obtained within the ten years preceding submittal of the application; or

(VI) A training certificate from a handgun training class obtained within the ten years preceding submittal of the application. The applicant shall submit the original training certificate or a photocopy thereof that includes the original signature of the class instructor. To the extent permitted by section 18-12-202(5), in obtaining a training certificate from a handgun training class, the applicant shall have discretion in selecting which handgun training class to complete.

(2) Regardless of whether an applicant meets the criteria specified in subsection (1) of this section, if the sheriff has a reasonable belief that documented previous behavior by the applicant makes it likely the applicant will present a danger to self

or others if the applicant receives a permit to carry a concealed handgun, the sheriff may deny the permit.

(3)

(a) The sheriff shall deny, revoke, or refuse to renew a permit if an applicant or a permittee fails to meet one of the criteria listed in subsection (1) of this section and may deny, revoke, or refuse to renew a permit on the grounds specified in subsection (2) of this section.

(b) Following issuance of a permit, if the issuing sheriff has a reasonable belief that a permittee no longer meets the criteria specified in subsection (1) of this section or that the permittee presents a danger as described in subsection (2) of this section, the sheriff shall suspend the permit until such time as the matter is resolved and the issuing sheriff determines that the permittee is eligible to possess a permit as provided in this section.

(c) If the sheriff suspends or revokes a permit, the sheriff shall notify the permittee in writing, stating the grounds for suspension or revocation and informing the permittee of the right to seek a second review by the sheriff, to submit additional information for the record, and to seek judicial review pursuant to section 18-12-207.

Colorado Revised Statutes § 18-12-204
PERMIT CONTENTS -- VALIDITY -- CARRYING REQUIREMENTS

(1)

(a) Each permit shall bear a color photograph of the permittee and shall display the signature of the sheriff who issues the permit. In addition, the sheriffs of this state shall ensure that all permits issued pursuant to this part 2 contain the same items of information and are the same size and the same color.

(b) A permit is valid for a period of five years after the date of issuance and may be renewed as provided in section 18-12-211. A permit issued pursuant to this part 2, including a temporary emergency permit issued pursuant to section 18-12-209, is effective in all areas of the state, except as otherwise provided in section 18-12-214.

(2)

(a) A permittee, in compliance with the terms of a permit, may carry a concealed handgun as allowed by state law. The permittee shall carry the permit, together with valid photo identification, at all times during which the permittee is in actual possession of a concealed handgun and shall produce both documents upon demand by a law enforcement officer. Failure to produce a permit upon demand by a law enforcement officer raises a rebuttable presumption that the person does not have a permit. Failure to carry and produce a permit and valid photo identification upon demand as required in this subsection (2) is a class 1 petty offense. A charge of failure to carry and produce a permit and valid photo identification upon demand pursuant to this subsection (2) shall be dismissed by the court if, at or before the permittee's scheduled court appearance, the permittee exhibits to the court a valid permit and valid photo identification, both of which were issued to the permittee prior to the date on which the permittee was charged with failure to carry and produce a permit and valid photo identification upon demand.

(b) The provisions of paragraph (a) of this subsection (2) apply to temporary emergency permits issued pursuant to section 18-12-209.

(3)

(a) A person who may lawfully possess a handgun may carry a handgun under the following circumstances without obtaining a permit and the handgun shall not be considered concealed:

(I) The handgun is in the possession of a person who is in a private automobile or in some other private means of conveyance and who carries the handgun for a legal use, including self-defense; or

(II) The handgun is in the possession of a person who is legally engaged in hunting activities within the state.

(b) The provisions of this subsection (3) shall not be construed to authorize the carrying of a handgun in violation of the provisions of section 18-12-105 or 18-12-105.5.

Colorado Revised Statutes § 18-12-205
SHERIFF -- APPLICATION -- PROCEDURE -- BACKGROUND CHECK

(1)

(a) To obtain a permit, a person shall submit a permit application on a statewide standardized form developed by the sheriffs and available from each sheriff. The permit application form shall solicit only the following information from the applicant:

(I) The applicant's full name, date of birth, and address;

(II) The applicant's birth name, if different from the name provided pursuant to subparagraph (I) of this paragraph (a), and any other names the applicant may have used or by which the applicant may have been known;

(III) The applicant's home address or addresses for the ten-year period immediately preceding submittal of the application;

(IV) Whether the applicant is a resident of this state as of the date of application and whether the applicant has a valid driver's license or other state-issued photo identification or military order proving residence; and

(V) Whether the applicant meets the criteria for obtaining a permit specified in section 18-12-203(1).

(b) The permit application form shall not require the applicant to waive or release a right or privilege, including but not limited to waiver or release of privileged or confidential information contained in medical records.

(2)

(a) An applicant shall complete the permit application form and return it, in person, to the sheriff of the county or city and county in which the applicant resides or to the sheriff of the county or city and county in which the applicant maintains a secondary residence or owns or leases real property used by the applicant in a business. The applicant shall sign the completed permit application form in person before the sheriff. The applicant shall provide his or her signature voluntarily upon a sworn oath that the applicant knows the contents of the permit application and that the information contained in the permit application is true and correct. An applicant who knowingly and intentionally makes a false or misleading statement on a permit application or deliberately omits any material information requested on the application commits perjury as described in section 18-8-503. Upon conviction, the applicant shall be punished as provided in section 18-1.3-501. In addition, the applicant shall be denied the right to obtain or possess a permit, and the sheriff shall revoke the applicant's permit if issued prior to conviction.

(b) An applicant shall also submit to the sheriff a permit fee not to exceed one hundred dollars for processing the permit application. The sheriff shall set the amount of the permit fee as provided in subsection (5) of this section. In addition, the applicant shall submit an amount specified by the director of the bureau, pursuant to section 24-72-306, C.R.S., for processing the applicant's fingerprints through the bureau and through the federal bureau of investigation. Neither the permit fee nor the fingerprint processing fee shall be refundable in the event the sheriff denies the applicant's permit application or suspends or revokes the permit subsequent to issuance.

(3) In addition to the items specified in subsection (2) of this section, an applicant, when submitting the completed permit application, shall submit the following items to the sheriff:

(a) Documentary evidence demonstrating competence with a handgun as specified in section 18-12-203(1)(h); and

(b) A full frontal view color photograph of the applicant's head taken within the thirty days immediately preceding submittal of the permit application; except that the applicant need not submit a photograph if the sheriff photographs the applicant for purposes of issuing a permit. Any photograph submitted shall show the applicant's full head, including hair and facial features, and the depiction of the applicant's head shall measure one and one-eighth inches wide and one and one-fourth inches high.

(4)

(a) The sheriff shall witness an applicant's signature on the permit application as provided in subsection (2) of this section and verify that the person making application for a permit is the same person who appears in any photograph submitted and the same person who signed the permit application form. To verify the applicant's identity, the applicant shall present to the sheriff the applicant's valid

Colorado driver's license or valid Colorado or military photo identification.

(b) After verifying the applicant's identity, the sheriff shall take two complete sets of the applicant's fingerprints. The sheriff shall submit both sets of fingerprints to the bureau, and the sheriff shall not retain a set of the applicant's fingerprints.

(c) After receipt of a permit application and the items specified in this section, the sheriff shall verify that the applicant meets the criteria specified in section 18-12-203(1) and is not a danger as described in section 18-12-203(2). The verification at a minimum shall include requesting the bureau to conduct a search of the national instant criminal background check system and a search of the state integrated criminal justice information system to determine whether the applicant meets the criteria specified in section 18-12-203(1). In addition, if the applicant resides in a municipality or town, the sheriff shall consult with the police department of the municipality or town in which the applicant resides, and the sheriff may consult with other local law enforcement agencies.

(5) The sheriff in each county or city and county in the state shall establish the amount of the new and renewal permit fees within his or her jurisdiction. The amount of the new and renewal permit fees shall comply with the limits specified in paragraph (b) of subsection (2) of this section and section 18-12-211(1), respectively. The fee amounts shall reflect the actual direct and indirect costs to the sheriff of processing permit applications and renewal applications pursuant to this part 2.

Colorado Revised Statutes § 18-12-206
SHERIFF -- ISSUANCE OR DENIAL OF PERMITS -- REPORT

(1) Within ninety days after the date of receipt of the items specified in section 18-12-205, a sheriff shall:

    (a) Approve the permit application and issue the permit; or

    (b) Deny the permit application based solely on the ground that the applicant fails to qualify under the criteria listed in section 18-12-203(1) or that the applicant would be a danger as described in section 18-12-203(2). If the sheriff denies the permit application, he or she shall notify the applicant in writing, stating the grounds for denial and informing the applicant of the right to seek a second review of the application by the sheriff, to submit additional information for the record, and to seek judicial review pursuant to section 18-12-207.

(2) If the sheriff does not receive the results of the fingerprint checks conducted by the bureau and by the federal bureau of investigation within ninety days after receiving a permit application, the sheriff shall determine whether to grant or deny the permit application without considering the fingerprint check information. If, upon receipt of the information, the sheriff finds that the permit was issued or denied erroneously, based on the criteria specified in section 18-12-203(1) and (2), the sheriff shall either revoke or issue the permit, whichever is appropriate.

(3)

    (a) Each sheriff shall maintain a list of the persons to whom he or she issues permits pursuant to this part 2. Upon request by another criminal justice agency for law enforcement purposes, the sheriff may, at his or her discretion, share information from the list of permittees with a law enforcement agency for the purpose of determining the validity of a permit. A database maintained pursuant to this subsection (3) and any database operated by a state agency that includes permittees shall be searchable only by name.

(b)

(I) Notwithstanding the provisions of paragraph (a) of this subsection (3), on and after July 1, 2011, a sheriff shall not share information from the list of permittees with a law enforcement agency for the purpose of creating a statewide database of permittees, and any law enforcement agency that receives information concerning permittees from a sheriff shall not use the information to create or maintain a statewide database of permittees. Any information concerning a permittee that is included in a statewide database pursuant to paragraph (a) of this subsection (3) shall be removed from the database no later than July 1, 2011.

(II) Prior to the repeal in subparagraph (I) of this paragraph (b), the state auditor's office shall conduct a performance audit of the statewide database of permittees as provided in section 2-3-118, C.R.S.

(c) Except for suspected violations of sections 18-12-105 and 18-12-105.5, a peace officer may not use or search a database of permittees maintained by a law enforcement agency to establish reasonable suspicion for a traffic stop, or when contacting an individual, to justify probable cause for a search or seizure of a person or a person's vehicle or property.

(4) Each sheriff shall annually prepare a report specifying, at a minimum, the number of permit applications received during the year for which the report was prepared, the number of permits issued during the year, the number of permits denied during the year, the reasons for denial, the number of revocations during the year, and the reasons for the revocations. The report shall not include the name of a person who applies for a permit, regardless of whether the person receives or is denied a permit. Each sheriff

shall submit the report on or before March 1, 2004, and on or before March 1 each year thereafter, to the members of the general assembly. In addition, each sheriff shall provide a copy of the annual report prepared pursuant to this subsection (4) to a member of the public upon request.

Colorado Revised Statutes § 18-12-207

JUDICIAL REVIEW -- PERMIT DENIAL -- PERMIT SUSPENSION -- PERMIT REVOCATION

(1) If a sheriff denies a permit application, refuses to renew a permit, or suspends or revokes a permit, the applicant or permittee may seek judicial review of the sheriff's decision. The applicant or permittee may seek judicial review either in lieu of or subsequent to the sheriff's second review.

(2) The procedure and time lines for filing a complaint, an answer, and briefs for judicial review pursuant to this section shall be in accordance with the procedures specified in rule 106(a)(4) and (b) of the Colorado rules of civil procedure.

(3) Notwithstanding any other provision of law to the contrary, at a judicial review sought pursuant to this section, the sheriff shall have the burden of proving by a preponderance of the evidence that the applicant or permittee is ineligible to possess a permit under the criteria listed in section 18-12-203(1) or, if the denial, suspension, or revocation was based on the sheriff's determination that the person would be a danger as provided in section 18-12-203(2), the sheriff shall have the burden of proving the determination by clear and convincing evidence. Following completion of the review, the court may award attorney fees to the prevailing party.

Colorado Revised Statutes § 18-12-208
COLORADO BUREAU OF INVESTIGATION -- DUTIES

(1) Upon receipt of a permit applicant's fingerprints from a sheriff pursuant to section 18-12-205(4) or upon a sheriff's request pursuant to section 18-12-211(1), the bureau shall process the full set of fingerprints to obtain any available state criminal justice information or federal information pursuant to section 16-21-103(5), C.R.S., and shall report any information received to the sheriff. In addition, within ten days after receiving the fingerprints, the bureau shall forward one set of the fingerprints to the federal bureau of investigation for processing to obtain any available state criminal justice information or federal information.

(2) The bureau shall use the fingerprints received pursuant to this part 2 solely for the purposes of:

(a) Obtaining information for the issuance or renewal of permits; and

(b) Notifying an issuing sheriff that a permittee has been arrested for or charged with an offense that would require revocation or suspension of the permit or that a permittee has been convicted of such an offense.

(3) On or before January 15, 2004, and on or before January 15 each year thereafter until January 15, 2007, the bureau shall provide to the general assembly a list of the jurisdictions in which the sheriff provides to the bureau the names of persons to whom the sheriff issues permits.

Colorado Revised Statutes § 18-12-209
ISSUANCE BY SHERIFFS OF TEMPORARY EMERGENCY PERMITS

(1) Notwithstanding any provisions of this part 2 to the contrary, a sheriff, as provided in this section, may issue a temporary emergency permit to carry a concealed handgun to a person

whom the sheriff has reason to believe may be in immediate danger.

(2)

(a) To receive a temporary emergency permit, a person shall submit to the sheriff of the county or city and county in which the person resides or in which the circumstances giving rise to the emergency exist the items specified in section 18-12-205; except that an applicant for a temporary emergency permit need not submit documentary evidence demonstrating competence with a handgun as required under section 18-12-205(3)(a), and the applicant shall submit a temporary permit fee not to exceed twenty-five dollars, as set by the sheriff. Upon receipt of the documents and fee, the sheriff shall request that the bureau conduct a criminal history record check of the bureau files and a search of the national instant criminal background check system. The sheriff may issue a temporary emergency permit to the applicant if the sheriff determines the person may be in immediate danger and the criminal history record check shows that the applicant meets the criteria specified in section 18-12-203; except that the applicant need not demonstrate competence with a handgun and the applicant may be 18 years of age or older.

(b)

(I) A temporary emergency permit issued pursuant to this section is valid for a period of ninety days after the date of issuance. Prior to or within ten days after expiration of a temporary emergency permit, the permittee may apply to the sheriff of the county or city and county in which the person resides or in which the circumstances giving rise to the emergency exist for renewal of the permit. The sheriff may renew a temporary emergency permit once for an additional ninety-day period; except that, if the permittee is younger than 21 years of age, the sheriff may renew the temporary emergency permit for subsequent ninety-day periods until the permittee reaches 21 years of age.

II) If the sheriff is not the same sheriff who issued the temporary emergency permit to the permittee:

(A) The permittee shall submit to the renewing sheriff, in addition to the materials described in section 18-12-205, a legible photocopy of the temporary emergency permit; and

(B) The renewing sheriff shall contact the office of the sheriff who issued the temporary emergency permit and confirm that the issuing sheriff has not revoked or suspended the temporary emergency permit.

Colorado Revised Statutes § 18-12-210
MAINTENANCE OF PERMIT -- ADDRESS CHANGE -- INVALIDITY OF PERMIT

(1) Within thirty days after a permittee changes the address specified on his or her permit or within three business days after his or her permit is lost, stolen, or destroyed, the permittee shall notify the issuing sheriff of the change of address or permit loss, theft, or destruction. Failure to notify the sheriff pursuant to this subsection (1) is a class 1 petty offense.

(2) If a permit is lost, stolen, or destroyed, the permit is automatically invalid. The person to whom the permit was issued may obtain a duplicate or substitute therefor upon payment of fifteen dollars to the issuing sheriff and upon submission of a notarized statement to the issuing sheriff that the permit has been lost, stolen, or destroyed.

(3) The provisions of this section apply to temporary emergency permits issued pursuant to section 18-12-209.

Colorado Revised Statutes § 18-12-211

RENEWAL OF PERMITS

(1)

(a) Within one hundred twenty days prior to expiration of a permit, the permittee may obtain a renewal form from the sheriff of the county or city and county in which the permittee resides or from the sheriff of the county or city and county in which the permittee maintains a secondary residence or owns or leases real property used by the permittee in a business and renew the permit by submitting to the sheriff a completed renewal form, a notarized affidavit stating that the permittee remains qualified pursuant to the criteria specified in section 18-12-203(1)(a) to (1)(g), and the required renewal fee not to exceed fifty dollars, as set by the sheriff pursuant to section 18-12-205(5). The renewal form must meet the requirements specified in section 18-12-205(1) for an application.

(b) If the sheriff is not the same sheriff who issued the permit to the permittee:

(I) The permittee shall submit to the renewing sheriff, in addition to the materials described in paragraph (a) of this subsection (1), a legible photocopy of the permit; and

(II) The renewing sheriff shall contact the office of the sheriff who issued the permit and confirm that the issuing sheriff has not revoked or suspended the permit.

(c) The sheriff shall verify pursuant to section 18-12-205(4) that the permittee meets the criteria specified in section 18-12-203(1)(a) to (1)(g) and is not a danger as described in section 18-12-203(2) and shall either renew or deny the renewal of the permit in accordance with the provisions of section 18-12-206(1). If the sheriff denies renewal of a permit, the permittee may seek a second review of the renewal application by the sheriff and may submit additional information for the record. The permittee may also seek judicial review as provided in section 18-12-207.

(2) A permittee who fails to file a renewal form on or before the permit expiration date may renew the permit by paying a late fee of fifteen dollars in addition to the renewal fee established pursuant to subsection (1) of this section. No permit shall be renewed six months or more after its expiration date, and the permit shall be deemed to have permanently expired. A person whose permit has permanently expired may reapply for a permit, but the person shall submit an application for a permit and the fee required pursuant to section 18-12-205. A person who knowingly and intentionally files false or misleading information or deliberately omits material information required under this section is subject to criminal prosecution for perjury under section 18-8-503.

Colorado Revised Statutes § 18-12-212
EXEMPTION

(1) This part 2 shall not apply to law enforcement officers employed by jurisdictions outside this state, so long as the foreign employing jurisdiction exempts peace officers employed by jurisdictions within Colorado from any concealed handgun or concealed weapons laws in effect in the foreign employing jurisdiction.

(2) Notwithstanding any provision of this part 2 to the contrary, a retired peace officer, level I or Ia, as defined in section 18-1-901(3)(l)(I) and (3)(l)(II), as said section existed prior to its repeal in 2003, within the first five years after retirement may obtain a permit by submitting to the sheriff of the jurisdiction in which the retired peace officer resides a letter signed by the sheriff or chief of police of the jurisdiction by which the peace officer was employed immediately prior to retirement attesting that the retired officer meets the criteria specified in section 18-12-203(1). A retired peace officer who submits a letter pursuant to this

subsection (2) is not subject to the fingerprint or criminal history check requirements specified in this part 2 and is not required to pay the permit application fee. Upon receipt of a letter submitted pursuant to this subsection (2), the sheriff shall issue the permit. A permit issued pursuant to this subsection (2) may not be renewed. Upon expiration of the permit, the permittee may apply for a new permit as provided in this part 2.

Colorado Revised Statutes § 18-12-213
RECIPROCITY

(1) A permit to carry a concealed handgun or a concealed weapon that is issued by a state that recognizes the validity of permits issued pursuant to this part 2 shall be valid in this state in all respects as a permit issued pursuant to this part 2 if the permit is issued to a person who is:

(a) 21 years of age or older; and

(b)

(I) A resident of the state that issued the permit, as demonstrated by the address stated on a valid picture identification that is issued by the state that issued the permit and is carried by the permit holder; or

(II) A resident of Colorado for no more than ninety days, as determined by the date of issuance on a valid picture identification issued by Colorado and carried by the permit holder.

(2) For purposes of this section, a "valid picture identification" means a driver's license or a state identification issued in lieu of a driver's license.

Colorado Revised Statutes § 18-12-214

AUTHORITY GRANTED BY PERMIT -- CARRYING RESTRICTIONS

(1)

(a) A permit to carry a concealed handgun authorizes the permittee to carry a concealed handgun in all areas of the state, except as specifically limited in this section. A permit does not authorize the permittee to use a handgun in a manner that would violate a provision of state law. A local government does not have authority to adopt or enforce an ordinance or resolution that would conflict with any provision of this part 2.

(b) A peace officer may temporarily disarm a permittee, incident to a lawful stop of the permittee. The peace officer shall return the handgun to the permittee prior to discharging the permittee from the scene.

(2) A permit issued pursuant to this part 2 does not authorize a person to carry a concealed handgun into a place where the carrying of firearms is prohibited by federal law.

(3) A permit issued pursuant to this part 2 does not authorize a person to carry a concealed handgun onto the real property, or into any improvements erected thereon, of a public elementary, middle, junior high, or high school; except that:

(a) A permittee may have a handgun on the real property of the public school so long as the handgun remains in his or her vehicle and, if the permittee is not in the vehicle, the handgun is in a compartment within the vehicle and the vehicle is locked;

(b) A permittee who is employed or retained by contract by a school district or charter school as a school security officer may carry a concealed handgun onto the real property, or into any improvement erected thereon, of a public elementary, middle, junior high, or high school while the permittee is on duty;

(c) A permittee may carry a concealed handgun on undeveloped real property owned by a school district that is used for hunting or other shooting sports.

(4) A permit issued pursuant to this part 2 does not authorize a person to carry a concealed handgun into a public building at which:

(a) Security personnel and electronic weapons screening devices are permanently in place at each entrance to the building;

(b) Security personnel electronically screen each person who enters the building to determine whether the person is carrying a weapon of any kind; and

(c) Security personnel require each person who is carrying a weapon of any kind to leave the weapon in possession of security personnel while the person is in the building.

(5) Nothing in this part 2 shall be construed to limit, restrict, or prohibit in any manner the existing rights of a private property owner, private tenant, private employer, or private business entity.

(6) The provisions of this section apply to temporary emergency permits issued pursuant to section 18-12-209.

Colorado Revised Statutes § 18-12-215
IMMUNITY

(1) The bureau and a local law enforcement agency and an individual employed by the bureau or a local law enforcement

agency shall not be liable for any damages that may result from good faith compliance with the provisions of this part 2.

(2) A law enforcement officer or agency, medical personnel, and an organization that offers handgun training classes and its personnel who in good faith provide information regarding an applicant shall not be liable for any damages that may result from issuance or denial of a permit.

Colorado Revised Statutes, Title 18, Article 12, Part 3
LARGE-CAPACITY AMMUNITION MAGAZINES

Colorado Revised Statutes § 18-12-301
DEFINITIONS

As used in this part 3, unless the context otherwise requires:

(1) "Bureau" means the Colorado bureau of investigation created and existing pursuant to section 24-33.5-401, C.R.S.

(2)
    (a) "Large-capacity magazine" means:

        (I) A fixed or detachable magazine, box, drum, feed strip, or similar device capable of accepting, or that is designed to be readily converted to accept, more than fifteen rounds of ammunition;

        (II) A fixed, tubular shotgun magazine that holds more than twenty-eight inches of shotgun shells, including any extension device that is attached to the magazine and holds additional shotgun shells; or

        (III) A nontubular, detachable magazine, box, drum, feed strip, or similar device that is capable of accepting more than eight shotgun shells when combined with a fixed magazine.

(b) "Large-capacity magazine" does not mean:

(I) A feeding device that has been permanently altered so that it cannot accommodate more than fifteen rounds of ammunition;

(II) An attached tubular device designed to accept, and capable of operating only with, .22 caliber rimfire ammunition; or

(III) A tubular magazine that is contained in a lever-action firearm.

Colorado Revised Statutes § 18-12-302
LARGE-CAPACITY MAGAZINES PROHIBITED -- PENALTIES -- EXCEPTIONS

(1)

(a) Except as otherwise provided in this section, on and after July 1, 2013, a person who sells, transfers, or possesses a large-capacity magazine commits a class 2 misdemeanor.

(b) Any person who violates this subsection (1) after having been convicted of a prior violation of said subsection (1) commits a class 1 misdemeanor.

(c) Any person who violates this subsection (1) commits a class 6 felony if the person possessed a large-capacity magazine during the commission of a felony or any crime of violence, as defined in section 18-1.3-406.

(2)

(a) A person may possess a large-capacity magazine if he or she:

(I) Owns the large-capacity magazine on July 1, 2013; and

(II) Maintains continuous possession of the large-capacity magazine.

(b) If a person who is alleged to have violated subsection (1) of this section asserts that he or she is permitted to legally possess a large-capacity magazine pursuant to paragraph (a) of this subsection (2), the prosecution has the burden of proof to refute the assertion.

(3) The offense described in subsection (1) of this section shall not apply to:

(a) An entity, or any employee thereof engaged in his or her employment duties, that manufactures large-capacity magazines within Colorado exclusively for transfer to, or any licensed gun dealer, as defined in section 12-26.1-106(6), C.R.S., or any employee thereof engaged in his or her official employment duties, that sells large-capacity magazines exclusively to:

(I) A branch of the armed forces of the United States;

(II) A department, agency, or political subdivision of the state of Colorado, or of any other state, or of the United States government;

(III) A firearms retailer for the purpose of firearms sales conducted outside the state;

(IV) A foreign national government that has been approved for such transfers by the United States government; or

(V) An out-of-state transferee who may legally possess a large-capacity magazine; or

(b) An employee of any of the following agencies who bears a firearm in the course of his or her official duties:

(I) A branch of the armed forces of the United States; or

(II) A department, agency, or political subdivision of the state of Colorado, or of any other state, or of the United States government; or

(c) A person who possesses the magazine for the sole purpose of transporting the magazine to an out-of-state entity on behalf of a manufacturer of large-capacity magazines within Colorado.

Colorado Revised Statutes § 18-12-303
IDENTIFICATION MARKINGS FOR LARGE-CAPACITY MAGAZINES -- RULES

(1) A large-capacity magazine that is manufactured in Colorado on or after July 1, 2013, must include a permanent stamp or marking indicating that the large-capacity magazine was manufactured or assembled after July 1, 2013. The stamp or marking must be legibly and conspicuously engraved or cast upon the outer surface of the large-capacity magazine.

(2) The bureau may promulgate such rules as may be necessary for the implementation of this section, including but not limited to rules requiring a large-capacity magazine that is manufactured on or after July 1, 2013, to bear identifying information in addition to the identifying information described in subsection (1) of this section.

(3) A person who manufactures a large-capacity magazine in Colorado in violation of subsection (1) of this section commits a class 2 misdemeanor and shall be punished in accordance with section 18-1.3-501.

Colorado Revised Statutes, Title 24, Article 33.5, Part 4
COLORADO BUREAU OF INVESTIGATIONS

Colorado Revised Statutes § 24-33.5-424

NATIONAL INSTANT CRIMINAL BACKGROUND CHECK SYSTEM -- STATE POINT OF CONTACT -- FEE -- GROUNDS FOR DENIAL OF FIREARM TRANSFER -- APPEAL -- RULE-MAKING -- UNLAWFUL ACTS -- INSTANT CRIMINAL BACKGROUND CHECK CASH FUND -- CREATION

(1) For purposes of this section:

(a) "18 U.S.C. sec. 922(t)" means 18 U.S.C. sec. 922(t) as it exists as of March 7, 2000, or as it may be amended.

(b) "Firearm" has the same meaning as set forth in 18 U.S.C. sec. 921(a)(3), as amended.

(c) "NICS system" means the national instant criminal background check system created by Public Law 103-159, known as the federal "Brady Handgun Violence Prevention Act", the relevant portion of which is codified at 18 U.S.C. sec. 922(t).

(d) "Transfer" means the sale or delivery of any firearm in this state by a transferor to a transferee. "Transfer" shall include redemption of a pawned firearm by any person who is not licensed as a federal firearms licensee by the federal bureau of alcohol, tobacco, and firearms or any of its successor agencies. "Transfer" shall not include the return or replacement of a firearm that had been delivered to a federal firearms licensee for the sole purpose of repair or customizing.

(e) "Transferee" means any person who is not licensed as a federal firearms licensee by the federal bureau of alcohol, tobacco, and firearms or any of its successor agencies, in accordance with the federal "Gun Control Act of 1968", chapter 44 of title 18 U.S.C., as amended, and to whom a transferor wishes to sell or deliver a firearm.

(f) "Transferor" means any licensed importer, licensed manufacturer, or licensed dealer as defined in 18 U.S.C. sec. 921(a)(9), (a)(10), and (a)(11), as amended, respectively.

(2) The bureau is hereby authorized to serve as a state point of contact for implementation of 18 U.S.C. sec. 922(t), all federal regulations and applicable guidelines adopted pursuant thereto, and the NICS system.

(3)

(a) The bureau, acting as the state point of contact for implementation of 18 U.S.C. sec. 922(t), shall transmit a request for a background check in connection with the prospective transfer of a firearm to the NICS system and may also search other databases. The bureau shall deny a transfer of a firearm to a prospective transferee if the transfer would violate 18 U.S.C. sec. 922(g) or (n) or result in the violation of any provision of state law, including but not limited to section 18-12-108(4)(c), C.R.S., involving acts which, if committed by an adult, would constitute a burglary, arson, or any felony involving the use of force or the use of a deadly weapon.

(b)

(I) In addition to the grounds for denial specified in paragraph (a) of this subsection (3), the bureau shall deny a transfer of a firearm if, at any time the bureau transmits the request or searches other databases, information indicates that the prospective transferee:

(A) Has been arrested for or charged with a crime for which the prospective transferee, if convicted, would be prohibited under state or federal law from purchasing, receiving, or possessing a firearm and either there has been no final disposition of the case or the final disposition is not noted in the other databases; or

(B) Is the subject of an indictment, an information, or a felony complaint alleging that the prospective transferee has committed a crime punishable by imprisonment for a term exceeding one year as defined in 18 U.S.C. sec. 921(a)(20), as amended, and either there has been no final disposition of the case or the final disposition is not noted in the other databases.

(c) The bureau is authorized to cooperate with federal, state, and local law enforcement agencies to perform or assist any other law enforcement agency in performing any firearm retrievals, and to assist in the prosecution of any rescinded transfers.

(3.5)

(a) On and after March 20, 2013, the bureau shall impose a fee for performing an instant criminal background check pursuant to this section. The amount of the fee shall not exceed the total amount of direct and indirect costs incurred by the bureau in performing the background check.

(b) The bureau shall transmit all moneys collected pursuant to this subsection (3.5) to the state treasurer, who shall credit the same to the instant criminal background check cash fund, which fund is hereby created and referred to in this subsection (3.5) as the "fund".

(c) The moneys in the fund shall be subject to annual appropriation by the general assembly for the direct costs associated with performing background checks pursuant to this section. The state treasurer may invest any moneys in the fund not expended for the purpose of this section as provided by law. The state treasurer shall credit any interest and income derived from the deposit and investment of moneys in the fund to the fund.

(d) Any unexpended and unencumbered moneys remaining in the fund at the end of a fiscal year shall remain in the fund and shall not be credited to any other fund. To the extent practicable, the bureau shall use any such remaining funds to reduce the amount of the fee described in paragraph (a) of this subsection (3.5).

(e) The bureau is authorized to contract with a public or private entity for services related to the collection of the fee described in paragraph (a) of this subsection (3.5).

(f) On January 15, 2014, and on January 15 of each calendar year thereafter, the bureau shall report to the joint budget committee concerning:

(I) The number of full-time employees used by the bureau in the preceding year for the purpose of performing background checks pursuant to this section; and

(II) The calculations used by the bureau to determine the amount of the fee imposed pursuant to this subsection (3.5).

(4) Pursuant to section 16-21-103(4)(c), C.R.S., and section 19-1-304(1)(b.8), C.R.S., the bureau shall receive and process information concerning final case disposition data of any cases prosecuted in a court in this state within 72 hours after the final disposition of the case for purposes of carrying out its duties under this section.

(5)

(a) Upon denial of a firearm transfer, the bureau shall notify the transferor and send notice of the denial to the NICS system, pursuant to 18 U.S.C. sec. 922(t). In addition, the bureau shall immediately send notification of such denial and the basis for the denial to the federal, state, and local law enforcement agencies having jurisdiction over the area in which the transferee resides and in which the transferor conducts any business.

(b) Upon denial of a firearm transfer, the transferor shall provide the transferee with written information prepared by the bureau concerning the procedure by which the transferee, within thirty days after the denial, may request a review of the denial and of the instant criminal background check records that prompted the denial. Within thirty days of receiving such a request, the bureau shall:

(I) Perform a thorough review of the instant criminal background check records that prompted the denial; and

(II) Render a final administrative decision regarding the denial within thirty days after receiving information from the transferee that alleges the transfer was improperly denied.

(c) In the case of any transfer denied pursuant to paragraph (b) of subsection (3) of this section, the inability of the bureau to obtain the final disposition of a case that is no longer pending shall not constitute the basis for the continued denial of the transfer.

(d) If the bureau reverses a denial, the bureau shall immediately request that the agency that provided the records prompting the denial make a permanent change to such records if necessary to reflect accurate information. In addition, the bureau shall provide immediate notification of such reversal to all agencies and entities that had been previously notified of a denial pursuant to paragraph (a) of this subsection (5).

(6) If in the course of conducting any background check pursuant to this section, whether the firearms transaction is approved or denied, the bureau obtains information that indicates the prospective transferee is the subject of an outstanding warrant, the bureau shall immediately provide notification of such warrant to the federal, state, and local law enforcement agencies having jurisdiction over the area in which the transferee resides and in which the transferor conducts any business.

(7)

(a) The executive director or his or her designee shall adopt such rules as are necessary to:

(I) Carry out the duties of the bureau as the state point of contact, as those duties are set forth in federal law, and assist in implementing 18 U.S.C. sec. 922(t), all federal regulations and applicable guidelines adopted pursuant thereto, and the NICS system; and

(II) Ensure the proper maintenance, confidentiality, and security of all records and data provided pursuant to this section.

(b) The rules adopted pursuant to paragraph (a) of this subsection (7) shall include, but need not be limited to:

(I) Procedures whereby a prospective transferee whose transfer is denied may request a review of the denial and of the instant criminal background check records that prompted the denial;

(II) Procedures regarding retention of records obtained or created for purposes of this section or for implementation of 18 U.S.C. sec. 922(t); except that the bureau shall not retain a record for more than forty-eight hours after the day on which the bureau approves the transfer;

(III) Procedures and forms adopted by the bureau that request information from and establish proper identification of a prospective transferee and that may correspond with any firearms transaction record required by 18 U.S.C. sec. 922(t). Such procedures and forms shall not preclude any person from making a lawful firearm transfer under this section.

(IV) Procedures for carrying out the duties under this section, including at a minimum:

(A) That the bureau shall be open for business at least twelve hours per day every calendar day, except Christmas day and Thanksgiving day, in order to transmit the requests for a background check to the NICS system and search other databases;

(B) That the bureau shall provide a toll-free telephone number for any person calling from within the state that is operational every day that the office is open for business for the purpose of responding to requests from transferors in accordance with this section; and

(C) That the bureau shall employ and train personnel at levels that ensure prompt processing of the reasonably anticipated volume of inquiries received under this section.

(8) Nothing in this section shall be construed to create any civil cause of action for damages in addition to that which is available under the "Colorado Governmental Immunity Act", Article 10 of this title.

(9) No act performed by the bureau or its agents in carrying out their lawful duties under this section shall be construed to be a violation of any provision of title 18, C.R.S.

(10)

    (a) It is unlawful for:

        (I) Any person, in connection with the acquisition or attempted acquisition of a firearm from any transferor, to willfully make any false or fictitious oral or written statement or to furnish or exhibit any false, fictitious, or misrepresented identification that is intended or likely to deceive such transferor with respect to any fact material to the lawfulness of the sale or other disposition of such firearm under federal or state law;

        (II) Any transferor knowingly to request criminal history record information or a background check under false pretenses or knowingly to disseminate criminal history record information to any person other than the subject of such information;

        (III) Any agent or employee or former agent or employee of the bureau knowingly to violate the provisions of this section.

    (b) Any person who violates the provisions of paragraph (a) of this subsection (10) commits a class 1 misdemeanor and shall be punished as provided in section 18-1.3-501, C.R.S.

(11) Any transferor who complies with the provisions of this section shall not be subject to any civil or criminal liability or regulatory sanction that may arise from the lawful transfer or lawful denial of the transfer of a firearm.

Colorado Revised Statutes, Title 25, Article 12, Part 1
NOISE ABATEMENT

Colorado Revised Statutes § 25-12-109

EXCEPTION -- SPORT SHOOTING RANGES -- LEGISLATIVE DECLARATION -- DEFINITIONS

(1) The general assembly hereby finds, determines, and declares that the imposition of inconsistent, outdated, and unnecessary noise restrictions on qualifying sport shooting ranges that meet specific, designated qualifications work to the detriment of the public health, welfare, and morale as well as to the detriment of the economic well-being of the state. The general assembly further finds, determines, and declares that a need exists for statewide uniformity with respect to exempting qualifying shooting ranges from the enforcement of laws, ordinances, rules, and orders regulating noise. As the gain associated with having a uniform statewide exemption for qualifying sport shooting ranges outweighs any gains associated with enforcing noise regulations against such ranges, the general assembly further declares that the provisions of this section, as enacted, are a matter of statewide concern and preempt any provisions of any law, ordinance, rule, or order to the contrary.

(2) As used in this section, unless the context otherwise requires:

(a) "Local government" means any county, city, city and county, town, or any governmental entity, board, council, or committee operating under the authority of any county, city, city and county, or town.

(b) "Local government official" means any elected, appointed, or employed individual or group of individuals acting on behalf of or exercising the authority of any local government.

(c) "Person" means an individual, proprietorship, partnership, corporation, club, or other legal entity.

(d) "Qualifying sport shooting range" or "qualifying range" means any public or private establishment, whether operating for profit or not for profit, that operates an area for the discharge or other use of firearms or other equipment for silhouette, skeet, trap, black powder, target, self-defense, recreational or competitive shooting, or professional training.

(3) Notwithstanding any other law or municipal or county ordinance, rule, or order regulating noise to the contrary:

(a) A local governmental official may not commence a civil action nor seek a criminal penalty against a qualifying sport shooting range or its owners or operators on the grounds of noise emanating from such range that results from the normal operation or use of the qualifying shooting range except upon a written complaint from a resident of the jurisdiction in which the range is located. The complaint shall state the name and address of the complainant, how long the complainant has resided at the address indicated, the times and dates on which the alleged excessive noise occurred, and such other information as the local government may require. The local government shall not proceed to seek a criminal penalty or pursue a civil action against a qualifying sport shooting range on the basis of such a noise complaint if the complainant established residence within the jurisdiction after January 1, 1985.

(b) No person may bring any suit in law or equity or any other claim for relief against a qualifying sport shooting range located in the vicinity of the person's property or against the owners or operators of such range on the grounds of noise emanating from the range if:

(I) The qualifying range was established before the person acquired the property;

(II) The qualifying range complies with all laws, ordinances, rules, or orders regulating noise that applied to the range and its operation at the time of its construction or initial operation;

(III) No law, ordinance, rule, or order regulating noise applied to the qualifying range at the time of its construction or initial operation.

Colorado Revised Statutes, Title 29, Article 7, Part 1
RECREATIONAL FACILITIES DISTRICTS

Colorado Revised Statutes § 29-7-101
CITY OR COUNTY MAY OWN AND OPERATE

(1) Any city, town, village, county, metropolitan recreational district, or park and recreation district organized under Article 1 of title 32, C.R.S., may acquire, sell, own, exchange, and operate public recreation facilities, open space and parklands, playgrounds, and television relay and translator facilities; acquire, equip, and maintain land, buildings, or other recreational facilities either within or without the corporate limits of such city, town, village, or county; and expend funds therefor and for all purposes connected therewith.

(2) Any county through its board of county commissioners shall have the power, authority, and jurisdiction to regulate and control public recreation lands and facilities owned or operated by the county by the promulgation of rules and regulations pursuant to a lawfully adopted resolution. The rules and regulations may include but are not limited to the following: Removal, destruction, mutilation, or defacing of any natural object or man-made object owned by the county; explosives or any form of firearm; animal control; any public use, including boating, fishing, camping, or hunting; and polluting or littering. Any person violating any rule or regulation lawfully adopted pursuant to this subsection (2) commits a class 2 petty offense

and, upon conviction thereof, shall be punished by a fine of not more than three hundred dollars. It is the duty of the sheriff and the sheriff's undersheriff and deputies, in their respective counties, as well as any county enforcement personnel authorized and appointed as described in subsection (3), to enforce the rules and regulations adopted pursuant to this subsection (2), and the county courts in their respective counties have jurisdiction in the prosecution of any violation of a rule or regulation adopted pursuant to this subsection (2). If authorized by resolution, the penalty assessment procedure provided in section 16-2-201, C.R.S., may be followed by any arresting law enforcement officer for any violation of a rule or regulation adopted pursuant to this subsection (2). As part of a resolution authorizing the penalty assessment procedure, the board of county commissioners may adopt a graduated fine schedule for violations. The graduated fine schedule may provide for increased penalty assessments for repeat offenses by the same person. All fines and forfeitures for the violation of county regulations adopted pursuant to this subsection (2) shall be paid into the treasury of the county at such times and in such manner as may be prescribed by resolution; or, if there is no resolution providing for the payment, it shall be paid to the county treasurer at once.

(3)

(a) In addition to the enforcement of the rules and regulations by the sheriff, an undersheriff, or a deputy sheriff, a board of county commissioners may by resolution designate specific other county personnel, however titled or administratively assigned, to enforce rules and regulations duly adopted by the county to control and regulate the use of county public lands and recreation facilities, by issuance of citations or summonses and complaints.

(b) Personnel designated pursuant to this subsection (3):

(I) Shall not be subject to peace officer certification or any other requirements of part 3 of article 31 of title 24, C.R.S.;

(II) Shall be included within the definition of "peace officer or firefighter engaged in the performance of his or her duties" found in section 18-3-201(2), C.R.S.; and

(III) Shall not have the power to arrest or to execute warrants and shall not have authority to enforce any other resolution, ordinance, or statute, unless otherwise provided by law.

Colorado Revised Statutes, Title 29, Article 11.7, Part 1
REGULATION OF FIREARMS

Colorado Revised Statutes § 29-11.7-102
FIREARMS DATABASE -- PROHIBITED

(1) A local government, including a law enforcement agency, shall not maintain a list or other form of record or database of:

(a) Persons who purchase or exchange firearms or who leave firearms for repair or sale on consignment;

(b) Persons who transfer firearms, unless the persons are federally licensed firearms dealers;

(c) The descriptions, including serial numbers, of firearms purchased, transferred, exchanged, or left for repair or sale on consignment.

Colorado Revised Statutes § 29-11.7-103
REGULATION -- TYPE OF FIREARM -- PROHIBITED

A local government may not enact an ordinance, regulation, or other law that prohibits the sale, purchase, or possession of a firearm that a person may lawfully sell, purchase, or possess under state or federal law. Any such ordinance, regulation, or other law enacted by a local government prior to March 18, 2003, is void and unenforceable.

Colorado Revised Statutes § 29-11.7-104
REGULATION -- CARRYING -- POSTING

A local government may enact an ordinance, regulation, or other law that prohibits the open carrying of a firearm in a building or specific area within the local government's jurisdiction. If a local government enacts an ordinance, regulation, or other law that prohibits the open carrying of a firearm in a building or specific area, the local government shall post signs at the public entrances to the building or specific area informing persons that the open carrying of firearms is prohibited in the building or specific area.

Colorado Revised Statutes, Title 30, Article 15, Part 3
UNINCORPORATED AREAS -- DISCHARGE OF FIREARMS PROHIBITED

Colorado Revised Statutes § 30-15-302
BOARD OF COUNTY COMMISSIONERS TO DESIGNATE AREA

(1) The board of county commissioners of any county in this state may designate, by resolution, areas in the unincorporated territory of such county in which it is unlawful for any person to discharge any firearms, except a duly authorized law enforcement officer acting in the line of duty, but nothing in this subsection (1) shall prevent the discharge of any firearm in shooting galleries or in any private grounds or residence under circumstances when such firearm can be discharged in such a manner as not to endanger persons or property and also in such a manner as to prevent the projectile from any such firearm from traversing any grounds or space outside the limits of such shooting gallery, grounds, or residence.

(2) No area shall be so designated under authority of subsection (1) of this section unless it has an average population density of not less than one hundred persons per square mile in the area designated, and, before making any such designation, the board of county commissioners shall hold a public hearing thereon at which any interested person shall have an opportunity to be heard. The provisions of article 3 of title 33, C.R.S., concerning the state's liability for damages done to property by wild animals protected by the game laws of the state shall not apply to any area designated by a board of county commissioners under authority of this part 3.

(3) Nothing in this section shall be construed to restrict or otherwise affect any person's constitutional right to bear arms or his right to the defense of his person, his family, or his property.

Colorado Revised Statutes § 30-15-303
VIOLATION -- PENALTY

Any person violating any provisions of this part 3 is guilty of a misdemeanor and, upon conviction thereof, shall be punished by a fine of not more than one hundred dollars.

Colorado Revised Statutes, Title 31, Article 15, Part 1
VESTING OF CORPORATE POWERS

Colorado Revised Statutes § 31-15-103
MAKING OF ORDINANCES

Municipalities shall have power to make and publish ordinances not inconsistent with the laws of this state, from time to time, for carrying into effect or discharging the powers and duties conferred by this title which are necessary and proper to provide for the safety, preserve the health, promote the prosperity, and improve the morals, order, comfort, and convenience of such municipality and the inhabitants thereof not inconsistent with the laws of this state.

Colorado Revised Statutes, Title 33, Article 3, Part 1
DAMAGE BY WILDLIFE -- GENERAL PROVISIONS

Colorado Revised Statutes § 33-3-106
EXCESSIVE DAMAGE TO PROPERTY -- PERMIT TO TAKE WILDLIFE --
WHEN -- HARASSMENT BY DOGS

(1)

(a) Where wildlife is causing excessive damage to property, as determined by the division after consultation with the property owner, the division is authorized to issue a permit to the property owner, the property owner's designee, or to such other person selected by the division to kill a specified number of the species of wildlife causing such excessive damage. Upon request by the property owner, whenever the wildlife causing the excessive damage exceeds the wildlife objective set by the division for that species for that geographical area for the current year, the division is encouraged to issue a permit under this section. Any determination by the division that the damage being caused is not excessive may, upon application by the property owner, be reviewed by the commission.

(b) No permit to take wildlife pursuant to this subsection (1) shall be issued or used in violation of any local restriction on firearm use.

(2) Any wildlife killed, as permitted under subsection (1) of this section, shall remain the property of the state and shall be field dressed promptly, and such killing shall be reported to the division within forty-eight hours; except that the killing of a bear or mountain lion shall be reported within five days.

(3) Nothing in this section shall make it unlawful to trap, kill, or otherwise dispose of bears, mountain lions, or dogs without a permit in situations when it is necessary to prevent them from inflicting death, damage, or injury to livestock, real property, a

motor vehicle, or human life and additionally, in the case of dogs, when it is necessary to prevent them from inflicting death or injury to big game and to small game, birds, and mammals. Any wildlife killed as permitted under this subsection (3) shall remain the property of the state, and such killing shall be reported to the division within five days. The division may bring a civil action against the owner of any dog inflicting death or injury to any big game and to small game, birds, and mammals for the value of each game animal injured or killed. The minimum value of each animal shall be as set forth in section 33-6-110.

Colorado Revised Statutes, Title 33, Article 6, Part 1
LAW ENFORCEMENT AND PENALTIES -- WILDLIFE -- GENERAL PROVISIONS

Colorado Revised Statutes § 33-6-123
HUNTING UNDER THE INFLUENCE

It is unlawful for any person who is under the influence of alcohol or any controlled substance, as defined in section 18-18-102(5), C.R.S., or any other drug to a degree that renders such person incapable of safely operating a firearm or bow and arrow to hunt or take any wildlife in this state. The fact that any person charged with a violation of this section is or has been entitled to use such controlled substance or drug under the laws of this state shall not constitute a defense against any charge of violating this section. For the purposes of this section, being under the influence of any drug shall include the use of glue-sniffing, aerosol inhalation, or the inhalation of any other toxic vapor. Any person who violates this section is guilty of a misdemeanor and, upon conviction thereof, shall be punished by a fine of not less than one hundred dollars nor more than one thousand dollars or by imprisonment in the county jail for not more than one year, or by both such fine and imprisonment, and an assessment of twenty license suspension points.

Colorado Revised Statutes, Title 35, Article 43, Part 1

BRANDING AND HERDING -- GENERAL AND ADMINISTRATIVE PROVISIONS

<u>Colorado Revised Statutes § 35-43-126</u>
DOG WORRYING STOCK

Any dog found running, worrying, or injuring sheep, cattle, or other livestock may be killed, and the owner or harborer of such dog shall be liable for all damages done by it.

APPENDIX B: SELECTED FEDERAL FORMS

ATF Form 4473 *Page 1*

OMB No. 1140-0020

U.S. Department of Justice
Bureau of Alcohol, Tobacco, Firearms and Explosives

**Firearms Transaction Record Part I -
Over-the-Counter**

WARNING: You may not receive a firearm if prohibited by Federal or State law. The information you provide will be used to determine whether you are prohibited under law from receiving a firearm. Certain violations of the Gun Control Act, 18 U.S.C. §§ 921 et. seq., are punishable by up to 10 years imprisonment and/or up to a $250,000 fine.	Transferors Transaction Serial Number (If any)

Prepare in original only. All entries must be handwritten in ink. Read the Notices, Instructions, and Definitions on this form. **"PLEASE PRINT."**

Section A - Must Be Completed Personally By Transferee (Buyer)

1. Transferee's Full Name

Last Name	First Name	Middle Name (If no middle name, state "NMN")

2. Current Residence Address (U.S. Postal abbreviations are acceptable. Cannot be a post office box.)

Number and Street Address	City	County	State	IP Code

3. Place of Birth		4. Height	5. Weight (Lbs.)	6. Gender	7. Birth Date		
U.S. City and State -OR-	Foreign Country	Ft. ____ In. ____		☐ Male ☐ Female	Month	Day	Year

8. Social Security Number (Optional, but will help prevent misidentification)	9. Unique Personal Identification Number (UPIN) if applicable (See Instructions for Question 9.)

10.a. Ethnicity	10.b. Race (Check one or more boxes.)
☐ Hispanic or Latino	☐ American Indian or Alaska Native ☐ Black or African American ☐ White
☐ Not Hispanic or Latino	☐ Asian ☐ Native Hawaiian or Other Pacific Islander

11. Answer questions 11.a. (see exceptions) through 11.l. and 12 (if applicable) by checking or marking "yes" or "no" in the boxes to the right of the questions.

		Yes	No
a.	Are you the actual transferee/buyer of the firearm(s) listed on this form Warning: You are not the actual buyer if you are acquiring the firearm(s) on behalf of another person. If you are not the actual buyer, the dealer cannot transfer the firearm(s) to you. (See Instructions for Question 11.a.) Exception: If you are picking up a repaired firearm(s) for another person, you are not required to answer 11.a. and may proceed to question 11.b.	☐	☐
b.	Are you under indictment or information in any court for a felony, or any other crime, for which the judge could imprison you for more than one year (See Instructions for Question 11.b.)	☐	☐
c.	Have you ever been convicted in any court of a felony, or any other crime, for which the judge could have imprisoned you for more than one year, even if you received a shorter sentence including probation (See Instructions for Question 11.c.)	☐	☐
d.	Are you a fugitive from justice	☐	☐
e.	Are you an unlawful user of, or addicted to, marijuana or any depressant, stimulant, narcotic drug, or any other controlled substance	☐	☐
f.	Have you ever been adjudicated mentally defective (which includes a determination by a court, board, commission, or other lawful authority that you are a danger to yourself or to others or are incompetent to manage your own affairs) OR have you ever been committed to a mental institution (See Instructions for Question 11.f.)	☐	☐
g.	Have you been discharged from the Armed Forces under dishonorable conditions	☐	☐
h.	Are you subject to a court order restraining you from harassing, stalking, or threatening your child or an intimate partner or child of such partner (See Instructions for Question 11.h.)	☐	☐
i.	Have you ever been convicted in any court of a misdemeanor crime of domestic violence (See Instructions for Question 11.i.)	☐	☐
j.	Have you ever renounced your United States citizenship	☐	☐
k.	Are you an alien illegally in the United States	☐	☐
l.	Are you an alien admitted to the United States under a nonimmigrant visa (See Instructions for Question 11.l.) If you answered "no" to this question, do NOT respond to question 12 and proceed to question 13.	☐	☐
12.	If you are an alien admitted to the United States under a nonimmigrant visa, do you fall within any of the exceptions set forth in the instructions (If "yes," the licensee must complete question 20c.) (See Instructions for Question 12.) If question 11.l. is answered with a "no" response, then do NOT respond to question 12 and proceed to question 13.	☐	☐

13. What is your State of residence (if any) (See Instructions for Question 13.)	14. What is your country of citizenship (List/check more than one, if applicable. If you are a citizen of the United States, proceed to question 16.) ☐ United States of America ☐ Other (Specify)_____	15. If you are not a citizen of the United States, what is your U.S.-issued alien number or admission number

Note: Previous Editions Are Obsolete

Transferee (Buyer) Continue to Next Page
STAPLE IF PAGES BECOME SEPARATED

ATF Form 4473 (5300.9) Part I
Revised April 2012

Page 1 of 6

I certify that my answers to Section A are true, correct, and complete. I have read and understand the Notices, Instructions, and Definitions on ATF Form 4473. I understand that answering "yes" to question 11.a. if I am not the actual buyer is a crime punishable as a felony under Federal law, and may also violate State and/or local law. I understand that a person who answers "yes" to any of the questions 11.b. through 11.k. is prohibited from purchasing or receiving a firearm. I understand that a person who answers "yes" to question 11.l. is prohibited from purchasing or receiving a firearm, unless the person also answers "Yes" to question 12. I also understand that making any false oral or written statement, or exhibiting any false or misrepresented identification with respect to this transaction, is a crime punishable as a felony under Federal law, and may also violate State and/or local law. I further understand that the repetitive purchase of firearms for the purpose of resale for livelihood and profit without a Federal firearms license is a violation of law (See Instructions for Question 16.)

16. Transferee's/Buyer's Signature	17. Certification Date

Section B - Must Be Completed By Transferor (Seller)

18. Type of firearm(s) to be transferred (check or mark all that apply):	19. If sale at a gun show or other qualifying event.
☐ Handgun ☐ Long Gun ☐ Other Firearm (Frame, Receiver, etc. (rifles or See Instructions for Question 18.) shotguns)	Name of Event _____ City, State _____

20a. Identification (e.g., Virginia Driver's license (VADL) or other valid government-issued photo identification.) (See Instructions for Question 20.a.)

Issuing Authority and Type of Identification	Number on Identification	Expiration Date of Identification (if any)		
		Month	Day	Year

20b. Alternate Documentation (if driver's license or other identification document does not show current residence address) (See Instructions for Question 20.b.)

20c. Aliens Admitted to the United States Under a Nonimmigrant Visa Must Provide: Type of documentation showing an exception to the nonimmigrant visa prohibition. (See Instructions for Question 20.c.)

Questions 21, 22, or 23 Must Be Completed Prior To The Transfer Of The Firearm(s) (See Instructions for Questions 21, 22 and 23.)

21a. Date the transferee's identifying information in Section A was transmitted to NICS or the appropriate State agency: (Month/Day/Year)	21b. The NICS or State transaction number (if provided) was:
Month Day Year	

21c. The response initially provided by NICS or the appropriate State agency was:	21d. If initial NICS or State response was "Delayed," the following response was received from NICS or the appropriate State agency:
☐ Proceed ☐ Delayed ☐ Denied The firearm(s) may be transferred on ☐ Cancelled _____ (Missing Disposition Information date provided by NICS) if State law permits (optional)	☐ Proceed _____ (date) ☐ Denied _____ (date) ☐ Cancelled _____ (date) ☐ No resolution was provided within 3 business days.

21e. (Complete if applicable.) After the firearm was transferred, the following response was received from NICS or the appropriate State agency on: _____ (date). ☐ Proceed   ☐ Denied   ☐ Cancelled

21f. The name and Brady identification number of the NICS examiner (Optional)

_____ (name)   _____ (number)

22.	☐ No NICS check was required because the transfer involved only National Firearms Act firearm(s). (See Instructions for Question 22.)

23. ☐ No NICS check was required because the buyer has a valid permit from the State where the transfer is to take place, which qualifies as an exemption to NICS (See Instructions for Question 23.)

Issuing State and Permit Type	Date of Issuance (if any)	Expiration Date (if any)	Permit Number (if any)

Section C - Must Be Completed Personally By Transferee (Buyer)

If the transfer of the firearm(s) takes place on a different day from the date that the transferee (buyer) signed Section A, the transferee must complete Section C immediately prior to the transfer of the firearm(s). (See Instructions for Question 24 and 25.)

I certify that my answers to the questions in Section A of this form are still true, correct and complete.

24. Transferee's/Buyer's Signature	25. Recertification Date

Transferor (Seller) Continue to Next Page
STAPLE IF PAGES BECOME SEPARATED

Page 2 of 6   ATF Form 4473 (5300.9) Part I
Revised April 2012

ATF Form 4473

		Section D - Must Be Completed By Transferor (Seller)		
26. Manufacturer and/or Importer (If the manufacturer and importer are different, the FFL should include both.)	**27.** Model	**28.** Serial Number	**29.** Type (pistol, revolver, rifle, shotgun, receiver, frame, etc.) (See Instructions for question 29)	**30.** Caliber or Gauge

30a. Total Number of Firearms (Please handwrite by printing e.g., one, two, three, etc. Do not use numerals.)

30b. Is any part of this transaction a Pawn Redemption ☐ Yes ☐ No

30c. For Use by FFL (See Instructions for Question 30c.)

Complete ATF Form 3310.4 For Multiple Purchases of Handguns Within 5 Consecutive Business Days

31. Trade/corporate name and address of transferor (seller) (Hand stamp may be used.)	32. Federal Firearms License Number (Must contain at least first three and last five digits of FFL Number X-XX-XXXXX.) (Hand stamp may be used.)

The Person Transferring The Firearm(s) Must Complete Questions 33-36. For Denied/Cancelled Transactions, The Person Who Completed Section B Must Complete Questions 33-35.

I certify that my answers in Sections B and D are true, correct, and complete. I have read and understand the Notices, Instructions, and Definitions on ATF Form 4473. On the basis of: (1) the statements in Section A (and Section C if the transfer does not occur on the day Section A was completed); (2) my verification of the identification noted in question 20a (and my reverification at the time of transfer if the transfer does not occur on the day Section A was completed); and (3) the information in the current State Laws and Published Ordinances, it is my belief that it is not unlawful for me to sell, deliver, transport, or otherwise dispose of the firearm(s) listed on this form to the person identified in Section A.

33. Transferor's/Seller's Name (Please print)	34. Transferor's/Seller's Signature	35. Transferor's/Seller's Title	36. Date Transferred

NOTICES, INSTRUCTIONS AND DEFINITIONS

Purpose of the Form: The information and certification on this form are designed so that a person licensed under 18 U.S.C. § 923 may determine if he or she may lawfully sell or deliver a firearm to the person identified in Section A, and to alert the buyer of certain restrictions on the receipt and possession of firearms. This form should only be used for sales or transfers where the seller is licensed under 18 U.S.C. § 923. The seller of a firearm must determine the lawfulness of the transaction and maintain proper records of the transaction. Consequently, the seller must be familiar with the provisions of 18 U.S.C. §§ 921-931 and the regulations in 27 CFR Part 478. In determining the lawfulness of the sale or delivery of a long gun (rifle or shotgun) to a resident of another State, the seller is presumed to know the applicable State laws and published ordinances in both the seller's State and the buyer's State.

After the seller has completed the firearms transaction, he or she must make the completed, original ATF Form 4473 (which includes the Notices, General Instructions, and Definitions), and any supporting documents, part of his or her permanent records. Such Forms 4473 must be retained for at least 20 years. Filing may be chronological (by date), alphabetical (by name), or numerical (by transaction serial number), as long as all of the seller's completed Forms 4473 are filed in the same manner. FORMS 4473 FOR DENIED/CANCELLED TRANSFERS MUST BE RETAINED: If the transfer of a firearm is denied/cancelled by NICS, or if for any other reason the transfer is not complete after a NICS check is initiated, the licensee must retain the ATF Form 4473 in his or her records for at least 5 years. Forms 4473 with respect to which a sale, delivery, or transfer did not take place shall be separately retained in alphabetical (by name) or chronological (by date of transferee's certification) order.

If you or the buyer discover that an ATF Form 4473 is incomplete or improperly completed after the firearm has been transferred, and you or the buyer wish to make a record of your discovery, then photocopy the inaccurate form and make any necessary additions or revisions to the photocopy. You only should make changes to Sections B and D. The buyer should only make changes to Sections A and C. Whoever made the changes should initial and date the changes. The corrected photocopy should be attached to the original Form 4473 and retained as part of your permanent records.

Over-the-Counter Transaction: The sale or other disposition of a firearm by a seller to a buyer, at the seller's licensed premises. This includes the sale or other disposition of a rifle or shotgun to a nonresident buyer on such premises.

State Laws and Published Ordinances: The publication (ATF P 5300.5) of State firearms laws and local ordinances ATF distributes to licensees.

Exportation of Firearms: The State or Commerce Department may require you to obtain a license prior to export.

Section A

Question 1. Transferee's Full Name: The buyer must personally complete Section A of this form and certify (sign) that the answers are true, correct, and complete. However, if the buyer is unable to read and/or write, the answers (other than the signature) may be completed by another person, excluding the seller. Two persons (other than the seller) must then sign as witnesses to the buyer's answers and signature.

When the buyer of a firearm is a corporation, company, association, partnership, or other such business entity, an officer authorized to act on behalf of the

ATF Form 4473 (5300.9) Part I
Revised April 2012

OMB No. 1140-0014 (01/31/2014)

U.S. Department of Justice
Bureau of Alcohol, Tobacco, Firearms and Explosives

Application for Tax Paid Transfer and Registration of Firearm

ATF Control Number

2a. Transferee's Name and Address *(Including tradename, if any) (See instruction 2)*

2b. County

Submit in Duplicate to:
National Firearms Act Branch
Bureau of Alcohol, Tobacco, Firearms
and Explosives, P.O. Box 530298
Atlanta, GA 30353-0298

1. Type of Transfer *(Check one)*
☐ $5   ☐ $200
Submit with your application a check or money order for the appropriate amount made payable to the Bureau of Alcohol, Tobacco, Firearms and Explosives. Upon approval of this application, this office will acquire, affix and cancel the required "National Firearms Act" stamp for you. *(See instructions 2h, 2i and 3.)*

3a. Transferor's Name and Address *(Including trade name, if any) (Executors: see instruction 2k)*

3b. Transferor's Telephone Number and Area Code

3d. Number, Street, City, State and Zip Code of Residence *(or Firearms Business Premises)* if Different from Item 3a.

3c. If Applicable: Decedent's Name, Address, and Date of Death

The above-named and undersigned transferor hereby makes application as required by Section 5812 of the National Firearms Act to transfer and register the firearm described below to the transferee.

4. Description of Firearm *(Complete items a through h)*

a. Name and Address of Manufacturer and/or Importer of Firearm

b. Type of Firearm *(See instruction 1c)*

c. Calibar, Gauge or Size *(Specify)*

d. Model

Length (Inches)	e. Of Barrel:	f. Overall:

g. Serial Number

h. Additional Description or Data Appearing on Firearm *(Attach additional sheet if necessary)*

5. Transferee's Federal Firearms License *(If any)*
(Give complete 15-digit number) (See instruction 2b)

First 6 digits	2 digits	2 digits	5 digits

6. Transferee's Special (Occupational) Tax Status *(If any)*

a. Employer Identification Number	b. Class

7. Transferor's Federal Firearms License *(If any)*
(Give complete 15-digit number) (See instruction 2b)

First 6 digits	2 digits	2 digits	5 digits

8. Transferor's Special (Occupational) Tax Status *(If any)*

a. Employer Identification Number	b. Class

Under Penalties of Perjury, I Declare that I have examined this application, and to the best of my knowledge and belief it is true, correct and complete, and that the transfer of the described firearm to the transferee and receipt and possession of it by the transferee are not prohibited by the provisions of Chapter 44, Title 18, United States Code; Chapter 53, Title 26, United States Code, or Title VII of the Omnibus Crime Control and Safe Streets Act, as amended, or any provisions of State or local law.

9. Consent to Disclosure of Information to Transferee *(See instruction 8)* . **I Do** or **Do Not** *(Circle one)* Authorize ATF to Provide Information Relating to this Application to the Above-Named Transferee .

10. Signature of Transferor *(or authorized official)*

11. Name and Title of Authorized Official *(Print or type)*

12. Date

The Space Below is for the use of the Bureau of Alcohol, Tobacco, Firearms and Explosives

By authority of the Director, This Application has been Examined, and the Transfer and Registration of the Firearm Described herein and the Interstate Movement of that Firearm, when Applicable, to the Transferee are:

Stamp Denomination

☐ Approved *(with the following conditions, if any)*

☐ Disapproved *(For the following reasons)*

Signature of Authorized ATF Official

Date

ATF Form 4 (5320.4)
Revised March 2006

Transferee Information

The following questions must be answered by any transferee who is not a Federal firearms licensee or government agency. The transferee shall give full details on a separate sheet for all "YES" answers. (See instruction 2d)

Are You:	Yes	No	14. Have You:	Yes	No
Charged by information or under indictment in any court for a crime punishable by imprisonment for a term exceeding one year?	☐	☐	a. Been convicted in any court of a crime for which the judge could have imprisoned you for more than one year, even if the judge actually gave you a shorter sentence?	☐	☐
A fugitive from justice?	☐	☐	b. Been discharged from the armed forces under dishonorable conditions?	☐	☐
An alien who is illegally or unlawfully in the United States?	☐	☐	c. Been adjudicated mentally defective or been committed to a mental institution?	☐	☐
Under 21 years of age?	☐	☐	d. Renounced your United States citizenship?	☐	☐
An unlawful user of or addicted to, marijuana, or any depressant, stimulant, or narcotic drug, or any other controlled substance?	☐	☐	e. Been convicted in any court of a misdemeanor crime of domestic violence? This includes any misdemeanor conviction involving the use or attempted use of physical force committed by a current or former spouse, parent, or guardian of the victim, or by a person with a similar relationship with the victim.	☐	☐
Subject to a court order restraining you from harassing, stalking or threatening an intimate partner or child of such partner?	☐	☐			

15. Transferee's Certification (See instruction 2e)

_____, have a reasonable necessity to
(Name of Transferee)

possess the machinegun, short-barreled rifle, short-barreled shotgun, or destructive device described on this application
for the following reason(s)_____

and my possession of the device or weapon would be consistent with public safety (18 U.S.C. 922(b) (4) and 27 CFR 478.98).

UNDER PENALTIES OF PERJURY, I declare that I have examined this application and the documents submitted in support thereof, and to the best of my knowledge and belief it is true, correct and complete.

_____   _____
(Signature of Transferee)   *(Date)*

16. Photograph

Affix
Recent Photograph Here
(Approximately 2" x 2")
(See instruction 2f.)

17. Law Enforcement Certification (See instruction 2e)

I certify that I am the chief law enforcement officer of the organization named below having jurisdiction in the area of residence of

_____. I have no information indicating that the transferee will use the firearm or device
(Name of Transferee)

described on this application for other lawful purposes. I have no information that the receipt or possession of the firearm or device described in item 4 would be place the transferee in violation of State or local law.

_____   _____
(Signature and Title of Chief Law Enforcement Officer)   *(Date)*

_____
(Organization and Street Address)

_____   _____
(County)   *(Telephone Number)*

Important Information for Currently Registered Firearms
If this registration document evidences the current registration of the firearm described on it, please note the following information.

Estate Procedures: For procedures regarding the transfer of firearms in an estate resulting from the death of the registrant identified in item 2a, the executor should contact the NFA Branch, Bureau of Alcohol, Tobacco, Firearms and Explosives, 244 Needy Road, Martinsburg, WV 25405.

Change of Address: Unless currently licensed under the Gun Control Act, the registrant shall notify the NFA Branch, Bureau of Alcohol, Tobacco, Firearms and Explosives, 244 Needy Road, Martinsburg, WV 25405, in writing, of any change to the address in Item 2a.

Change of Description: The registrant shall notify the NFA Branch, Bureau of Alcohol, Tobacco, Firearms and Explosives, 244 Needy Road, Martinsburg, WV 25405, in writing, of any change to the description of the firearm in Item 4.

Interstate Movement: If the firearm identified in item 4 is a machinegun, short-barreled rifle, short-barreled shotgun, or destructive device, the registrant may be required by 18 U.S.C. § 922(a)(4) to obtain permission from ATF prior to any transportation in interstate or foreign commerce.

Restrictions on Possession: Any restriction *(see approval block on face of form)* on the possession of the firearm identified in item 4 continues with the further transfer of the firearm.

Persons Prohibited from Possessing Firearms: If the registrant becomes prohibited by 18 U.S.C. § 922 from possessing a firearm, the registrant shall notify the NFA Branch, Bureau of Alcohol, Tobacco, Firearms and Explosives, 244 Needy Road, Martinsburg, WV 25405, in writing, immediately upon becoming prohibited for guidance on the disposal of the firearm.

Proof of Registration: This approved application is the registrant's proof of registration and it shall be made available to any ATF officer upon request.

ATF Form 4 (5320.4)
Revised March 2006

ATF Form 1

U.S. Department of Justice
Bureau of Alcohol, Tobacco, Firearms and Explosives

OMB No. 1140-0011 (06/30/2016)

Application to Make and Register a Firearm

ATF Control Number

To: National Firearms Act Branch, Bureau of Alcohol, Tobacco, Firearms and Explosives, P.O. Box 530298, Atlanta, GA 30353-0298

(Submit in duplicate. See Instructions attached.)

As required by Sections 5821(b), 5822, and 5841 of the National Firearms Act, Title 26 U.S.C., Chapter 53, the undersigned hereby submits application to make and register the firearm described below.

1. Type of Application (check one)

    a. Tax Paid. Submit your tax payment of $200 with the application. The tax may be paid by credit or debit card, check, or money order. Please complete item 17. Upon approval of the application, we will affix and cancel the required National Firearms Act Stamp. (See instructions 2c and 3)

    b. Tax Exempt because firearm is being made on behalf of the United States, or any department, independent establishment, or agency thereof.

    c. Tax Exempt because firearm is being made by or on behalf of any State or possession of the United States, or any political subdivision thereof, or any official police organization of such a government entity engaged in criminal investigations.

2. Application is made by:
   ☐ Individual ☐ Corporation or Other Legal Entity ☐ Government Entity

3a. Trade Name (If any)

3b. Applicant's Name and Mailing Address (Type or print below and between the dots) (See instruction 2d)

3c. If P.O. Box is Shown Above, Street Address Must Be Given Here

3d. County

3e. Telephone Area Code and Number

4. Description of Firearm (complete items a through i) (See instruction 2j)

a. Name and Location of Original Manufacturer of Firearm (Receiver) (If prototype, furnish plans and specifications)

b. Type of Firearm to be made (See instruction 1c)

c. Caliber or Gauge (Specify one)

d. Model

e. Length (Inches) Of Barrel:

f. Overall:

g. Serial Number

h. Additional Description (Include all numbers and other identifying data to include maker's name, city and state which will appear on the firearm) (use additional sheet if necessary)

i. State Why You Intend To Make Firearm (Use additional sheet if necessary)

j. Is this firearm being reactivated? ☐ Yes ☐ No (See Definition 1k)

5. Applicant's Federal Firearms License (If any)

(Give complete 15-digit Number)

6. Special (Occupational) Tax Status (If applicable) (See definition 1f)

a. Employer Identification Number

b. Class

Important: All individual applicants (including Federally Licensed Collectors) must complete the reverse side of this form and submit, in duplicate, FBI Form FD-258, Fingerprint Card.

Under Penalties of Perjury, I Declare that I have examined this application, including accompanying documents, and to the best of my knowledge and belief it is true, accurate and complete and the making and possession of the firearm described above would not constitute a violation of Chapter 44, Title 18, U.S.C., Chapter 53, Title 26, U.S.C., or any provisions of State or local law.

7. Signature of Applicant

8. Name and Title of Authorized Official

9. Date

The space below is for the use of the Bureau of Alcohol, Tobacco, Firearms and Explosives

By authority of the Director, Bureau of Alcohol, Tobacco, Firearms and Explosives, this application has been examined and the applicant's making and registration of the firearm described above is:

☐ Approved (With the following conditions, if any)

☐ Disapproved (For the following reasons)

Authorized ATF Official

Date

ATF Form 1 (5320.1)
Revised June 2014

ATF Form 1

---

10. Law Enforcement Certification (See instruction 2g)

certify that I am the chief law enforcement officer of the organization named below having jurisdiction in the area of residence of _____

(Name of maker)

have no information that the maker will use the firearm or device described on this application for other than lawful purposes. I have no information that Possession the firearm described in Item 4 on the front of this form would place the maker in Violation of State or Local Law.

Signature of Chief Law Enforcement Officer)   (Printed name)   (Title and agency name)

Street address, city, State and zip code)

Telephone Number)   (Date)

y (if delegated authority to sign for the chief law enforcement official):

Signature)   (Printed name)   (Title and agency name)

Street address, city, State and zip code)

Telephone Number)   (Date)

Maker's Certification

maker who is an individual must complete this Section.

1. Answer questions 11.a. through 11.j. Answer questions 13 through 16 if applicable. For any YES answer (other than for 11.i.), the applicant shall provide details on a separate sheet. (See instructions 7c and definitions)

	Yes	No	12. Photograph
Are you under indictment or information in any court for a felony, or any other crime, for which the judge could imprison you for more than one year?			
Have you ever been convicted in any court for a felony, or any other crime, for which the judge could imprison you for more than one year, even if you received a shorter sentence including probation?			Affix Recent Photograph Here (Approximately 2" x 2") (See instruction 2e)
Are you a fugitive from justice?			
Are you an unlawful user of, or addicted to, marijuana or any depressant, stimulant, narcotic drug, or any other controlled substance?			
Have you ever been adjudicated mentally defective (which includes a determination by a court, board, commission, or other lawful authority that you are a danger to yourself or others or are incompetent to manage your own affairs) OR have you ever been committed to a mental institution?			
Have you been discharged from the Armed Forces under dishonorable conditions?			
Are you subject to a court order restraining you from harassing, stalking, or threatening your child or an intimate partner or child of such partner?			
a. Have you ever been convicted in any court of a misdemeanor crime of domestic violence?			
i. Are you a United States citizen?			
j. Have you ever renounced your United States citizenship?			

f you answered "NO" to question 11.i., please answer questions 13, 14, 15 and 16.

3. Answer questions 13.a. through 13.b., and 14 by checking or marking "Yes or "No" or "NA" in the boxes to the right of the questions.

	Yes	No
Are you an alien illegally in the United States?		
Are you an alien admitted to the United States under a nonimmigrant visa? If the answer is "NO", do not respond to question 14 and proceed to questions 15 and 16.		

4. If you are an alien admitted to the United States under a nonimmigrant visa, do you fall within any of the exceptions set forth in the instructions (see definition 2.u.)? If the answer is "YES", a copy of the Documentation must be attached to the Application. ☐ Yes ☐ No ☐ N/A

5. What is your country of Citizenship if other than the United States? (Specify Country)

6. If you are not a Citizen of the United States, what is your U.S.-issued alien number or admission number?

CERTIFICATION: Under penalties imposed by 26 U.S.C. 5861, I certify that the statements contained in this Certification, and any attached documents in support thereof, are true and correct to the best of my knowledge and belief.

Signature of Maker _____   Date _____

ATF Form 1 (5320.1)
Revised June 2014

ATF Form 1

17. Method of Payment Check one) See Instruction 2h)						
☐ Check Enclosed)	☐ Cashier's Check or Money Order Enclosed)	☐ Visa	☐ Mastercard	☐ American Express	☐ Discover	☐ Diners Club

Credit/Debit Card Number No dashes)	Name as Printed on the Credit/Debit Card	Expiration Date Month year)

Credit/Debit Card Billing Address:	Address:		
	City:	State:	lp Code:

Please Complete to Ensure Payment is Credited to the Correct Application:

I am Paying the making Tax for the Applicant:	Total Amount:

I Authori e ATF to Charge my Credit/Debit Card the Above Amount.

_____   _____
Signature of Cardholder   Date

Your credit/debit card will be charged the above stated amount upon receipt of your application. The charge will be reflected on your credit/debit card statement. In the event your application is NOT approved, the above amount will be credited to the credit/debit card noted above.

Important Information for Currently Registered Firearms

If this registration document evidences the current registration of the firearm described on it, please note the following information.

Estate Procedures: For procedures regarding the transfer of firearms in an estate resulting from the death of the registrant identified in item , the executor should contact the NFA Branch, Bureau of ATF, 244 Needy Road, Martinsburg, WV 25405.

Interstate Movement: If the firearm identified in item 4 is a machinegun, short barreled rifle, short barreled shotgun, or destructive device, the registrant may be required by 18 U.S.C. 22 a) 4) to obtain permission from ATF prior to any transportation in interstate or foreign commerce.

Change of Description or Address: The registrant shall notify the NFA Branch, Bureau of Alcohol, Tobacco, Firearms and Explosives, 244 Needy Road, Martinsburg, WV 25405, in writing, of any change to the description of the firearms in item 4, or any change to the address of the registrant.

Restrictions on Possession: Any restriction see approval block on face of form) on the possession of the firearm identified in item 4 continues with the further transfer of the firearm.

Persons Prohibited from Possessing Firearms: If the registrant becomes prohibited from possessing a firearm, please contact the NFA Branch for procedures on how to dispose of the firearm.

Proof of Registration: A person possessing a firearm registered as required by the NFA shall retain proof of registration which shall be made available to an ATF officer upon request.

Paperwork Reduction Act Notice

This form is in accordance with the Paperwork Reduction Act of 1 5. The information you provide is used to establish that a transferee's receipt and possession of the firearm will be in conformance with Federal, State, and local law. The data is used as proof of lawful registration of a firearm to the manufacturer. The furnishing of this information is mandatory 26 U.S.C. 5822).

The estimated average burden associated with this collection of information 1.6 hours per respondent or recordkeeper, depending on individual circumstances. Comments concerning the accuracy of this burden estimate and suggestions for reducing this burden should be addressed to Reports Management Officer, Information Technology Coordination Staff, Bureau of Alcohol, Tobacco, Firearms and Explosives, Washington, DC 20226.

An agency may not conduct or sponsor, and a person is not required to respond to, a collection of information unless it displays a currently valid OMB control number.

Privacy Act Information

1. **Authority.** Solicitation of this information is made pursuant to the National Firearms Act 26 U.S.C. 5821 and 5822). Disclosure of this information by the applicant is mandatory for any person other than a manufacturer qualified under the National Firearms Act) making a firearm as defined in the National Firearms Act.

2. **Purpose.** To verify payment of the tax imposed by 26 U.S.C. 5821 to determine that the making would not be in violation of law and to effect registration of the firearm.

. **Routine Uses.** The information will be used by ATF to make the determinations set forth in paragraph 2. In addition, to effect registration of the firearm, information as to the identification of the firearm, date of registration, and the identification and address of person entitled to possess the firearm will be entered into the National Firearms Registration and Transfer Record. No information obtained from a application, registration, or records required to be submitted by a natural person in order to comply with any provision of the National Firearms Act or regulations issued thereunder, shall, except in connection with prosecution or other action for furnishing false information, be used, directly or indirectly, as evidence against that person in any criminal proceeding with respect to a violation of law occurring prior to or concurrently with the filing of the application. The information from this application may only be disclosed to Federal authorities for purpose of prosecution for violation of the National Firearms Act.

4. **Effects of not Supplying Information Requested.** Failure to supply complete information will delay processing and may cause denial of the application.

ATF Form 1 5 20.1)
Revised June 2014

ABOUT THE ATTORNEY AUTHORS

DOUGLAS I. RICHARDS
CO-AUTHOR

Douglas began his career as a prosecutor in the Harris County District Attorney's Office in Houston, Texas. There he handled cases ranging from murder, armed robbery, sexual assaults of adults and children, kidnapping, and drug distribution. Doug was then hired by the Department of Justice as an Assistant United States Attorney. As a federal prosecutor Doug worked closely with Special Agents from the FBI, ATF and DEA to investigate and prosecute international criminal travel networks, international drug trafficking organizations, public corruption, white-collar crime and cases involving national security. Since 2010 Doug has been in private practice defending clients accused of violating criminal laws and fiercely advocating for their Second Amendment rights.

STANLEY H. MARKS
CO-AUTHOR

Stanley has been a practicing criminal law attorney for in excess of 40 years. He is one of the Founders of the Colorado Defense Bar, the largest criminal defense organization in Colorado. He has been admitted by motion in over 35 state and federal jurisdictions in the United States wherein he has handled a wide variety of criminal cases including cases involving the use of firearms and other deadly weapons. In defense of these cases he has utilized affirmative defenses related to self-defense, defense of property and various state "Make My Day Laws."

CHRISTOPHER FERRARO
CO-AUTHOR

Christopher graduated in May 2015 from the University of Denver Sturm College Of Law and joined the Colorado Bar in November of that year. In his short time in the legal field, he has dedicated much time to the protection of Second Amendment rights in Colorado. In addition to co-authoring this book, while in law school, Chris supported David Kopel of the Independence Institute in challenging the constitutionality of the various gun control measures passed by the Colorado Legislature in 2013, on behalf of Colorado's sheriffs.